HOLT McDOUGAL LITERATURE

Adapted
Interactive Reader

GRADE 7

HOLT McDOUGAL
a division of Houghton Mifflin Harcourt

ISBN-13 978-0-547-28035-6

ISBN-10 0-547-28035-1

2 3 4 5 6 7 8 9 10   0928   18 17 16 15 14 13 12 11 10

TABLE OF CONTENTS

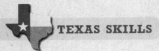

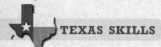

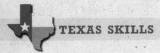

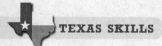**TEXAS SKILLS**

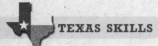

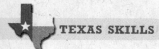 **TEXAS SKILLS**

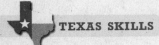

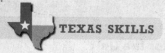**TEXAS SKILLS**

Academic Vocabulary for Unit 1

You will see these Academic Vocabulary words as you work through this book. You will also be asked to use them as you write and talk about the selections in this unit.

Contemporary (kuhn TEM puh rer ee) is an adjective that means *from the present time.*
Her brother likes oldies, but Ana prefers **contemporary** music.

How are contemporary clothes different from older styles? _____
_____

Element (EL uh muhnt) is a noun that means *a needed or basic part of something.*
One key **element** of a winning team is everyone working together.

Describe the most important element of a good movie: _____
_____

Identify (eye DEN tuh fy) is a verb that means *to point out or recognize something.*
Will needed to look closely to **identify** the tiny bug as a mite.

When might it be important to identify something or someone? _____
_____

Influence (IN floo uhns) is a noun that means *the power of a person or thing to affect others.*
Abe tried to **influence** the school election by giving voters snacks.

Tell about someone who has a strong influence on your life: _____
_____

Structure (STRUHK chuhr) is a noun that means *something made of parts put together or the way something is put together.*
The school's strong **structure** helped it withstand a tornado.

List each type of structure you spend part of your day in: _____
_____

ACADEMIC VOCABULARY   3

Academic Vocabulary for the Unit

Academic vocabulary is the language you use to talk and write about the subjects you are studying, including math, science, social studies, and language arts. Understanding and using academic vocabulary correctly will help you succeed in your classes and on tests.

Each unit in this book introduces five academic vocabulary words. You will practice each word on this page by writing a sentence about your life using the word. You will also have a chance to study these words in more depth later in the unit.

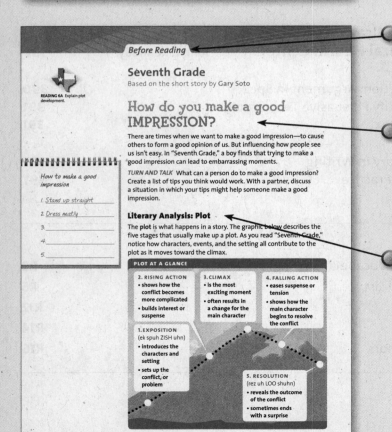

Before Reading

READING 6A Explain plot development.

Seventh Grade
Based on the short story by Gary Soto

How do you make a good IMPRESSION?

There are times when we want to make a good impression—to cause others to form a good opinion of us. But influencing how people see us isn't easy. In "Seventh Grade," a boy finds that trying to make a good impression can lead to embarrassing moments.

TURN AND TALK What can a person do to make a good impression? Create a list of tips you think would work. With a partner, discuss a situation in which your tips might help someone make a good impression.

How to make a good impression
1. Stand up straight
2. Dress neatly
3. _____
4. _____
5. _____

Literary Analysis: Plot
The **plot** is what happens in a story. The graphic below describes the five stages that usually make up a plot. As you read "Seventh Grade," notice how characters, events, and the setting all contribute to the plot as it moves toward the climax.

PLOT AT A GLANCE

1. EXPOSITION (ek spuh ZISH uhn)
- introduces the characters and setting
- sets up the conflict, or problem

2. RISING ACTION
- shows how the conflict becomes more complicated
- builds interest or suspense

3. CLIMAX
- is the most exciting moment
- often results in a change for the main character

4. FALLING ACTION
- eases suspense or tension
- shows how the main character begins to resolve the conflict

5. RESOLUTION (rez uh LOO shuhn)
- reveals the outcome of the conflict
- sometimes ends with a surprise

4   ADAPTED INTERACTIVE READER / UNIT 1: PLOT, CONFLICT, AND SETTING

Before Reading
The **Before Reading** pages will prepare you to read the selection. Here you can preview the skills and vocabulary you will need as you read.

Big Question
This activity will get you thinking about a real-life question the selection addresses, and how that question connects to what is important to you. Sometimes you'll work in a group or with a partner to complete this activity. After reading, you'll return to this activity.

Literary Analysis
This section presents a brief, easy-to-understand lesson that introduces an important literary element and explains what to look for in the selection you are about to read.

Reading Strategy: Connect

When you **connect** to a story, you think about how it relates to your own knowledge and experience. Connecting "Seventh Grade" to your own life will help you understand the characters in the story and the events they go through. As you read, you will use a chart like this one to keep track of the connections you make.

RC-7(C) Monitor comprehension by making personal connections.

In the Story	Connection to My Life
Victor feels foolish after saying the wrong thing to Teresa.	I've said things that I immediately wanted to take back.

Vocabulary in Context

Note: Words are listed in the order in which they appear in the story.

Ferocity (fuh ROS ih tee) is a noun that means *wildness* or *intensity.*
Michael thinks he looks cool when he stares at his classmates with **ferocity.**

Linger (LING guhr) is a verb that means *to be slow to leave a place.*
Victor decides to **linger,** waiting for Teresa.

Unison (YOO nih suhn) is a noun that means *at the same time* or *together.*
In **unison,** everyone recites the same answer.

Sheepishly (SHEE pish lee) is an adverb that means *in an embarrassed way.*
Not knowing how to speak French, Victor mumbles the words **sheepishly.**

Vocabulary Practice

Review the words and sample sentence above. Based on these words and sentences, what do you think the characters of Michael and Victor will be like? Explain your thoughts below.

_____
_____
_____
_____

SEVENTH GRADE   5

Reading Skill or Strategy

This lesson presents a reading skill or strategy that will help your reading comprehension. You will learn why this skill is important, and how it can help you become a better reader. A graphic organizer will help you put the strategy into practice.

Vocabulary in Context

Through this feature you will be introduced to key Vocabulary words in the selection. Each entry gives the pronunciation and definition as well as an example sentence.

Vocabulary Practice

This activity gives you a chance to practice the selection Vocabulary words.

Monitor Your Comprehension

SET A PURPOSE FOR READING
Read "Seventh Grade" to learn how Victor tries to impress a girl he likes.

Seventh Grade

Based on the short story by
GARY SOTO

○ PLOT: EXPOSITION
The exposition (EK spuh ZISH uhn) introduces the main characters, setting, and conflict. Reread lines 1–10. Underline the setting, and circle the name of the main character. What conflict does the main character face?

_____
_____
_____
_____
_____

VISUAL VOCABULARY
To **scowl** (skowl) is to make a frowning, unhappy expression.

French

BACKGROUND "Seventh Grade" is set in Fresno, California, where author Gary Soto grew up. Fresno's hot, dry summers and cool, wet winters are excellent for growing grapes. A large number of Latinos, whose families are originally from Spanish-speaking countries, work in Fresno's fields of grapes, or vineyards.

On the first day of school, Victor signed up for French. He already spoke Spanish and English, but he thought some day he might travel to France, where it was cooler than Fresno.

Besides, Teresa, a girl he had liked for a long time, was taking French, too. With any luck they would be in the same class. Teresa is going to be my girl this year, he promised himself. She was cute. And good in math, too. On his way to his homeroom, he ran into his friend, Michael Torres. "How come you're making a face?" asked
10 Victor. **○**

"I'm not making a face, man. This *is* my face." In magazines, Michael pointed out, handsome male models all had the same look on their faces. No matter what they did or where they were, they **scowled.**

6   ADAPTED INTERACTIVE READER / UNIT 1: PLOT, CONFLICT, AND SETTING

Reading the Selection

Notes in the side column of each selection will guide you as you read. Many notes ask you to underline or circle in the text itself. Others provide lines on which you can write your responses.

Set a Purpose for Reading

This feature gives you a reason for reading the selection.

Background

This paragraph gives you helpful information about the selection you are about to read. You may learn more about the author; the time period the selection was written; or other facts that will help you better understand the selection.

Literary Analysis or Reading Skill or Strategy

Notes help you identify and analyze the literary element or reading skill you learned about on the Before Reading pages.

Visual Vocabulary

This feature illustrates the meaning of words when it helps to picture a word's meaning.

A Walk Through the Book

Side notes provide a variety of activities for you to complete as you read the selection.

Vocabulary words

The vocabulary words introduced on the Before Reading page are defined in the side column and appear underlined in bltue within the selection.

In Other Words

These summaries will help you understand what you have just read.

Language Coach

These notes will help you master the finer points of the English language.

Pause & Reflect

These notes give you a chance to think about what you have just read.

Monitor Your Comprehension

"I think it works," Michael said. He scowled with <u>ferocity</u>, putting a lot of effort into it. "Belinda Reyes walked by a while ago and looked at me."

Victor didn't say anything. He thought his friend looked very strange.

20 He thought, man, that's weird. Michael thinks making a face makes him handsome. The two boys went to their homerooms.

On the way there, Victor tried a scowl. He felt foolish, until he saw a girl looking at him. He thought, maybe it does work. He scowled even harder.

IN OTHER WORDS It is the first day of school. Victor likes Teresa, a girl in the same grade, and he hopes to impress her. One of the reasons he takes French is that Teresa is taking French, too. He hopes that they'll have class together. Before class, Michael, one of Victor's friends, tells him that scowling will impress girls. Victor scowls.

In homeroom, the principal spoke over the intercom, welcoming the students to a new year. Victor sat thinking of Teresa. She sat two rows away. This would be his lucky year. She and Victor were in some classes together,
30 including French.

The bell rang for first period, and the students moved noisily through the door. Only Teresa <u>lingered</u>, hanging around to talk with the homeroom teacher about a dance class she wanted to take.

Victor also lingered, keeping his head down and staring at his desk. He wanted to leave when Teresa did so he could say something clever to her.

He secretly watched her. As she turned to leave, he managed to catch her eye. Noticing him, she smiled and
40 said, "Hi, Victor." ◎

VOCABULARY
The word **ferocity** (fuh ROS ih tee) is a noun that means *wildness* or *intensity*.

VOCABULARY
The word **linger** (LING guhr) is a verb that means *to be slow to leave a place*.

<u>Underline</u> the reason why Teresa *lingered*.

◎ LANGUAGE COACH
Idioms are expressions with special meanings. An idiom cannot be understood from the meanings of its separate words but must be learned as a whole. In line 39, "catch her eye" is an idiom. <u>Underline</u> the clue in the next sentence that tells you what this idiom means.

SEVENTH GRADE **7**

After Reading

After Reading pages feature graphic organizers. Use them to review the skills you have practiced throughout the selection.

Literary Analysis

Here you can review the literary element you have been practicing throughout the selection.

After Reading

Literary Analysis: Plot

The plot of "Seventh Grade" centers on Victor's wish to impress Teresa. In the chart below, answer the questions about each plot stage.

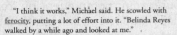

READING 6A Explain plot development

PLOT STRUCTURE OF "SEVENTH GRADE"

2. RISING ACTION
Which events in the story build suspense or get you interested?

3. CLIMAX
How does the climax—the most exciting part—change Victor?

4. FALLING ACTION
How is the conflict or problem resolved?

1. EXPOSITION
Where is the story set? Who are the main characters?

5. RESOLUTION
How does the story end?

SEVENTH GRADE **13**

After Reading

RC-7(C) Monitor comprehension by making personal connections.

Reading Strategy: Connect

Use these sentence starters to connect to the text.

Victor is like me because _____

_____

I understood how Victor felt when _____

_____

Victor reminds me of _____

_____

How do you make a good IMPRESSION?

Victor has made a good impression on Teresa. Unfortunately, the impression is based on something that is not true.

TURN AND TALK Do you think Victor should admit to Teresa that he doesn't know how to speak French? What would you do if you were Victor? Share your thoughts—and your reasons for them—in a discussion with a classmate.

Vocabulary Practice

If the sentence is true, write a T after it. If it is false, write an F.

1. A group sings in unison when each member sings at the same time. ___

2. People tend to linger when they are in a rush. ___

3. A student might behave sheepishly after he made a mistake. ___

4. A basketball team that plays with ferocity is determined to win. ___

Reading Skill or Reading Strategy

The Reading Skill or Strategy activity follows up on the skill you used to understand the text.

Big Question

Here's a chance to think again about the Big Question you examined before reading. It offers an opportunity to consider whether your thoughts have changed now that you have read the selection.

Vocabulary Practice

Complete this activity to practice the selection Vocabulary words.

Academic Vocabulary in Speaking

The word contemporary (kuhn TEM puh rer ee) is an adjective that means *from the present time*.
  Alex prefers **contemporary** popular music to the 1980s bands that some of his friends like.

READING 6A Explain plot development.

TURN AND TALK When do you think "Seventh Grade" takes place—roughly in the present or in an earlier time? Discuss your thoughts with a partner. Use details from the story to support your opinion, and be sure to use the word **contemporary** in your conversation.

Texas Assessment Practice

DIRECTIONS Use "Seventh Grade" to answer questions 1–5.

1. Which phrase best describes Victor's personality?
   - (A) Charming and talkative
   - (B) Hopeful but awkward
   - (C) Confident and brave
   - (D) Quiet but funny

2. When does the conflict of the story begin?
   - (F) When Victor signs up for French
   - (G) When Victor promises himself he will go out with Teresa
   - (H) When the first-period bell rings
   - (J) When Victor tries to speak French in class

3. Victor thinks Michael's scowling is strange, but —
   - (A) he tells Michael that it makes him look handsome
   - (B) he just laughs and shakes his head
   - (C) he pretends not to notice
   - (D) he tries it himself anyway

4. Why does Mr. Bueller allow Teresa to think Victor speaks French?
   - (F) Because he recalls doing something foolish to impress a girl
   - (G) Because he wants Victor to clean his erasers
   - (H) Because he was also fooled by Victor's French
   - (J) Because Victor is his favorite student

5. When Victor says, "Oh no, I like being bothered" in line 135, it shows that —
   - (A) he has decided to take French because it will be challenging
   - (B) Michael's scowling bothered him
   - (C) he likes Teresa but still feels uncomfortable around her
   - (D) he doesn't really plan to study with Teresa

Academic Vocabulary

In this activity, you use the Academic Vocabulary words for the unit in a speaking or writing activity about the selection.

Texas Assessment Practice

Finally, after each selection, multiple-choice questions assess your knowledge of the selection and the skill taught with it.

UNIT 1

Weaving a Story
PLOT, CONFLICT, AND SETTING

Be sure to read the Reader's Workshop on pages 28–33 in *Holt McDougal Literature*.

Academic Vocabulary for Unit 1

You will see these Academic Vocabulary words as you work through this book. You will also be asked to use them as you write and talk about the selections in this unit.

Contemporary (kuhn TEM puh rair ee) is an adjective that means *from the present time*.
Her brother likes oldies, but Ana prefers **contemporary** music.

How are **contemporary** clothes different from older styles? _____

_____

Element (EL uh muhnt) is a noun that means *a needed or basic part of something*.
One key **element** of a winning team is everyone working together.

Describe the most important **element** of a good movie: _____

_____

Identify (eye DEN tuh fy) is a verb that means *to point out or recognize something*.
Will needed to look closely to **identify** the tiny bug as a mite.

When might it be important to **identify** something or someone? ____

_____

Influence (IN floo uhns) is a noun that means *the power of a person or thing to affect others*.
Abe tried to **influence** the school election by giving voters snacks.

Tell about someone who has a strong **influence** on your life: _____

_____

Structure (STRUHK chuhr) is a noun that means *something made of parts put together or the way something is put together*.
The school's strong **structure** helped it withstand a tornado.

List each type of **structure** you spend part of your day in: _____

_____

READING 6A Explain plot development.

Seventh Grade

Based on the short story by **Gary Soto**

How do you make a good IMPRESSION?

There are times when we want to make a good impression—to cause others to form a good opinion of us. But influencing how people see us isn't easy. In "Seventh Grade," a boy finds that trying to make a good impression can lead to embarrassing moments.

TURN AND TALK What can a person do to make a good impression? Create a list of tips you think would work. With a partner, discuss a situation in which your tips might help someone make a good impression.

Literary Analysis: Plot

The **plot** is what happens in a story. The graphic below describes the five stages that usually make up a plot. As you read "Seventh Grade," notice how characters, events, and the setting all contribute to the plot as it moves toward the climax.

How to make a good impression

1. Stand up straight
2. Dress neatly
3. _____
4. _____
5. _____

PLOT AT A GLANCE

2. RISING ACTION
- shows how the conflict becomes more complicated
- builds interest or suspense

3. CLIMAX
- is the most exciting moment
- often results in a change for the main character

4. FALLING ACTION
- eases suspense or tension
- shows how the main character begins to resolve the conflict

1. EXPOSITION
(ek spuh ZISH uhn)
- introduces the characters and setting
- sets up the conflict, or problem

5. RESOLUTION
(rez uh LOO shuhn)
- reveals the outcome of the conflict
- sometimes ends with a surprise

Reading Strategy: Connect

When you **connect** to a story, you think about how it relates to your own knowledge and experience. Connecting "Seventh Grade" to your own life will help you understand the characters in the story and the events they go through. As you read, you will use a chart like this one to keep track of the connections you make.

RC-7(C) Monitor comprehension by making personal connections.

In the Story	Connection to My Life
Victor feels foolish after saying the wrong thing to Teresa.	I've said things that I immediately wanted to take back.

Vocabulary in Context

Note: Words are listed in the order in which they appear in the story.

Ferocity (fuh ROS ih tee) is a noun that means *wildness* or *intensity*.
  Michael thinks he looks cool when he stares at his classmates with **ferocity.**

Linger (LING guhr) is a verb that means *to be slow to leave a place*.
  Victor decides to **linger,** waiting for Teresa.

Unison (YOO nih suhn) is a noun that means *at the same time or together*.
  In **unison,** everyone recites the same answer.

Sheepishly (SHEE pish lee) is an adverb that means *in an embarrassed way*.
  Not knowing how to speak French, Victor mumbles the words **sheepishly.**

Vocabulary Practice

Review the words and sample sentence above. Based on these words and sentences, what do you think the characters of Michael and Victor will be like? Explain your thoughts below.

_____

_____

_____

_____

SET A PURPOSE FOR READING
Read "Seventh Grade" to learn how Victor tries to impress a girl he likes.

Ⓐ PLOT: EXPOSITION
The exposition (EK spuh ZISH uhn) introduces the main characters, setting, and conflict. Reread lines 1–10. Underline the setting, and circle the name of the main character. What conflict does the main character face?

_____

_____

_____

_____

_____

VISUAL VOCABULARY
To **scowl** (skowl) is to make a frowning, unhappy expression.

Seventh Grade

Based on the short story by
GARY SOTO

BACKGROUND "Seventh Grade" is set in Fresno, California, where author Gary Soto grew up. Fresno's hot, dry summers and cool, wet winters are excellent for growing grapes. A large number of Latinos, whose families are originally from Spanish-speaking countries, work in Fresno's fields of grapes, or vineyards.

On the first day of school, Victor signed up for French. He already spoke Spanish and English, but he thought some day he might travel to France, where it was cooler than Fresno.

Besides, Teresa, a girl he had liked for a long time, was taking French, too. With any luck they would be in the same class. Teresa is going to be my girl this year, he promised himself. She was cute. And good in math, too. On his way to his homeroom, he ran into his friend, Michael Torres. "How come you're making a face?" asked

10 Victor. Ⓐ

"I'm not making a face, man. This *is* my face." In magazines, Michael pointed out, handsome male models all had the same look on their faces. No matter what they did or where they were, they **scowled**.

"I think it works," Michael said. He scowled with **ferocity**, putting a lot of effort into it. "Belinda Reyes walked by a while ago and looked at me."

Victor didn't say anything. He thought his friend looked very strange.

20   He thought, man, that's weird. Michael thinks making a face makes him handsome. The two boys went to their homerooms.

On the way there, Victor tried a scowl. He felt foolish, until he saw a girl looking at him. He thought, maybe it does work. He scowled even harder.

IN OTHER WORDS It is the first day of school. Victor likes Teresa, a girl in the same grade, and he hopes to impress her. One of the reasons he takes French is that Teresa is taking French, too. He hopes that they'll have class together. Before class, Michael, one of Victor's friends, tells him that scowling will impress girls. Victor scowls.

In homeroom, the principal spoke over the intercom, welcoming the students to a new year. Victor sat thinking of Teresa. She sat two rows away. This would be his lucky year. She and Victor were in some classes together,
30 including French.

The bell rang for first period, and the students moved noisily through the door. Only Teresa **lingered**, hanging around to talk with the homeroom teacher about a dance class she wanted to take.

Victor also lingered, keeping his head down and staring at his desk. He wanted to leave when Teresa did so he could say something clever to her.

He secretly watched her. As she turned to leave, he managed to catch her eye. Noticing him, she smiled and
40 said, "Hi, Victor." ℬ

VOCABULARY
The word **linger** (LING guhr) is a verb that means *to be slow to leave a place*.

Underline the reason why Teresa *lingered*.

ℬ LANGUAGE COACH
Idioms are expressions with special meanings. An idiom cannot be understood from the meanings of its separate words but must be learned as a whole. In line 39, "catch her eye" is an idiom. Underline the clue in the next sentence that tells you what this idiom means.

He smiled back and said, "Yeah, that's me." He blushed, his face turning red. Why hadn't he said, "Hi, Teresa," or something nice?

So much for being in the same class, he thought.

In English they reviewed
50 the parts of speech. Their teacher, Mr. Lucas, asked, "What is a noun?"

"A person, place, or thing," the class said in **unison**, as if everyone shared a single voice.

"Yes, now somebody give me an example of a person— you, Victor Rodriguez."

"Teresa," Victor said right away. Some of the girls giggled. They knew he liked Teresa. He blushed again.

"Correct," Mr. Lucas said. "Now name a place."

Another kid answered, "Teresa's house with a kitchen
60 full of big brothers."

IN OTHER WORDS Victor and Teresa are in homeroom together. She greets him happily, but his response sounds rude, so he feels embarrassed. Later, Victor's teacher asks him to name a person. He answers, "Teresa." Other students laugh.

▶ Why does Victor's answer make his classmates laugh? Underline the reason.

At lunch, Victor sat with Michael, who practiced scowling again, frowning between bites.

Girls walked by and looked at him.

"See what I mean, Vic?" Michael scowled. "They love it."

VOCABULARY

The word **unison** (YOO nih suhn) is a noun that means *at the same time* or *together*.

"Yeah, I guess so."

Victor looked for Teresa. He didn't see her. She must be eating outside.

Victor hurried outside. He sat down and opened his math book. He raised his eyes slowly and looked around. 70 No Teresa.

He lowered his eyes, pretending to study, and then looked slowly to the left. No Teresa. **C**

Then he saw her. She was sitting with a girlfriend. Victor moved to a table near her. He daydreamed about taking her to a movie. When the bell sounded, Teresa looked up, and their eyes met. She smiled sweetly and gathered her books. Her next class was French, the same as Victor's. **PAUSE & REFLECT**

In French, Victor sat near the front of the class, a few desks away from Teresa. Mr. Bueller wrote French words 80 on the chalkboard. The bell rang, and Mr. Bueller turned to the class and said, *"Bonjour."*[1]

"Bonjour," said a few brave students.

"Bonjour," Victor whispered. He wondered if Teresa heard him.

Mr. Bueller asked if anyone knew French. Victor didn't speak French, but he raised his hand, wanting to impress Teresa. The teacher smiled and said, *"Très bien. Parlez-vous français?"*[2]

Victor didn't know what to say. The teacher asked 90 something else in French. The room grew silent. Victor tried to pretend he knew the language by making noises that sounded French. At least he thought they sounded French.

"La me vave me con le grandma," Victor said slowly and uncertainly.

---

1. *Bonjour* (bon ZHOOR): French word meaning "Good day," or "hello."
2. *Très bien* (treh byan). *Parlez-vous* (PAR lay voo) *français?* (frahn SEH): French expressions meaning "Very good" and "Do you speak French?"

C PLOT: RISING ACTION

Complications (kom plih KAY shuhnz) are plot events that make resolving the conflict more difficult. What complications are getting in the way of Victor making Teresa "his girl"?

_____

_____

_____

_____

_____

PAUSE & REFLECT

With a partner, discuss how Victor might be feeling now that he has found Teresa. What about his earlier behavior helps you imagine his feelings now?

Ⓓ CONNECT
Victor says he can speak French even though he cannot. Think about what he hopes to gain by being dishonest. Then think of a time when you or someone you know pretended something in a similar way and why. Fill in your thoughts in the chart below.

In the Story
Victor says he can speak
French because . . .

↓

Connection to My Life

VOCABULARY
The word **sheepishly** (SHEE pish lee) is an adverb that means *in an embarrassed way.*

Mr. Bueller, confused by Victor's words, asked him to speak up.

Victor's face grew red. As he blushed, great rosebushes of red bloomed on his cheeks. He felt awful. Teresa sat a few desks away, probably thinking he was a fool. Without looking 100 at Mr. Bueller, Victor mumbled, "Frenchie oh wewe gee in September." Mr. Bueller asked Victor to repeat what he said.

"Frenchie oh wewe gee in September," Victor repeated. **Ⓓ**

Mr. Bueller understood that the boy didn't know French and turned away. He went on with the lesson. He asked the class to read aloud some French words from the board.

Victor was too weak from failure to join the class. He stared at the board and wished he had taken Spanish, not French. Better yet, he wished he could start his life over. He had never been so embarrassed.

IN OTHER WORDS In French class, Victor pretends that he can speak French. Victor's teacher, Mr. Bueller, realizes that Victor does not know the language. Victor feels silly and embarrassed.

▶ With a partner, discuss how Mr. Bueller reacts to Victor's "French."

110 The bell sounded for fifth period. Victor rushed out of the room, forgetting his book. He went back to get it and looked **sheepishly** at the teacher, who was erasing the board. He felt shy and awkward about looking so foolish in class. Then, when Teresa suddenly walked in, Victor looked frightened. "I didn't know you knew French," Teresa said. "That was good." **Ⓔ**

Mr. Bueller looked at Victor, and Victor looked back. Without saying a word, Victor begged with his eyes, Oh please, don't say anything. I'll wash your car, mow your

¹²⁰ lawn, walk your dog—anything! I'll be your best student, and I'll clean your erasers after school.

Mr. Bueller smiled. He remembered his college years when he had borrowed cars from different friends to take out a girl. The girl thought Mr. Bueller was rich because he had picked her up in a different car each time they went out. It was fun until he had spent all of his money on her. Finally he had to write home to his parents because he had no money left.

Victor couldn't stand to look at Teresa. He was sweaty
¹³⁰ with shame. "Yeah, well, I picked up a few things from movies and books." They left the class together. Teresa asked him if he would help her study French.

"Sure, anytime," Victor said.

"I won't be bothering you, will I?"

"Oh no, I like being bothered."

"*Bonjour*," Teresa said, leaving him outside her next class. She smiled.

"Yeah, right, *bonjour*," Victor said. The rosebushes of shame on his face became **bouquets** of love, beautiful
¹⁴⁰ flowers. Teresa is a great girl, he thought. And Mr. Bueller is a good guy.

ⓔ PLOT: CLIMAX
Place brackets [ ] around what Teresa says to Victor in lines 115–116. Explain whether you think this is the **climax**—the turning point and most exciting moment in the story.

_____

_____

_____

_____

VISUAL VOCABULARY
A **bouquet** (boh KAY) is a bunch of flowers.

He ran happily to his next class. Then, after school, he ran to the public library. He checked out three French textbooks.

He was going to like seventh grade. **F**

F PLOT: RESOLUTION

Underline the details that reveal Victor's mood at the end of the day. How has his mood changed throughout the story?

_____

_____

_____

_____

_____

_____

_____

_____

_____

_____

IN OTHER WORDS Teresa doesn't realize that Victor only pretended to speak French. In front of Mr. Bueller, she tells him she is impressed. Mr. Bueller doesn't tell Teresa that Victor can't actually speak the language. When Teresa asks Victor to help her study French, he agrees. After school, he runs to the library and checks out books to help him learn French for real.

Literary Analysis: Plot

The plot of "Seventh Grade" centers on Victor's wish to impress Teresa. In the chart below, answer the questions about each plot stage.

READING 6A Explain plot development.

PLOT STRUCTURE OF "SEVENTH GRADE"

2. RISING ACTION
Which events in the story build suspense or get you interested?

_____
_____
_____
_____

3. CLIMAX
How does the climax—the most exciting part—change Victor?

_____
_____
_____
_____

4. FALLING ACTION
How is the conflict or problem resolved?

_____
_____
_____
_____

1. EXPOSITION
Where is the story set? Who are the main characters?

_____
_____
_____
_____

5. RESOLUTION
How does the story end?

_____
_____
_____
_____

RC-7(C) Monitor comprehension by making personal connections.

Reading Strategy: Connect

Use these sentence starters to connect to the text.

Victor is like me because _____

_____

I understood how Victor felt when _____

_____

Victor reminds me of _____

_____

How do you make a good IMPRESSION?

Victor has made a good impression on Teresa. Unfortunately, the impression is based on something that is not true.

TURN AND TALK Do you think Victor should admit to Teresa that he doesn't know how to speak French? What would you do if you were Victor? Share your thoughts—and your reasons for them—in a discussion with a classmate.

Vocabulary Practice

If the sentence is true, write a T after it. If it is false, write an F.

1. A group sings in **unison** when each member sings at the same time. ____

2. People tend to **linger** when they are in a rush. ____

3. A student might behave **sheepishly** after he made a mistake. ____

4. A basketball team that plays with **ferocity** is determined to win. ____

Academic Vocabulary in Speaking

The word **contemporary** (kuhn TEM puh rair ee) is an adjective that means *from the present time*.

> Alex prefers **contemporary** popular music to the 1980s bands that some of his friends like.

TURN AND TALK When do you think "Seventh Grade" takes place— roughly in the present or in an earlier time? Discuss your thoughts with a partner. Use details from the story to support your opinion, and be sure to use the word **contemporary** in your conversation.

READING 6A Explain plot development.

Texas Assessment Practice

DIRECTIONS Use "Seventh Grade" to answer questions 1–5.

1. Which phrase best describes Victor's personality?
   - A Charming and talkative
   - B Hopeful but awkward
   - C Confident and brave
   - D Quiet but funny

2. When does the conflict of the story begin?
   - F When Victor signs up for French
   - G When Victor promises himself he will go out with Teresa
   - H When the first-period bell rings
   - J When Victor tries to speak French in class

3. Victor thinks Michael's scowling is strange, but —
   - A he tells Michael that it makes him look handsome
   - B he just laughs and shakes his head
   - C he pretends not to notice
   - D he tries it himself anyway

4. Why does Mr. Bueller allow Teresa to think Victor speaks French?
   - F Because he recalls doing something foolish to impress a girl
   - G Because he wants Victor to clean his erasers
   - H Because he was also fooled by Victor's French
   - J Because Victor is his favorite student

5. When Victor says, "Oh no, I like being bothered" in line 135, it shows that —
   - A he has decided to take French because it will be challenging
   - B Michael's scowling bothered him
   - C he likes Teresa but still feels uncomfortable around her
   - D he doesn't really plan to study with Teresa

READING 6A Explain the influence of the setting on plot development.

The Last Dog
Based on the short story by Katherine Paterson

Why are pets good COMPANIONS?

For many of us, pets are an important part of our lives. We feed them and care for them and often think of them as part of the family, but what do we get in return? Some would say that pets reward us with their companionship—their affection, loyalty, and good company. In "The Last Dog," a boy's powerful bond with a puppy teaches him an important lesson.

LIST IT Make a list of reasons pets are good companions. Write down a list like the one on the lines to the left.

Literary Analysis: Setting

Setting is where and when a story happens. A story may take place in a variety of places, from a house to a boat to another planet. Its events may occur in the past, present, or future. Setting often has a major effect on plot events.

"The Last Dog" is set far in the future on an Earth where life is very different from what it is today. Look for details about the setting to help you understand how it affects what happens in the story. These details can include

• details about the landscape and weather

• details about clothing, food, buildings, and technology

Why are pets good COMPANIONS?

1. *Pets are fun to play with.*

2. _____

3. _____

4. _____

5. _____

Reading Skill: Identify Sequence in Plot

The plot's **sequence,** or order of events, helps you understand the story. Words and phrases such as *first, last, later,* and *in the past* are often clues to the order of events in a story. Sometimes a scene from the past interrupts, or breaks into, the order of events. This is called a **flashback,** and it often provides important information.

As you read, you will record the sequence of important events in the story in a chart like the one below. When a flashback occurs, you will need to decide where in the sequence of events the flashback event actually happened.

READING 6 Draw conclusions about the structure and elements of fiction.

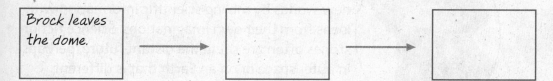

Brock leaves the dome. → →

Vocabulary in Context

Note: Words are listed in the order in which they appear in the story.

Disembodied (dis em BOD eed) is an adjective that means *separated from a body.*

The computer's **disembodied** voice gave him information.

Evasive (ih VAY siv) is an adjective that means *trying to avoid.*

Instead of answering him right away, she was **evasive.**

Posterity (pos TAIR ih tee) is a noun that means *people in the future.*

The important discovery could be saved for **posterity.**

Vocabulary Practice

Identify each statement as true or false. On the line below the statement, write a sentence explaining your choice.

1. If you enjoyed a trip, you would be **evasive** when asked about it.

_____

2. Someone would seem **disembodied** if you could hear but not see the person.

_____

3. If you worry about **posterity,** you are thinking about the future.

_____

SET A PURPOSE FOR READING
Read to discover what happens when a boy learns that the world is a very different place than he was taught.

THE LAST DOG

Based on the short story by
KATHERINE PATERSON

BACKGROUND In science fiction, writers create new worlds by mixing scientific information with ideas from their own imaginations. Science fiction stories often are set in the distant future, perhaps in outer space or on an Earth that is different from ours. Science fiction plots are often about challenges created by unusual settings.

VOCABULARY
The word **disembodied** (dis em BOD eed) is an adjective that means *separated from a body*.

Ⓐ SEQUENCE IN PLOT
What does Brock have to do before he leaves the dome?

_____

_____

_____

_____

Brock walked up to the computer at the customs gate. People wanting to leave or come back had to stop there to check in or out. "This is highly unusual, Brock," the **disembodied** voice said. "What is your reason for travel outside the dome?"

"Scientific research," he replied. He had never heard of anyone leaving the dome to do research. "The Research Team gave me permission to go."

"Are you wearing the protective suit with helmet
10 and gloves?"

"Yes—affirmative."

"You have enough liquid and food tablets for only one day of travel."

"Affirmative."

"Brock, walk to the gate." Ⓐ

Why weren't they asking him more questions? Ever since he had said he wanted to go outside the dome, people had treated him strangely. Did they think he was a deviant— someone who acted strangely? Deviants sometimes
20 disappeared. There were stories that deviants had "gone

outside," but no one really knew. They said that no deviant had ever returned to the dome.

The gate opened and Brock stepped outside. He blinked. The sun was too bright for his eyes. He turned and looked at the dome one last time. Then, he started to walk toward the mountains he saw in the distance. He recognized them from **holograms**.

Brock didn't know of anyone who had left the <u>dome</u>, but there were <u>protective suits</u> and equipment, like his, 30 to protect anyone who did. He also carried a <u>scanner</u>, a computer that could warn him of dangers and describe his emotions to him. He asked the person who gave him the suit and scanner about why they had equipment like this, but she was <u>evasive</u>. She said that people used to go outside the dome, but the world was too frightening. Hardly anyone ever used the equipment anymore. **B**

Was Brock, then, the only person who was still curious? Or had all of the people who had gone outside died, scaring people out of further attempts?

40 If Brock never returned, he'd have no one to blame but himself. While his podfellows—others about his age living inside the dome—had played games on computers, he had spent time reading "ancient fictions," or "novels." Their characters seemed *real* to Brock. They had strange names like Huck Finn and M. C. Higgins the Great.[1] He had read the stories again and again. The novels made him wonder about the world outside the dome.

IN OTHER WORDS Far in the future, people live inside a protective dome. They believe that the outside world is too dangerous for people to live in. Brock gets permission to go on a research trip outside the dome. Reading novels makes Brock interested in the world outside the dome. No one has returned from such a trip.

► Why do the novels make Brock interested in the world outside the dome? Bracket [ ] the sentence that tells you.

---

1. **Huck Finn and M.C. Higgins the Great:** the main characters in two novels that are often read by young adults.

VISUAL VOCABULARY
Holograms are three-dimensional pictures made by laser light.

VOCABULARY
The word **evasive** (ih VAY siv) is an adjective that means *trying to avoid.*

B **SETTING**
Look at the underlined words in lines 28–30. What do these items suggest about what the world outside the dome is like?

_____

_____

_____

_____

_____

_____

_____

_____

_____

_____

Now Brock was in that world, and he could see its mountains.

50 Close to the dome, the land was clear, but after he walked for an hour or so, he passed ruins. The wrecked buildings may have been places where people lived long ago.

He had an unfamiliar feeling. The scanner told him that the feeling was "loneliness." He liked having names for new feelings.

He was alone for the first time in his life. Perhaps he should have taken one of the other podfellows along. But they all laughed when he spoke of going outside. Ever since he started reading the ancient fictions, his podfellows 60 thought he was odd—not like them. Perhaps he should have taken a robopet, a robot in the form of a pet, along for company. But he didn't really like the robopet his pod shared. **ⓒ**

He had not understood how far he needed to walk to reach the mountains. It was now well past noon, and he had nearly two miles to go. Should he send a signal that he would be late, or should he head home now? He had only a day's supply of water and food pellets. Still, he was closer to the mountains than to the dome. He felt what the 70 scanner told him was "excitement" and kept going.

Actual trees grew on the first hill. The leader of Brock's pod, the podmaster, had said that trees no longer existed, that they had become extinct. Brock pulled off a leaf. It was green and had veins. In some ways, it looked like his hand. He put the leaf in his pack so that he could study it later. He didn't want anyone saying he had started paying more attention to his feelings. He didn't want anyone saying he had stopped using scientific information. Only deviants did that.

80 Then he heard the sound of water running. He checked the scanner. There was no danger signal. He hurried toward the sound. It was a "brook"—he was sure of it!

ⓒ SEQUENCE IN PLOT
Underline the **flashback** in the paragraph. With a partner, discuss what this flashback tells you about Brock's relationship with his "podfellows."

In the dome, he was taught that these small streams had become poisonous and then dried up when the world grew hot. But here was a brook. **D**

He first wanted to take off his glove and dip a finger in the brook, but he didn't. He had been trained to avoid danger. He sat down on the ground. Yes, this must be grass. There were even some small flowers. Would the air 90 poison him if he took off his helmet and breathed it? He decided not to try. **E**

He pushed some buttons. A tube appeared in his mouth. It dropped a food pellet on his tongue. Then he sucked in some liquid and swallowed his meal. What did novels call eating outside? *Picnic?* He was having a *picnic* in the *woods* by a *brook*. The scanner told him that he felt "pleasure."

It was then that he heard the new sound. The scanner did not indicate danger, so he went toward it. Something was lying under a tree's shadow. It was three feet long and 100 furry, but it wasn't moving.

Then he saw the puppy. With its nose, it was poking the stiff body of what must have been its mother. It was making the little crying sounds he had heard.

IN OTHER WORDS As he walks toward the mountains, Brock finds out that he was not taught the truth about the world outside the dome. He had been told that trees and running water no longer existed. He finds both and a puppy, too.

Brock could guess the puppy was "sad." But he didn't know what missing a mother would feel like. There were no mothers in the dome. Instead, children were born in a laboratory and raised together. Computers and a podmaster—not parents—watched over them.

Brock had never seen a dog, but he had learned about 110 them. There had been many dogs once. They filled the stories he had read. They even had names—Lassie, Toto,

D LANGUAGE COACH
Depending on what it refers to, the word *running* may have different meanings. In line 80, when Brock hears water *running*, the word refers to the sound the flowing water of the brook makes. In a small group discuss what else the word *running* can describe.

E SETTING
With a partner, discuss why Brock is surprised by the scenery he sees on his trip outside the dome. What does this tell you about what the setting may be like inside the dome?

F SEQUENCE IN PLOT

Brock remembers what he was taught about dogs and humans who lived outside the dome. Put brackets [ ] around the lines that tell you what Brock was told happened to them. Is this paragraph a flashback or not? Why or why not?

_____

_____

_____

_____

_____

_____

_____

G SETTING

Reread lines 133–141. With a partner, discuss what Brock learns when the dog drinks from the stream.

Sounder.[2] Now there were no dogs at all. The people who stayed outside the domes had killed all the animals for food. After that, the people had died out. **F**

Obviously, dogs still existed, though. Brock moved toward the puppy.

"Alert. Alert. Scanning unknown object."

Brock pushed the off button. "Are you sure you want to turn off scanner?"

120   "Yes. Affirmative."

The puppy looked at him as if deciding whether to run or stay.

"It's all right, dog," Brock said. "I won't hurt you." He stayed still. He didn't want to frighten it.

He held out his gloved hand. The dog backed away. But when Brock kept his hand out, the puppy slowly crept toward him and sniffed, making soft crying noises. It was looking for food.

Brock looked first at the dead mother who could no 130 longer feed her puppy, then around the landscape. What would a puppy eat? He took out one of his food pellets. Moving slowly so he would not scare the dog, he held it out.

The puppy gulped down the pellet. Then, it ran over to the brook. Brock watched in horror as it drank from the poisoned stream.

"Don't!" Brock yelled.

The puppy turned for a second, but then kept drinking, as if it was the most normal thing in the world. The puppy was breathing the poisoned air too, wasn't it? Why hadn't 140 Brock thought of it before? The puppy lived outside the dome *without any protective gear.* What could it mean? **G**

The puppy made more crying noises and looked up at Brock with large, trusting eyes. For the first time in his life, Brock felt something for another living thing, an emotion.

---

2. **Lassie, Toto, and Sounder:** three famous fictional dogs. Lassie appeared in the novel *Lassie Come-Home* and the television series *Lassie*. Toto was Dorothy's pet dog in *The Wizard of Oz*. Sounder was a hunting dog in the novel and film of the same name.

The thought of the puppy suffering here next to its dead parent until the puppy died of hunger was terrible.

"Your name is Brog, all right?" Brock said to the puppy. "Don't worry, Brog. I won't let you starve. I'll get food for you."

150 That's why Brock returned to the dome's entrance after dark, carrying a lively and wriggling *Canis familiaris*. Those words, Brock knew, were the scientific name for "dog." **PAUSE & REFLECT**

PAUSE & REFLECT
Discuss with a partner what makes Brock feel "something for another living thing" for the first time. What does this tell you about Brock's life in the dome?

IN OTHER WORDS Brock finds and makes friends with a puppy whose mother has died. He worries that the puppy will starve if he leaves it alone. He names the dog Brog and takes it with him when he returns to the dome.

The voice of the customs monitor spoke to him:

"Welcome back, Brock. You're late."

"Affirmative."

"Computer detects something warm-blooded. It is not on the list."

"I found a dog," Brock mumbled.

160 "*Canis familiaris* is extinct. Dogs no longer exist."

"Well, maybe it's just a robopet that got out."

"Correction. Robopets are bloodless. Proceed to quarantine[3] inspection."

The inspectors, who rarely had anything to check, were nervous at first. Then they watched the puppy happily licking Brock's face and became interested. An actual dog! None of them had ever seen one. Brock's dog was lively, unlike a robopet. They knew they should have killed the dog or sent it back outside the dome, but they couldn't do it.

170 "It will have to go to Research," the chief inspector finally said.

---

3. **quarantine** (KWAHR uhn teen): a place where travelers are kept for a short time to prevent them from bringing dangerous diseases into a country.

The scientists in Research were amazed to see a live *Canis familiaris,* but they stayed back. Only one scientist, dressed in protective clothing, came into the laboratory. He poked and prodded the poor dog until it began to whimper. He learned that Brog was female.

"Brog needs to rest," said Brock, stopping the scientist in the middle of his inspection. "She's had a hard day. And she needs actual food. She's not used to pellets."

180   One of the scientists in the observation booth answered through a speaker. "Send someone out for a McLike burger without sauce. She may think it is meat." ⊕

Brock realized that the scientists wanted him to give them advice about Brog. He was, after all, the person who had discovered the last dog. They treated him as someone who was important and smart, and Brock took advantage and made the most of it. He insisted on staying with Brog. "She's not like us," he explained. "In the old stories, puppies cried all night long if they were separated from their

190 families. She needs to have contact with another warm-blooded animal or she might die of 'loneliness.'"

The scientists agreed.

IN OTHER WORDS Scientists in the dome stay away from the dog because she is from outside the dome. Brock persuades them to let him stay with Brog in the research center. He tells them that puppies need to be with other living things.

For nearly a week, Brock lived with Brog in the research center. The dog quickly learned to obey Brock's commands, but it wasn't the automatic response of a robopet. Brog enjoyed obedience. She wanted to please Brock. Those few times when she did not obey Brock, Brog looked up with sorrowful eyes, begging to be forgiven. He put his arms around her and held her. He noticed that

200 one of the scientists was watching. Well, let him watch.

⊕ **SETTING**
Reread lines 172–182. List details about clothing, food, and buildings that show how the scientists react to Brog.

_____

_____

_____

_____

_____

Share your list with a partner. Discuss how you would describe the scientists' reaction to Brog.

Nothing was as wonderful as feeling this warmth toward another creature.

Then Brock woke in the middle of the night. He heard an argument. One of the researchers had forgotten to turn off the speaker.

"Cloning[4]—it's the only thing to do. If she's the last, we owe it to **posterity** to keep producing dogs."

"And how are we going to raise a pack of dogs in a dome? We don't have enough food for them. We have

210　to be realistic. Besides, no one has had the chance to do experiments on such an animal in the dome."

"What about the boy? He won't agree. He's with the dog all the time. He's developed strong feelings for it."

"Can you think of what a disaster it would be if a flood of emotions happened in a controlled environment such **as** ours? Creatures like dogs inspire powerful emotions," another said.

"Shh. Not now. The speaker is—" The system clicked off. But Brock had already heard. He knew he had lost

220　his scientific objectivity, his ability to focus on facts, not feelings. He was no longer sure he wanted it. He enjoyed being flooded by "emotions." But he was more worried for Brog than for himself. Cloning would be bad enough. Ten dogs who looked just like Brog so no one would know **how unique Brog was.** But experiments! They'd cut her open and examine her insides. They'd try to change her personality, who Brog was. ❶

IN OTHER WORDS Brock hears the scientists talking about what to do with Brog. He worries that they will clone her or perform experiments on her. He cares about Brog and does not want her to suffer or to have her personality changed.

► With a partner, discuss why the scientists are worried about Brog.

---

4. **cloning** (KLOH ning): a scientific way to make identical copies of an animal or plant.

VOCABULARY

The word **posterity** (pos TAIR ih tee) is a noun that means *people in the future.*

❶ **SEQUENCE IN PLOT**

Reread lines 219–223. Discuss with a partner how Brock's feelings about living in the dome have changed.

The next day Brock pretended to be sick. Brog stayed with him. The scientists didn't care. They were too busy
230 thinking about what they might do with Brog.

Brock crept to the nearest computer in the lab. The scientists had been studying dog diseases. Brock looked down the list. What he needed was a disease that might affect people as well as dogs. Here it was! "Rabies (RAY beez): A disease occurring in animals and humans, especially in dogs and wolves. Passed along by bite or scratch. The early stages of the disease are the most dangerous, for an otherwise healthy and friendly animal will suddenly bite."

240 Rabies was it! He would have to make Brog bite him. In the dome, there was no medicine to cure rabies. They'd be so afraid of spreading the disease that they'd make both Brog and him leave. No matter what was outside, Brock couldn't stand to go back to the life he had lived in the dome before he met Brog.

He waited until the right moment. All the scientists had gathered in the lab. They were explaining to Brock and Brog what must be done.

"It has to be done for the sake of science," they began,
250 "and for the sake of the dome community, which is always short on food and water. It won't be as if she'll be gone, you know. We've made computer copies of her. You can play with her on your computer whenever you like."

That was all Brock needed to hear. He turned and bit Brog on the tail so hard it bled. Brog, surprised and angry, spun around and bit Brock on the nose.

There was a shocked silence.

"I—I don't know what got into me," Brock said. "I've been feeling strange."

260 All of the scientists ran out of the room as fast as they could. When Brock offered to take Brog out of the dome to let her loose in the mountains, no one argued. No one

came close as he packed some water and food pellets. The customs gate monitor asked him no questions. ❶

IN OTHER WORDS Brock wants to save Brog from the scientists. He plans to escape from the dome by pretending that he and Brog have rabies. He bites Brog so the dog will bite him back. Frightened, the scientists let Brock and the dog leave the dome.

Out of sight of the dome, Brog was full of joy. She ran in circles around Brock's boots. If the air was as poisonous as people in the dome said, why wasn't it choking Brog? Brock unscrewed his helmet a little. Nothing happened. In fact, he seemed to be breathing normally. He took off
270 the helmet. He was still breathing freely. He waited to start choking, as he had been warned. It didn't happen. Could people in the dome be wrong? Could the outside world have healed itself?

Could fear have kept them prisoners many years longer than a poisoned environment would have?

He unfastened the protective suit and slowly stepped out of it into the sunlight.

"Who knows?" Brock said to Brog. "Maybe out here you aren't the last dog. Your mother had to come from
280 somewhere."

Brog barked happily.

❶ SEQUENCE IN PLOT
How does Brock get the scientists to let him and Brog leave the dome? List the sequence of events in this chart.

First

↓

Then

↓

Then

↓

Then

Ⓚ SETTING

With a partner, discuss how this setting differs from what people inside the dome think the outside world is like.

"And maybe, just maybe, where there are dogs, there are people, too."

They stopped at the brook where they'd met. Both of them took a long drink. Brock no longer carried a scanner, but he knew that he felt excitement. The water was delicious. Ⓚ

IN OTHER WORDS Outside, Brock discovers that the air is safe to breathe and the water is safe to drink. He wonders whether there are people living outside the dome.

Literary Analysis: Setting

Review the details you noted about the story's setting as you read.
What is the difference between life inside the dome and outside the
dome? Why does Brock decide to live outside the dome? Use the chart
below to plan your answer by listing details from the two settings.
Then answer the question on the lines below the chart.

READING 6A Explain the influence of the setting on plot development.

Inside the Dome	Outside the Dome
No grass, flowers, or trees	Grass, flowers, trees

Why does Brock choose to live outside the dome instead of remaining
in the dome? Write your answer on these lines:

_____

_____

_____

_____

_____

_____

_____

_____

_____

_____

_____

Reading Skill: Identify Sequence in Plot

Complete the sequence chart below for the plot of "The Last Dog." Begin by identifying the important events in the story. Look back at the story and decide whether the story would have turned out the same way without a particular event. If the event must happen for the story to turn out as it does, number it and then list it below in order. Be sure to place any flashbacks where they occur in time rather than when you learn about them in the story.

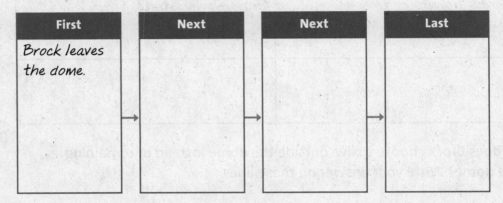

First	Next	Next	Last
Brock leaves the dome.			

Why Are Pets Good COMPANIONS?

Brock's life changes after a dog becomes his companion. By the end of the story, how has Brog changed the way Brock feels about his life? Use your chart to answer this question on the lines below:

_____

_____

_____

_____

Vocabulary Practice

Circle the word or phrase in each sentence that answers the question.

1. If you hear someone speaking in a **disembodied** voice, can you see who is speaking or not?

2. Does someone who is **evasive** toward you want to see you or prefer to avoid you?

3. If a plan is good for **posterity,** will people benefit from it now or in the future?

Academic Vocabulary in Speaking

The word **element** (EL uh muhnt) is a noun that means *a needed or basic part of something.*

> Fast-paced action is an important **element** in all of Jorge's favorite movies.

The word **influence** (IN floo uhns) is a noun that means *the power of a person or thing to affect others.*

> Amelia's supportive third-grade teacher had a lasting **influence** on her life.

TURN AND TALK Discuss the ending of the story with a partner. After they leave the dome, what might happen to Brock and Brog? Think about the **influence** that **elements** outside the dome might have on their lives. Be sure to use **element** and **influence** in your discussion.

Texas Assessment Practice

DIRECTIONS Use "The Last Dog" to answer questions 1–4.

1. The setting of the story is —
   - (A) not revealed
   - (B) Earth in the past
   - (C) Earth in the future
   - (D) the moon

2. Which event occurs first?
   - (F) Brock finds the puppy's mother.
   - (G) The scientists study the puppy for a week.
   - (H) Brock steps into the bright sunlight.
   - (J) Brock drinks water from the brook.

3.

Brock brings Brog to the dome.	Scientists decide to clone Brog.	

   Which event would you place in the next box to show the correct sequence of events?
   - (A) Brock goes back outside the dome to get the puppy's mother.
   - (B) Brock agrees with the scientists' plan.
   - (C) The dog bites the scientists.
   - (D) Brock creates a plan to save the puppy.

4. The end of the story suggests that —
   - (F) Brock and Brog may not live long.
   - (G) Brock and Brog will return to the dome.
   - (H) Brock and Brog may meet other humans and dogs.
   - (J) Other people from the dome will search for Brock and Brog.

READING 6 Draw conclusions about the elements of fiction. **6B** Analyze the development of plot.

Rikki-Tikki-Tavi

Based on the short story by **Rudyard Kipling**

What makes you BRAVE?

You have to stand up to a bully . . . You get a chance to sing in front of a thousand people . . . You are able to stop a bad accident. Any of these can make you feel brave—full of courage and able to meet a challenge. In the story you're about to read, you will see bravery in action.

TURN AND TALK Make a list of times when you felt you were brave. Then choose one time and discuss it with a partner.

When I Was Brave

1. Played drums in a talent show

2. _____

3. _____

4. _____

Literary Analysis: Suspense and Foreshadowing

A story is exciting when you read page after page without wanting to stop. An important part of an exciting story is suspense—the feeling of nervousness and uncertainty that makes you want to keep reading.

Writers create suspense with foreshadowing: hints or clues about what might happen later in the story. As you read "Rikki-tikki-tavi," notice how Kipling creates suspense and uses foreshadowing to make you want to keep reading.

Suspense and Foreshadowing	Example
Suspense The nervousness and uncertainty you feel	"Just then, Nag himself appeared. He was a huge cobra, five feet long."
Foreshadowing Hints or clues about what might happen	"But Teddy's father convinced her that a mongoose was the perfect house pet. After all, they had deadly snakes living right in their garden, and mongooses were snake killers."

Reading Strategy: Predict

A **prediction** is a good guess about what will happen in a story.
To make predictions, ask yourself:

- What do I know about what's happening in the story?

- What have I learned about the characters?

As you read "Rikki-tikki-tavi," notes in the side column will ask you to
make predictions in a chart like the one below.

RC-7(B) Ask interpretive questions
of text.

Details from the Story	My Prediction
Rikki-tikki knows that a mongoose's job is to fight snakes.	Rikki-tikki is going to get in a fight with a snake.

Vocabulary in Context

Note: Words are listed in the order in which they appear in the story.

Revive (rih VYV) is a verb that means *to come back to life*.
   The mongoose was able to **revive** after nearly drowning.

Fledgling (FLEJ ling) is a noun that means *a young bird*.
   Nag eats the bird Darzee's **fledgling** in its nest.

Singe (sinj) is a verb that means *to burn a little*.
   Teddy's father does not mean to **singe** Rikki's fur when he fires at
   Nag.

Valiant (VAL yuhnt) is an adjective that means *being brave* or *having
courage*.
   Rikki is always **valiant** in the face of danger.

Cunningly (KUHN ing lee) is an adverb that means *in a clever way that
is meant to trick or deceive*.
   Darzee's wife **cunningly** pretends her wing is broken.

Vocabulary Practice

Review the words and sample sentences above. Then, with a partner,
discuss what you can guess about the animals in this story.

Rikki-tikki-tavi

Based on the short story by
RUDYARD KIPLING

BACKGROUND The mongoose
(MONG goos) and the poisonous
snake called a cobra (KOH bruh) are
natural enemies. A mongoose, only 16
inches long, can move quickly enough
to win a fight with a six-foot cobra. In
this story, set in the late 1800s when
India was part of the British Empire,
many British families living in India
had homes that snakes could enter
easily. A mongoose could be very
helpful by keeping snakes away.

Ⓐ PREDICT

Think about what you
read in the **Background**
section. What enemy might
Rikki-tikki face in battle?

_____

_____

VOCABULARY

The word **revive** (rih VYV) is
a verb that means _to come
back to life._

This is the story of a great war. Rikki-tikki-tavi fought
this war in an English family's home in India. He had
some help, but he was the one who did the real fighting.

Rikki-tikki was a mongoose. His name came from the
sound he made going into battle: Rikk-tikk-tikki-tikki-tchk! Ⓐ

When Rikki was small, a flood swept him away from
his home and family. A little boy named Teddy found him
half dead and brought him home. Teddy and his mother
warmed the mongoose till he **revived** and looked as if he
10 would live after all.

Although the mother really liked animals, she wasn't
sure she wanted a wild animal in her house. But Teddy's
father convinced her that a mongoose was the perfect house

pet. After all, they had deadly snakes living right in their garden, and mongooses were snake killers.

IN OTHER WORDS Rikki-tikki-tavi was a mongoose—a small, furry, snake-eating animal—who lived with an English family in India. This is the story of how he won a war that he fought in their home. Teddy, the little boy, found Rikki-tikki-tavi and brought him home one day. Teddy's parents agreed to keep the mongoose because they had snakes in their garden. They thought that Rikki-tikki might protect them.

Rikki-tikki soon felt better, and he spent the rest of the day and the next morning exploring Teddy's house. In the yard he heard the sad voices of two birds, Darzee and his wife. The birds were crying because a cobra named
20 Nag had eaten one of their babies. Just then, Nag himself appeared. He was a huge cobra, five feet long. **B**

"I am Nag," he said. "Look, and be afraid!"

Though Rikki had never met a cobra, he knew that a mongoose's job was to kill snakes. Nag knew that, too, and he was secretly afraid.

Rikki-tikki replied, "Well. Do you think it is right to eat **fledglings** in their nest? They are just helpless babies."

Nag then glanced past Rikki-tikki and saw that he could play a trick on the mongoose.

30 "Let's talk," he said. "If you eat eggs, why shouldn't I eat birds?"

"Behind you! Look behind you!" cried Darzee the bird.

Rikki-tikki jumped high up in the air. He just missed being struck by Nag's wife Nagaina, who had slithered up behind him. Rikki landed on Nagaina's back and bit her, but she struggled and got free.

B SUSPENSE AND FORESHADOWING

Descriptions of characters help build **suspense** in the story. Circle three things you learn about Nag in lines 19–22. Explain whether these things make you curious about what might happen.

_____

_____

_____

_____

_____

VOCABULARY

The word **fledgling** (FLEJ ling) is a noun that means *a young bird*.

C LANGUAGE COACH

In line 37, notice how Rikki-tikki's eyes "grew very red." This is an **idiom**—a phrase that has a meaning different from the meaning of its individual words. With a partner discuss what you think "grew red" means here.

Now Rikki-tikki's eyes grew very red. But Nag and Nagaina were gone. **C**

IN OTHER WORDS Rikki-tikki-tavi meets Nag and Nagaina, two cobras who live in the garden. Nag has just killed a baby bird. Nag distracts Rikki so that Nagaina, Nag's wife, can attack him. Rikki escapes and bites Nagaina, but the two cobras get away. Rikki-tikki is very angry.

Teddy ran down the path to pet Rikki-tikki. But as
40 Teddy bent down, something moved in the dust. It was Karait, a small but deadly brown snake. Rikki's eyes glowed red.

Teddy shouted to his parents. His father ran out with a stick, but Rikki-tikki had already killed Karait.

Teddy's father beat the dead Karait.

"Why is he doing that?" thought Rikki-tikki. "I have already killed the snake."

The family treated Rikki like a hero. He enjoyed the attention, but he did not forget about Nag and Nagaina. **D**

IN OTHER WORDS Rikki-tikki fights and kills another snake named Karait. Teddy's family treats Rikki-tikki like a hero, but he does not forget about the two cobras, Nag and Nagaina.

D SUSPENSE AND FORESHADOWING

Recall that **foreshadowing** includes hints or clues about what might happen later in the story. Reread lines 48–49. <u>Underline</u> the detail that foreshadows a future fight between Rikki-tikki and Nag and Nagaina.

50 That night, Rikki wandered around inside the house. He met Chuchundra the **muskrat**. Chuchundra was very scared.

"Don't kill me!" cried Chuchundra.

"Why would I bother to kill you?" said Rikki-tikki scornfully.

"I don't know," said Chuchundra. "Maybe Nag will think I am you some dark night, and he will kill me. My cousin Chua, the rat, told me."

VISUAL VOCABULARY

A **muskrat** (MUS krat) is a small animal that lives in the water. It has brown fur, a long tail, and webbed hind feet.

"Told you what?" said Rikki-tikki.

60 Chuchundra was terrified, but he told Rikki that Nag and Nagaina were planning an attack that very night.

Just then, Rikki-tikki heard a soft scratch-scratch coming from the bathroom. Rikki-tikki moved quietly into the bathroom. There he heard Nag and Nagaina whispering in the drainpipe.

"Go in quietly, and kill the big man first," said Nagaina.

"Are you sure we should kill the people?" said Nag.

"Of course. The mongoose will leave if we kill them. Then we can be king and queen of the garden, and we will 70 have a safe hatching ground for our eggs," said Nagaina. She and Nag had eggs that were almost ready to hatch. **ⓔ**

Nag slipped through the drain into the bathroom. His head came first, then his five feet of scaly body. Rikki-tikki was angry, but also afraid. He stayed very still for an hour. Then, he moved slowly toward Nag. He knew he had to kill Nag with his first bite. Rikki jumped on Nag's head. Nag shook him fiercely, trying to make Rikki let go. Though Rikki was dizzy and he hurt all over, he held on tightly.

Then Rikki felt a blast. His fur was <u>singed</u> by red hot 80 fire. The fight had awakened Teddy's father, who shot Nag.

The man picked up Rikki. He shouted, "It's the mongoose again! This time, the <u>valiant</u> little animal has bravely saved our lives!"

Exhausted, Rikki-tikki dragged himself to Teddy's bedroom.

IN OTHER WORDS Nag and Nagaina enter the house at night, planning to kill Teddy's parents. Rikki-tikki bites Nag on the head and shakes him back and forth until Teddy's father shoots Nag and kills him. Again, Teddy's family treats Rikki as a hero.

Monitor Your Comprehension

ⓔ PREDICT
Remember that a **prediction** is a good guess about what will happen in a story. Reread lines 66–71. Think about what Nag and Nagaina are planning to do. How do you think Rikki-tikki might respond?

_____

_____

_____

_____

VOCABULARY
The word **singe** (sinj) is a verb that means *to burn a little.*

VOCABULARY
The word **valiant** (VAL yuhnt) is an adjective that means *being brave* or *having courage.*

Circle the clues that tell you why Teddy's father calls Rikki-tikki *valiant.*

Ⓕ PREDICT
Pause at line 102. Complete the
chart below by predicting the
outcome of Rikki-tikki's fight
with Nagaina.

Details from the Story

↓

My Prediction

When morning came, Rikki-tikki knew he had a job to
finish. Nagaina was still alive. Rikki went to Darzee the
bird for help. Darzee told Rikki that Nagaina was by the
trash pile, crying over Nag's body. Her eggs were in the
90 melon garden. But the foolish Darzee refused to help Rikki
get rid of the cobra's eggs. Darzee didn't think it was fair to
destroy eggs.

Darzee's wife had more common sense. She didn't want
young cobras around. She helped Rikki by fluttering
around, pretending her wing was broken. Nagaina couldn't
resist such an easy target, so she chased the bird.

Meanwhile, Rikki-tikki found Nagaina's twenty-five
soft, white eggs, **cunningly** hidden near the melon patch
by the clever snake. He had crushed all but one when he
100 heard Darzee's wife screaming:

"Rikki-tikki, I led Nagaina toward the house. Now she
is going in! Hurry! She is going to kill!" Ⓕ

Holding the last egg in his mouth, Rikki-tikki hurried
to the porch.

IN OTHER WORDS The next morning, the birds help Rikki-tikki
find and smash the cobras' eggs. He smashes all but one. Then he
hears that Nagaina is entering the house to kill the family.

There, Teddy and his parents sat at the breakfast table.
They were as still as stones, hardly daring to breathe.
Nagaina was coiled up on the floor by Teddy's chair.

Rikki-tikki came up and cried, "Turn round and fight,
Nagaina!"

110 "I will fight you soon," she said, but she didn't turn away
from Teddy's bare leg.

Rikki-tikki's eyes were blood-red. "Look what I have
here," he said. "Your last egg. I have smashed all the others."

Nagaina spun around. Teddy's father grabbed Teddy and pulled him across the table to safety.

"Tricked! Rikk-tck-tck!" laughed Rikki-tikki. "Rikki-tikki-tck-tck! Now come and fight with me."

Nagaina looked at her egg. "Give me the egg, Rikki-tikki. I will go away and never come back," she said, 120 lowering her hood.

"Yes, you will go away—to the trash pile. Fight!" said Rikki-tikki.

They circled each other in a deadly dance. But Rikki had forgotten the egg. Nagaina quickly caught her last egg in her mouth and raced away with it. Rikki-tikki followed her and caught her tail in his sharp little teeth. Together they disappeared down a rat hole. **G**

IN OTHER WORDS Rikki-tikki stops Nagaina from biting Teddy's leg, but she escapes. She grabs her last egg back from Rikki-tikki, and he chases her into a rat hole.

Darzee, who was watching the battle, cried, "A mongoose has no chance against a snake down there. 130 Brave Rikki is dead!"

Suddenly, the grass moved again. There was Rikki-tikki. He dragged himself out of the hole.

"It is all over," Rikki said. "Nagaina is dead."

> **PAUSE & REFLECT**

Then he curled up right there and slept until late afternoon. When he woke up he asked that the coppersmith, a little bird whose job it was to shout out the news, announce to the garden what had happened.

G **SUSPENSE AND FORESHADOWING**
Reread lines 123–127. <u>Underline</u> the details that help build suspense.

> **PAUSE & REFLECT**

At this point in the story, how do you feel about Rikki-tikki? Is he brave or cruel? With a partner, discuss how his actions are different from the snakes' actions.

That night at the house, Rikki ate a feast. He was amused by all the fuss.

140   "Just think, he saved our lives and Teddy's life," said Teddy's mother.

"What are they worried about?" Rikki-tikki wondered. "The cobras are all dead. And if any more come, I'm here."

But Rikki-tikki was proud, and he had a right to be. From then on, he protected the yard. No cobra dared to enter it ever again. ❶

IN OTHER WORDS Rikki-tikki kills Nagaina in the rat hole. The family celebrates his victory. Rikki-tikki protects the yard from then on, and no cobra ever bothers the family again.

---

❶ **PREDICT**

Reflect on the predictions you made as you read. Did anything about the end of the story surprise you? What was it?

_____

_____

_____

_____

_____

_____

_____

_____

_____

Literary Analysis: Suspense and Foreshadowing

Sometimes writers use **foreshadowing,** hints or clues about events that will happen later. Review "Rikki-tikki-tavi," focusing on clues that foreshadow later events. Then fill in the chart below. In each box on the left, fill in an example of a foreshadowing clue from the story. In each box on the right, describe the event that clue foreshadowed.

READING 6 Draw conclusions about the elements of fiction. **6B** Analyze the development of plot.

Foreshadowing Clue	Events Foreshadowed
Clue 1:	
Clue 2:	
Clue 3:	

Think about how these examples of foreshadowing helped create suspense—keeping you involved in the story and anxious about what would happen next. Which example of foreshadowing created the most suspense? Why?

_____

_____

_____

What makes you BRAVE?

Choose two characters from the story and explain why you think they behaved bravely. What would you do if you were in their place?

_____

_____

_____

RC-7(B) Ask interpretive questions of text.

Reading Strategy: Predict

Review the predictions you made in notes A, E, and F as you read. Record your predictions in the chart below. Then confirm the outcome of your predictions. If they didn't come true, explain what actually happened in the story.

My Prediction	What Really Happened

Vocabulary Practice

Complete each sentence below with the correct vocabulary word.

revive   cunningly   singe   valiant   fledgling

1. Rikki-tikki is able to _____ after he rests from the long battle.

2. Nag ate another _____.

3. Rikki-tikki's eyes seemed red hot, as if they might _____ whomever he looked at.

4. Rikki-tikki's _____ effort saved Teddy's life.

5. Nagaina _____ hides the eggs from Rikki-tikki.

Academic Vocabulary in Speaking

The word identify (eye DEN tuh fy) is a verb that means *to point out or recognize something.*

It was easy for Juan to **identify** his locker because it was painted bright orange.

The word structure (STRUHK chuhr) is a noun that means *something made of parts put together* or *the way something is put together.*

The **structure** of the tent was so weak that it fell over in the first gust of wind.

TURN AND TALK With a partner, talk about how you can identify what's going to happen throughout "Rikki-tikki-tavi." How does the author reveal the story through its **structure**—its beginning, middle, and end? Be sure to use the words **identify** and **structure** in your discussion.

Texas Assessment Practice

DIRECTIONS Use "Rikki-tikki-tavi" to answer questions 1–4.

1 The story's action begins when —
- A Nag meets Rikki-tikki in the garden
- B Rikki-tikki steals Nagaina's last egg
- C the snakes sneak into the house
- D Darzee talks too much

2. Which words foreshadow Rikki-tikki's battle with the snakes?
- F *When Rikki was small, a flood swept him away from his home and family.*
- G *A mongoose was the perfect house pet.*
- H *Mongooses were snake killers.*
- J *In the yard he heard the sad voices of two birds.*

3. Which words does the author use to build suspense?
- A *Rikki's eyes grew very red.*
- B *Teddy ran down the path to pet Rikki-tikki.*
- C *Teddy's father beat the dead Karait.*
- D *I have already killed the snake.*

4. At the end of the story, you can tell that —
- F Darzee has learned to keep quiet.
- G Rikki-tikki will be killed by a snake.
- H Teddy and his family will be safe.
- J Nag will return to the garden.

Included in this unit: TEKS 6B, 6C, 10A, RC-7(B), RC-7(C), RC-7(D), RC-7(E)

UNIT 2

Personality Tests

ANALYZING CHARACTER AND POINT OF VIEW

Be sure to read the Reader's Workshop on pages 184–189 in *Holt McDougal Literature*.

Academic Vocabulary for Unit 2

You will see these Academic Vocabulary words as you work through this book. You will also be asked to use them as you write and talk about the selections in this unit.

Analyze (AN uh lyz) is a verb that means *to examine something by looking critically or closely at it*.
For his science project, Eli decided to **analyze** how CDs work.

Explain why it helps to **analyze** a problem before trying to solve it: __

_____

Aware (uh WAIR) is an adjective that means *realizing or knowing about*.
Keisha suddenly became **aware** that a storm was coming.

Describe a time when you should be **aware** of your surroundings: ___

_____

Develop (dih VEL uhp) is a verb that means *to grow in a way that seems natural*.
The new plant began to **develop** tiny flowers as it grew.

How do you **develop** your talent at a sport or hobby? _____

_____

React (ree AKT) is a verb that means *to act in response to someone or something*.
If the volcano starts to erupt, visitors will **react** by running away.

How do you **react** when someone does or says something nice? _____

_____

Respond (rih SPOND) is a verb that means *to answer or reply*.
Max tries to **respond** to every comment posted on his blog.

List ways you might **respond** to a party invitation: _____

_____

READING 6B Analyze the development of plot through the internal and external responses of the characters, including their motivation and conflicts.

Zebra
Short story by **Chaim Potok**

What has the power to HEAL?

Both physical and emotional wounds can cause damage. An argument with a friend can hurt as much as a broken leg. A physical injury can also wound the spirit. In "Zebra," you will read about a boy who needs to heal both his body and his mind.

LIST IT With a partner, create two lists. List three ways people deal with physical injuries. Then list three ways people deal with emotional pain.

Literary Analysis: Character and Plot

People who appear in stories are called **characters.** A story usually focuses on one or two **main characters** who change during the story. The chart below shows some ways writers bring their **characters** to life.

Words, Thoughts, and Actions	"Zebra stood near the tall fence, looking out at the street and listening to the noises behind him."
Physical Appearance	"Zebra noticed that the left sleeve of his jacket was empty."
How Other Characters React	"'You always tell such sad stories,' Andrea said."

Plot—the series of events in a story—affects how the characters change. The actions a character takes also affect the plot.

Dealing with physical injuries

1. Go to the doctor

2. _____

3. _____

Dealing with emotional pain

1. Talk to a friend

2. _____

3. _____

Reading Strategy: Monitor

To be sure you understand what you are reading, it helps to check, or **monitor,** your reading. For example, you might make notes or record questions and answers, as in these examples:

RC-7(C) Reflect on understanding to monitor comprehension.

Note
Zebra isn't playing with his friends.

Question
What really happened to Zebra?

Vocabulary in Context

Note: Words are listed in the order in which they appear in the story.

Gaunt (gawnt) is an adjective that means *thin and bony*.
  The man's **gaunt** face was so thin that his cheekbones stood out.

Wince (wins) is a verb that means *to pull back, as in pain*.
  The doctor touching his hand made Zebra **wince** in pain.

Grimace (GRIM is) is a verb that means *to twist one's face to show pain or disgust*.
  Zebra didn't like his first drawing; his failure made him **grimace** with disappointment.

Vocabulary Practice

Review the words and sample sentences above. Then answer the questions below by using the boldfaced blue vocabulary words.

1. Why might someone **wince** and **grimace** at the same time?

_____

2. What can you guess about the life of someone who appears **gaunt**?

_____

SET A PURPOSE
FOR READING
Read "Zebra" to discover
some different ways
people heal.

Zebra

Short story by
CHAIM POTOK

BACKGROUND One of the characters in this story flew helicopters in the Vietnam War. About 58,000 Americans died in that war, and more than 300,000 were wounded. The Vietnam Veterans Memorial in Washington, D.C., is a black granite wall carved with the names of those who died in the war.

He couldn't remember when he began to be called by that name. Perhaps they started to call him Zebra when he first began running. Or maybe he began running when they started to call him Zebra.

He loved the name and he loved to run.

When he was very young, his parents took him to a zoo, where he saw zebras for the first time. They were odd-looking creatures, like stubby horses, short-legged, thick-necked, with dark and white stripes.

10 Then one day he went with his parents to a movie about Africa, and he saw zebras, hundreds of them, thundering across a grassy plain, dust rising in boiling brown clouds.

Was he already running before he saw that movie, or did he begin to run afterward? No one seemed able to remember.

He would go running through the neighborhood for the sheer joy of feeling the wind on his face. People said that when he ran he arched his head up and back, and his face kind of flattened out. One of his teachers told him it was clever to run that way, his balance was better. But the truth 20 was he ran that way, his head thrown back, because he loved to feel the wind rushing across his neck.

Each time, after only a few minutes of running, his legs would begin to feel wondrously light. He would run past the school and the homes on the street beyond the church. All the neighbors knew him and would wave and call out, "Go, Zebra!" And sometimes one or two of their dogs would run with him awhile, barking.

He would imagine himself a zebra on the African plain. Running.

30 There was a hill on Franklin Avenue, a steep hill. By the time he reached that hill, he would feel his legs so light it was as if he had no legs at all and was flying. He would begin to descend the hill, certain as he ran that he needed only to give himself the slightest push and off he would go, and instead of a zebra he would become the bird he had once seen in a movie about Alaska, he would swiftly change into an eagle, soaring higher and higher, as light as the gentlest breeze, the cool wind caressing his arms and legs and neck. Ⓐ

IN OTHER WORDS The main character is a boy called Zebra who loves to run. He often runs through his neighborhood and down a steep hill on Franklin Avenue.

40 Then, a year ago, racing down Franklin Avenue, he had given himself that push and had begun to turn into an eagle, when a huge rushing shadow appeared in his line

Ⓐ **CHARACTER AND PLOT**
How does Zebra feel about running? Reread lines 22–39. Underline three sentences that show how Zebra feels when he runs.

B LANGUAGE COACH

In line 45 the word "never" appears in *italics*. Italics are often used to add emphasis to words in a story. Watch for italics used in other places in the story.

of vision and crashed into him and plunged him into a darkness from which he emerged very, very slowly. . . .

"Never, never, *never* run down that hill so fast that you can't stop at the corner," his mother had warned him again and again. **B**

His schoolmates and friends kept calling him Zebra even after they all knew that the doctors had told him he
50 would never be able to run like that again.

His leg would heal in time, the doctors said, and perhaps in a year or so the brace would come off. But they were not at all certain about his hand. From time to time his injured hand, which he still wore in a sling, would begin to hurt. The doctors said they could find no cause for the pain.

IN OTHER WORDS Zebra is hurt in an accident as he is running on Franklin Avenue. His injuries have not yet healed.

▶ What caused Zebra's accident? Discuss your answer with a partner.

One morning, during Mr. Morgan's geography class, Zebra's hand began to hurt badly. He sat staring out the window at the sky. Mr. Morgan, a stiff-mannered person in
60 his early fifties, given to smart suits and dapper bow ties, called on him to respond to a question. Zebra stumbled about in vain for the answer. Mr. Morgan told him to pay attention to the geography inside the classroom and not to the geography outside.

"In this class, young man, you will concentrate your attention upon the earth, not upon the sky," Mr. Morgan said.

Later, in the schoolyard during the midmorning recess, Zebra stood near the tall fence, looking out at the street and listening to the noises behind him.

His schoolmates were racing about, playing exuberantly,[1] shouting and laughing with full voices. Their joyous sounds went ringing through the quiet street.

Most times Zebra would stand alongside the basketball court or behind the wire screen at home plate and watch the games. That day, because his hand hurt so badly, he stood alone behind the chain-link fence of the schoolyard.

That's how he happened to see the man. And that's how the man happened to see him. **PAUSE & REFLECT**

One minute the side street on which the school stood was strangely empty, without people or traffic, without even any of the dogs that often roamed about the neighborhood—vacant and silent, as if it were already in the full heat of summer. The red-brick ranch house that belonged to Mr. Morgan, and the white clapboard two-story house in which Mrs. English lived, and the other homes on the street, with their columned front porches and their back patios, and the tall oaks—all stood curiously still in the warm golden light of the mid-morning sun.

Then a man emerged from wide and busy Franklin Avenue at the far end of the street.

Zebra saw the man stop at the corner and stand looking at a public trash can. He watched as the man poked his hand into the can and fished about but seemed to find nothing he wanted. He withdrew the hand and, raising it to shield his eyes from the sunlight, glanced at the street sign on the lamppost.

He started to walk up the street in the direction of the school.

PAUSE & REFLECT

Reread lines 68–80. Then, think about the description of Zebra at the very beginning of the story. How has Zebra changed because of his accident? Discuss your answer with a partner.

---

1. **exuberantly** (ig ZOO buhr uhnt lee): in a manner showing great joy.

IN OTHER WORDS Zebra's hand hurts him so much that he is unable to focus his attention during class. At recess, Zebra doesn't play with the other students. Instead, he watches from the sidelines.

► With a partner, discuss what Zebra sees on Franklin Avenue one day.

VOCABULARY

The word **gaunt** (gawnt) is an adjective that means *thin and bony.*

He was tall and wiry, and looked to be about forty years old. In his right hand he carried a bulging brown plastic bag. He wore a khaki army jacket, a blue denim shirt, blue jeans, and brown cowboy boots. His **gaunt** face and muscular neck were reddened by exposure to the sun. Long brown hair spilled out below his dark-blue farmer's cap. On the front of the cap, in large orange letters, were the words LAND ROVER.[2]

He walked with his eyes on the sidewalk and the curb,
110 as if looking for something, and he went right past Zebra without noticing him.

Zebra's hand hurt very much. He was about to turn away when he saw the man stop and look around and peer up at the red-brick wall of the school. The man set down the bag and took off his cap and stuffed it into a pocket of his jacket. From one of his jeans pockets he removed a handkerchief, with which he then wiped his face. He shoved the handkerchief back into the pocket and put the cap back on his head.

120 Then he turned and saw Zebra.

He picked up the bag and started down the street to where Zebra was standing. When the man was about ten feet away, Zebra noticed that the left sleeve of his jacket was empty. **C**

The man came up to Zebra and said in a low, friendly, shy voice, "Hello."

C MONITOR

Reread lines 109–123. What questions do you have about the man? Write two questions.

My Questions
1.
2.

---

2. **Land Rover:** British automaker known for producing four-wheel-drive vehicles that can travel on rough roads.

Zebra answered with a cautious "Hello," trying not to look at the empty sleeve, which had been tucked into the man's jacket pocket.

The man asked, with a distinct Southern accent,
130 "What's your name, son?"

Zebra said, "Adam."

"What kind of school is this here school, Adam?"

"It's a good school," Zebra answered.

"How long before you-all begin your summer vacation?"

"Three days," Zebra said.

"Anything special happen here during the summer?"

"During the summer? Nothing goes on here. There are no classes."

"What do you-all do during the summer?"

140 "Some of us go to camp. Some of us hang around. We find things to do."

Zebra's hand had begun to tingle and throb. Why was the man asking all those questions? Zebra thought maybe he shouldn't be talking to him at all. He seemed vaguely menacing in that army jacket, the dark-blue cap with the words LAND ROVER on it in orange letters, and the empty sleeve. Yet there was kindness in his gray eyes and ruddy features.

The man gazed past Zebra at the students playing in
150 the yard. "Adam, do you think your school would be interested in having someone teach an art class during the summer?"

That took Zebra by surprise. "An *art* class?"

"Drawing, sculpting, things like that."

Zebra was trying *very hard* not to look at the man's empty sleeve. "I don't know. . . ."

IN OTHER WORDS Zebra meets a man who has lost an arm. The man asks Zebra if he thinks the school might want a summer art class.

VOCABULARY

The word **wince** (wins) is a verb that means *to pull back, as in pain.*

ⓓ CHARACTER AND PLOT

Reread lines 142–169. What are some things you know or can guess about the man at this point in the story? Write some ideas on the lines below.

He has kind eyes.

_____

_____

_____

ⓔ CHARACTER AND PLOT

Motivation is the reason for a character's actions. Reread lines 173–183. What is Zebra's **motivation** for helping John Wilson?

_____

_____

_____

"Where's the school office, Adam?"

"On Washington Avenue. Go to the end of the street and turn right."

160   "Thanks," the man said. He hesitated a moment. Then he asked, in a quiet voice, "What happened to you, Adam?"

"A car hit me," Zebra said. "It was my fault."

The man seemed to **wince**.

For a flash of a second, Zebra thought to ask the man what had happened to *him*. The words were on his tongue. But he kept himself from saying anything.

The man started back up the street, carrying the brown plastic bag. ⓓ

170   Zebra suddenly called, "Hey, mister."

The man stopped and turned. "My name is John Wilson," he said softly.

"Mr. Wilson, when you go into the school office, you'll see signs on two doors. One says 'Dr. Winter,' and the other says 'Mrs. English.' Ask for Mrs. English."

Dr. Winter, the principal, was a disciplinarian[3] and a grump. Mrs. English, the assistant principal, was generous and kind. Dr. Winter would probably tell the man to call his secretary for an appointment. Mrs. English might invite

180 him into her office and offer him a cup of coffee and listen to what he had to say.

The man hesitated, looking at Zebra.

"Appreciate the advice," he said. ⓔ

Zebra watched him walk to the corner.

Under the lamppost was a trash can. Zebra saw the man set down the plastic bag and stick his hand into the can and haul out a battered umbrella.

The man tried to open the umbrella, but its metal ribs were broken. The black fabric dangled flat and limp from

190 the pole. He put the umbrella into the plastic bag and headed for the entrance to the school.

_____

3. **disciplinarian** (dis uh pluh NAYR ee uhn): someone who enforces strict rules.

A moment later, Zebra heard the whistle that signaled the end of recess. He followed his classmates at a distance, careful to avoid anyone's bumping against his hand.

IN OTHER WORDS Zebra learns that the man's name is John Wilson. Wilson asks Zebra what happened to him. Zebra tells him that a car hit him. Zebra wonders what happened to John Wilson's arm.

He sat through his algebra class, copying the problems on the blackboard while holding down his notebook with his left elbow. The sling chafed[4] his neck and felt warm and clumsy on his bare arm. There were sharp pains now in the two curled fingers of his hand.

200   Right after the class he went downstairs to the office of Mrs. Walsh, a cheerful, gray-haired woman in a white nurse's uniform.

She said, "I'm sorry I can't do very much for you, Adam, except give you two Tylenols."

He swallowed the Tylenols down with water.

On his way back up to the second floor, he saw the man with the dark-blue cap emerge from the school office with Mrs. English. He stopped on the stairs and watched as the man and Mrs. English stood talking

210 together. Mrs. English nodded and smiled and shook the man's hand.

The man walked down the corridor, carrying the plastic bag, and left the school building.

Zebra went slowly to his next class.

The class was taught by Mrs. English, who came hurrying into the room some minutes after the bell had rung.

"I apologize for being late," she said, sounding a little out of breath. "There was an important matter I had to

220 attend to."

---

4. **chafed** (chayfd): irritated by rubbing.

Mrs. English was a tall, gracious woman in her forties. It was common knowledge that early in her life she had been a journalist on a Chicago newspaper and had written short stories, which she could not get published. Soon after her marriage to a doctor, she had become a teacher.

This was the only class Mrs. English taught.

Ten students from the upper school—seventh and eighth grades—were chosen every year for this class. They met for an hour three times a week and told one another
230 stories. Each story would be discussed and analyzed by Mrs. English and the class.

Mrs. English called it a class in the *imagination*.

PAUSE & REFLECT

PAUSE & REFLECT

Imagination, line 232, means "the ability to create new things by thinking." With a partner, discuss what you think you might learn in a class like this one.

Zebra was grateful he did not have to take notes in this class. He had only to listen to the stories.

That day, Andrea, the freckle-faced, redheaded girl with very thick glasses who sat next to Zebra, told about a woman scientist who discovered a method of healing trees that had been blasted apart by lightning.

Mark, who had something wrong with his upper lip,
240 told in his quavery[5] voice about a selfish space cadet who stepped into a time machine and met his future self, who turned out to be a hateful person, and how the cadet then returned to the present and changed himself.

Kevin talked in blurred, high-pitched tones and often related parts of his stories with his hands. Mrs. English would quietly repeat many of his sentences. Today he told about an explorer who set out on a journey through a valley filled with yellow stones and surrounded by red mountains, where he encountered an army of green
250 shadows that had been at war for hundreds of years with an army of purple shadows. The explorer showed them how to make peace.

---

5. **quavery** (KWAY vuhr ee): quivering or trembling.

When it was Zebra's turn, he told a story about a bird that one day crashed against a closed windowpane and broke a wing. A boy tried to heal the wing but couldn't. The bird died, and the boy buried it under a tree on his lawn.

When he had finished, there was silence. Everyone in the class was looking at him.

260   "You always tell such sad stories," Andrea said.

The bell rang. Mrs. English dismissed the class.

In the hallway, Andrea said to Zebra, "You know, you are a very gloomy life form." **F**

"Andrea, get off my case," Zebra said.

IN OTHER WORDS Zebra is in a class where students tell each other stories. Zebra tells a sad story about an injured bird that dies because its broken wing won't heal. Andrea, a classmate, tells Zebra that he is a gloomy person.

► With a partner, discuss Zebra's story and what it tells you about him.

He went out to the schoolyard for the midafternoon recess. On the other side of the chain-link fence was the man in the dark-blue cap.

Zebra went over to him.

"Hello again, Adam," the man said. "I've been waiting
270 for you."

"Hello," said Zebra.

"Thanks much for suggesting I talk to Mrs. English."

"You're welcome."

"Adam, you at all interested in art?"

"No."

"You ever try your hand at it?"

"I've made drawings for class. I don't like it."

"Well, just in case you change your mind, I'm giving an art class in your school during the summer."

F CHARACTER AND PLOT
Reread lines 260–263. Draw arrows ⟶ pointing to Andrea's comments about Zebra. What do these comments tell you about Zebra?

_____

_____

_____

_____

_____

280   "I'm going to camp in August," Zebra said.

"There's the big long month of July."

"I don't think so," Zebra said.

"Well, okay, suit yourself. I'd like to give you something, a little thank-you gift."

He reached into an inside pocket and drew out a small pad and a pen. He placed the pad against the fence.

"Adam, you want to help me out a little bit here? Put your fingers through the fence and grab hold of the pad."

Extending the fingers of his right hand, Zebra held the
290 pad to the fence and watched as the man began to work with the pen. He felt the pad move slightly.

"I need you to hold it real still," the man said.

IN OTHER WORDS At recess, Zebra sees John Wilson again. The man tells Zebra that he is giving a summer art class at school, but Zebra says he isn't interested. Then, Wilson asks Zebra to hold a pad while he draws on it.

He was standing bent over, very close to Zebra. The words LAND ROVER on his cap shone in the afternoon sunlight. As he worked, he glanced often at Zebra. His tongue kept pushing up against the insides of his cheeks, making tiny hills rise and fall on his face. Wrinkles formed intricate[6] spidery webs in the skin below his gray eyes.
On his smooth forehead, in the blue and purple shadows
300 beneath the peak of his cap, lay glistening beads of sweat. And his hand—how dirty it was, the fingers and palm smudged with black ink and encrusted with colors.

Then Zebra glanced down and noticed the plastic bag near the man's feet. It lay partly open. Zebra was able to see a large pink armless doll, a dull metallic object that looked like a dented frying pan, old newspapers, strings of cord, crumpled pieces of red and blue cloth, and the broken umbrella. **G**

G MONITOR

What are your own questions at this point? Write down two questions.

My Questions
1.
2.

---

6. **intricate** (IN trih kit): arranged in a complex way; elaborate.

"One more minute is all I need," the man said.

310   He stepped back, looked at the pad, and nodded slowly. He put the pen back into his pocket and tore the top page from the pad. He rolled up the page and pushed it through the fence. Then he took the pad from Zebra.

"See you around, Adam," the man said, picking up the plastic bag.

Zebra unrolled the sheet of paper and saw a line drawing, a perfect image of his face.

He was looking at himself as if in a mirror. His long straight nose and thin lips and sad eyes and gaunt face;
320 his dark hair and smallish ears and the scar on his forehead where he had hurt himself years before while roller skating.

In the lower right-hand corner of the page the man had written: "To Adam, with thanks. John Wilson."

Zebra raised his eyes from the drawing. The man was walking away.

Zebra called out, "Mr. Wilson, all my friends call me Zebra."

The man turned, looking surprised.

330   "From my last name," Adam said. "Zebrin. Adam Martin Zebrin. They call me Zebra."

"Is that right?" the man said, starting back toward the fence. "Well, in that case you want to give me back that piece of paper."

He took the pad and pen from his pocket, placed the page on the pad, and, with Zebra holding the pad to the fence, did something to the page and then handed it back. **PAUSE & REFLECT**

"You take real good care of yourself, Zebra," the man said.
340   He went off toward Franklin Avenue.

PAUSE & REFLECT

Based on lines 327–338, what do you think John Wilson added to the drawing? Discuss your answer with a partner.

ⓗ CHARACTER AND PLOT
Reread lines 341–346. In
addition to wanting to give
a thank-you gift, what might
be Mr. Wilson's **motivation**
for giving Zebra the picture?

_____

_____

_____

_____

Zebra looked at the drawing. The man had crossed out
Adam and over it had drawn an animal with a stubby neck
and short legs and a striped body.

A zebra!

Its legs were in full gallop. It seemed as if it would gallop
right off the page. ⓗ

A strong breeze rippled across the drawing, causing it to
flutter like a flag in Zebra's hand. He looked out at the street.

350 The man was walking slowly in the shadows of the
tall oaks. Zebra had the odd sensation that all the houses
on the street had turned toward the man and were
watching him as he walked along. How strange that
was: the windows and porches and columns and front
doors following intently the slow walk of that tall, one-
armed man—until he turned into Franklin Avenue and
was gone.

IN OTHER WORDS As a thank-you gift, the man draws a picture
of Zebra's face. After Zebra tells him his nickname, Wilson adds a
drawing of a zebra.

The whistle blew, and Zebra went inside. Seated at
his desk, he slipped the drawing carefully into one of his
notebooks.

360 From time to time he glanced at it.

Just before the bell signaled the end of the school day,
he looked at it again.

Now *that* was strange!

He thought he remembered that the zebra had been
drawn directly over his name: the head over the A and the
tail over the M. Didn't it seem now to have moved a little
beyond the A?

Probably he was running a fever again. He would run mysterious fevers off and on for about three weeks after 370 each operation on his hand. Fevers sometimes did that to him: excited his imagination.

He lived four blocks from the school. The school bus dropped him off at his corner. In his schoolbag he carried his books and the notebook with the drawing.

His mother offered him a snack, but he said he wasn't hungry. Up in his room, he looked again at the drawing and was astonished to discover that the zebra had reached the edge of his name and appeared poised to leap off.

380 It *had* to be a fever that was causing him to see the zebra that way. And sure enough, when his mother took his temperature, the thermometer registered 102.6 degrees.

She gave him his medicine, but it didn't seem to have much effect, because when he woke at night and switched on his desk light and peered at the drawing, he saw the little zebra galloping across the page, along the contours[7] of his face, over the hills and valleys of his eyes and nose and mouth, and he heard the tiny clickings of its hooves as 390 cloudlets of dust rose in its wake.

He knew he was asleep. He knew it was the fever working upon his imagination.

But it was so real.

The little zebra running . . .

When he woke in the morning the fever was gone, and the zebra was quietly in its place over ADAM.

---

7. **contours** (KON turs): the outlines of figures or objects.

Later, as he entered the school, he noticed a large sign on the bulletin board in the hallway:

SUMMER ART CLASS

The well-known American artist Mr. John Wilson
will conduct an art class during the summer
for students in 7th and 8th grades.

For details, speak to Mrs. English.
There will be no tuition fee for this class.

During the morning, between classes, Zebra ran into
400 Mrs. English in the second-floor hallway.

"Mrs. English, about the summer art class . . . is it okay to ask where—um—where Mr. Wilson is from?"

"He is from a small town in Virginia. Are you thinking of signing up for his class?"

"I can't draw," Zebra said.

"Drawing is something you can learn."

"Mrs. English, is it okay to ask how did Mr. Wilson—um—get hurt?" ❶

The school corridors were always crowded between
410 classes. Zebra and Mrs. English formed a little island in the bustling, student-jammed hallway.

"Mr. Wilson was wounded in the war in Vietnam," Mrs. English said. "I would urge you to join his class. You will get to use your imagination."

IN OTHER WORDS Zebra becomes sick and imagines the zebra drawn by John Wilson running off the page. The next day he asks Mrs. English questions about John Wilson. He learns that Wilson was injured during the Vietnam War.

---

❶ **LANGUAGE COACH**
In lines 402 and 408, Zebra's words include the spoken pause –*um*–. Writers use spoken pauses such as *er*, *uh*, and *um* to show that the character is shy or cautious about speaking. Why might Zebra be shy about asking his teacher these questions?

_____

_____

_____

For the next hour, Zebra sat impatiently through Mr. Morgan's geography class, and afterward he went up to the teacher.

"Mr. Morgan, could I—um—ask where is Vietnam?"

Mr. Morgan smoothed down the jacket of his beige
420 summer suit, touched his bow tie, rolled down a wall map, picked up his pointer, and cleared his throat.

"Vietnam is this long, narrow country in southeast Asia, bordered by China, Laos, and Cambodia.[8] It is a land of valleys in the north, coastal plains in the center, and marshes in the south. There are barren mountains and tropical rain forests. Its chief crops are rice, rubber, fruits, and vegetables. The population numbers close to seventy million people. Between 1962 and 1973, America fought a terrible war there to prevent the south from
430 falling into the hands of the communist north. We lost the war." **J**

"Thank you."

"I am impressed by your suddenly awakened interest in geography, young man, though I must remind you that your class is studying the Mediterranean," said Mr. Morgan.

During the afternoon recess, Zebra was watching a heated basketball game, when he looked across the yard and saw John Wilson walk by, carrying a laden plastic
440 bag. Some while later, he came back along the street, empty-handed.

Over supper that evening, Zebra told his parents he was thinking of taking a summer art class offered by the school.

His father said, "Well, I think that's a fine idea."

"Wait a minute. I'm not so sure," his mother said.

J CHARACTER AND PLOT
Reread lines 418–431. What might be **motivating** Zebra to find out more about Mr. Wilson?

_____

_____

_____

_____

_____

---

8. **Laos** (lows) . . . **Cambodia** (kam BOH dee uh): countries in southeast Asia.

"It'll get him off the streets," his father said. "He'll become a Matisse[9] instead of a lawyer like his dad. Right, Adam?"

450 "Just you be very careful," his mother said to Adam. "Don't do anything that might injure your hand."

"How can drawing hurt his left hand, for heaven's sake?" said his father.

That night, Zebra lay in bed looking at his hand. It was a dread and a mystery to him, his own hand. The fingers were all there, but like dead leaves that never fell, the ring and little fingers were rigid and curled, the others barely moved. The doctors said it would take time to bring them back to life. So many broken bones. So many torn muscles 460 and tendons. So many injured nerves. The dark shadow had sprung upon him so suddenly. How stupid, stupid, *stupid* he had been!

He couldn't sleep. He went over to his desk and looked at John Wilson's drawing. The galloping little zebra stood very still over ADAM.

IN OTHER WORDS Because of John Wilson, Zebra is interested in Vietnam and asks his geography teacher about that country. Later, Zebra tells his parents that he's thinking of taking an art class.

▶ In lines 454–465, circle the two things Zebra looks at. Then, with a partner, discuss what Zebra might be thinking as he looks at these two things.

Early the following afternoon, on the last day of school, Zebra went to Mrs. English's office and signed up for John Wilson's summer art class.

"The class will meet every weekday from ten in 470 the morning until one," said Mrs. English. "Starting Monday."

---

9. **Matisse** (muh TEES) (1869–1954): a French painter who was one of the best-known artists of the 20th century.

Zebra noticed the three plastic bags in a corner of the office.

"Mrs. English, is it okay to ask what Mr. Wilson—um—did in Vietnam?"

"He told me he was a helicopter pilot," Mrs. English said. "Oh, I neglected to mention that you are to bring an unlined notebook and a pencil to the class."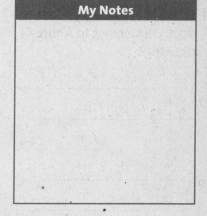

"That's all? A notebook and a pencil?"

480 Mrs. English smiled. "And your imagination."

When Zebra entered the art class the next Monday morning, he found about fifteen students there—including Andrea from his class with Mrs. English.

The walls of the room were bare. Everything had been removed for the summer. Zebra noticed two plastic bags on the floor beneath the blackboard.

He sat down at the desk next to Andrea's.

She wore blue jeans and a yellow summer blouse with blue stripes. Her long red hair was tied behind her head

490 with a dark-blue ribbon. She gazed at Zebra through her thick glasses, leaned over, and said, "Are you going to make gloomy drawings, too?"

Just then John Wilson walked in, carrying a plastic bag, which he put down on the floor next to the two others.

He stood alongside the front desk, wearing a light-blue long-sleeved shirt and jeans. The left shirtsleeve had been folded back and pinned to the shirt.

The dark-blue cap with the words LAND ROVER sat jauntily[10] on his head.

500 "Good morning to you-all," he said, with a shy smile. "Mighty glad you're here. We're going to do two things this summer. We're going to make paper into faces and garbage into people. I can see by your expressions that you don't know what I'm talking about, right? Well, I'm about to show you."

---

10. **jauntily** (JAWN tih lee): in a light and carefree way.

MONITOR

What ideas do you have about the cause of Mr. Wilson's injury? Reread lines 474–478 and make your notes below.

My Notes

VOCABULARY

The word **grimace** (GRIM is) is a verb that means *to twist one's face to show pain or disgust*.

Why does Andrea *grimace*? (Circle) the answer.

● CHARACTER AND PLOT

Reread lines 512–513. How does Zebra react to Andrea's drawing?

_____

_____

_____

_____

He asked everyone to draw the face of someone sitting nearby.

Zebra hesitated, looked around, then made a drawing of Andrea. Andrea carefully drew Zebra.

510   He showed Andrea his drawing.

"It's awful." She **grimaced**. "I look like a mouse."

Her drawing of him was good. But was his face really so sad? **●**

John Wilson went from desk to desk, peering intently at the drawings. He paused a long moment over Zebra's drawing. Then he spent more than an hour demonstrating with chalk on the blackboard how they should not be thinking *eyes* or *lips* or *hands* while drawing, but should think only *lines* and *curves* and *shapes*; how they should

520 be looking at where everything was situated in relation to the edge of the paper; and how they should not be looking *directly* at the edges of what they were drawing but at the space *outside* the edges.

Zebra stared in wonder at how fast John Wilson's hand raced across the blackboard, and at the empty sleeve rising and falling lightly against the shirt.

"You-all are going to learn how to *see* in a new way," John Wilson said.

They made another drawing of the same face.

530   "Now I look like a horse," Andrea said. "Are you going to add stripes?"

"You are one big pain, Andrea," Zebra said.

IN OTHER WORDS On the last day of school, Zebra signs up for the art class. During class, Mr. Wilson has the students draw people's faces. Zebra is unhappy with his drawings.

Shortly before noon, John Wilson laid out on his desk the contents of the plastic bags: a clutter of junked broken objects, including the doll and the umbrella.

Using strips of cloth, some lengths of string, crumpled newspaper, his pen, and his one hand, he swiftly transformed the battered doll into a red-nosed, umbrella-carrying clown, with baggy pants, a tattered coat, a derby hat, and a somber[11]
540 smile. Turning over the battered frying pan, he made it into a pedestal, on which he placed the clown.

"That's a sculpture," John Wilson said, with his shy smile. "Garbage into people."

The class burst into applause. The clown on the frying pan looked as if it might take a bow.

"You-all will be doing that, too, before we're done," John Wilson said. "Now I would like you to sign and date your drawings and give them to me."

When they returned the next morning the drawings
550 were on a wall.

Gradually, in the days that followed, the walls began to fill with drawings. Sculptures made by the students were looked at with care, discussed by John Wilson and the class, and then placed on shelves along the walls: a miniature bicycle made of wire; a parrot made of an old sofa cushion; a cowboy made of rope and string; a fat lady made of a dented metal pitcher; a zebra made of glued-together scraps of cardboard.

"I like your zebra," Andrea said.

560 "Thanks," Zebra said. "I like your parrot."

One morning John Wilson asked the class members to make a contour drawing of their right or left hand. Zebra felt himself sweating and trembling as he worked.

"That's real nice," John Wilson said, when he saw Andrea's drawing.

He gazed at the drawing made by Zebra.

"You-all were looking at your hand," he said. "You ought to have been looking at the edge of your hand and at the space outside."

---

11. **somber** (SOM buhr): serious; gloomy.

570   Zebra drew his hand again. Strange and ugly, the two fingers lay rigid and curled. But astonishingly, it looked like a hand this time.

IN OTHER WORDS John Wilson teaches the class how to see things in a new way. He places all the drawings and sculptures along the walls of the classroom.

▶ In lines 551–572, what kinds of art are the students in the class creating? Put check marks ✔ beside the words that tell you this.

    One day, a few minutes before the end of class, John Wilson gave everyone an assignment: draw or make something at home, something very special that each person *felt deeply* about. And bring it to class.

    Zebra remembered seeing a book titled *Incredible Cross-Sections* on a shelf in the family room at home. He found the book and took it into his room.

580   There was a color drawing of a rescue helicopter on one of the Contents pages. On pages 30 and 31, the helicopter was shown in pieces, its complicated insides displayed in detailed drawings. Rotor blades, control rods, electronics equipment, radar scanner, tail rotor, engine, lifeline, winch—all its many parts.

    Zebra sat at his desk, gazing intently at the space outside the edges of the helicopter on the Contents page.

    He made an outline drawing and brought it to class the next morning.

590   John Wilson looked at it. Was there a stiffening of his muscular neck, a sudden tensing of the hand that held the drawing?

    He took the drawing and tacked it to the wall.

The next day he gave them all the same home assignment: draw or make something they *felt very deeply* about.

That afternoon, Zebra went rummaging through the trash bin in his kitchen and the garbage cans that stood near the back door of his home. He found some sardine 600 cans, a broken **eggbeater**, pieces of cardboard, chipped buttons, bent bobby pins, and other odds and ends.

With the help of epoxy glue, he began to make of those bits of garbage a kind of helicopter. For support, he used his desktop, the floor, his knees, the elbow of his left arm, at one point even his chin. Struggling with the last piece—a button he wanted to position as a wheel—he realized that without thinking he had been using his left hand, and the two curled fingers had straightened slightly to his needs.

610 His heart beat thunderously. There had been so many hope-filled moments before, all of them ending in bitter disappointment. He would say nothing. Let the therapist or the doctors tell him. . . . **ⓜ**

The following morning, he brought the helicopter to the class.

"Eeewwww, what is *that*?" Andrea grimaced.

"Something to eat you with," Zebra said.

"Get human, Zebra. Mr. Wilson will have a laughing fit over that."

620 But John Wilson didn't laugh. He held the helicopter in his hand a long moment, turning it this way and that, nodded at Zebra, and placed it on a windowsill, where it shimmered in the summer sunlight. **ⓝ**

IN OTHER WORDS John Wilson asks the students to draw or make something that they feel deeply about. Zebra draws a helicopter, and the next day he makes a helicopter sculpture. Zebra notices that his hand seems to be getting better. Meanwhile, John Wilson seems to care about Zebra's art.

VISUAL VOCABULARY

An **eggbeater** (EG bee tuhr) is a kitchen tool used to beat eggs. It has a handle and metal blades that turn.

ⓜ CHARACTER AND PLOT
Reread lines 602–613. How is the art class affecting Zebra?

_____

_____

_____

_____

_____

ⓝ MONITOR
Reread lines 620–623. What questions do you have about Mr. Wilson's reaction to the helicopter? Write at least one question.

My Question

The next day, John Wilson informed everyone that three students would be leaving the class at the end of July. He asked each of those students to make a drawing for him that he would get to keep. Something to remember them by. All their other drawings and sculptures they could take home.

630   Zebra lay awake a long time that night, staring into the darkness of his room. He could think of nothing to draw for John Wilson.

In the morning, he sat gazing out the classroom window at the sky and at the helicopter on the sill.

"What are you going to draw for him?" Andrea asked.

Zebra shrugged and said he didn't know.

"Use your imagination," she said. Then she said, "Wait, what am I seeing here? Are you able to move those fingers?"

640   "I think so."

"You *think* so?"

"The doctors said there was some improvement."

Her eyes glistened behind the thick lenses. She seemed genuinely happy.

He sat looking out the window. Dark birds wheeled and soared. There was the sound of traffic. The helicopter sat on the windowsill, its eggbeater rotor blades ready to move to full throttle.

Later that day, Zebra sat at his desk at home, working

650 on a drawing. He held the large sheet of paper in place by pressing down on it with the palm and fingers of his left hand. He drew a landscape: hills and valleys, forests and flatlands, rivers and plateaus. Oddly, it all seemed to resemble a face.

Racing together over that landscape were a helicopter and a zebra.

It was all he could think to draw. It was not a very good drawing. He signed it: "To John Wilson, with thanks. Zebra." ◎

660   The next morning, John Wilson looked at the drawing and asked Zebra to write on top of the name "John Wilson" the name "Leon."

"He was an old buddy of mine, an artist. We were in Vietnam together. Would've been a much better artist than I'll ever be."

Zebra wrote in the new name.

"Thank you kindly," John Wilson said, taking the drawing. "Zebra, you have yourself a good time in camp and a good life. It was real nice knowing you."

670   He shook Zebra's hand. How strong his fingers felt!

"I think I'm going to miss you a little," Andrea said to Zebra after the class.

"I'll only be away a month."

"Can I help you carry some of those drawings?"

"Sure. I'll carry the helicopter." ℗

IN OTHER WORDS John Wilson asks Zebra to make a drawing for him. Zebra draws a helicopter and a zebra flying over a landscape of hills, valleys, forests, and rivers. Zebra signs the drawing "To John Wilson," but John Wilson asks Zebra to add the name "Leon." He tells Zebra that Leon was an artist friend that he knew in Vietnam.

    Zebra went off to a camp in the Adirondack Mountains.[12] He hiked and read and watched others playing ball. In the arts and crafts program he made some good drawings and even got to learn a little bit about 680 watercolors. He put together clowns and airplanes and helicopters out of discarded cardboard and wood and clothing. From time to time his hand hurt, but the fingers seemed slowly to be coming back to life.

12. **Adirondack** (ad uh RON dak) **Mountains:** mountains covering a large area of northeast New York State.

◎ **CHARACTER AND PLOT**
Reread lines 657–659. Why does Zebra thank Mr. Wilson?

_____

_____

_____

_____

_____

℗ **CHARACTER AND PLOT**
Reread lines 671–675. How have Andrea's feelings about Zebra changed since the art class started?

_____

_____

_____

_____

_____

"Patience, young man," the doctors told him when he returned to the city. "You're getting there."

One or two additional operations were still necessary. But there was no urgency. And he no longer needed the leg brace. PAUSE & REFLECT

690 On the first day of school, one of the secretaries found him in the hallway and told him to report to Mrs. English.

"Did you have a good summer?" Mrs. English asked.

"It was okay," Zebra said.

"This came for you in the mail."

She handed him a large brown envelope. It was addressed to Adam Zebrin, Eighth Grade, at the school. The sender was John Wilson, with a return address in Virginia.

"Adam, I admit I'm very curious to see what's inside," Mrs. English said.

700 She helped Zebra open the envelope.

Between two pieces of cardboard were a letter and a large color photograph.

The photograph showed John Wilson down on his right knee before a glistening dark wall. He wore his army jacket and blue jeans and boots, and the cap with the words LAND ROVER. Leaning against the wall to his right was Zebra's drawing of the helicopter and the zebra racing together across a facelike landscape. The drawing was enclosed in a narrow frame.

710 The wall behind John Wilson seemed to glitter with a strange black light. **Q**

IN OTHER WORDS While at summer camp, Zebra notices his hand is getting better. When he returns to school, he receives a letter and a photograph from John Wilson.

Zebra read the letter and showed it to Mrs. English.

Dear Zebra,

    *One of the people whose names are on this wall
was among my very closest friends. He was an artist
named Leon Kellner. Each year I visit him and leave a
gift—something very special that someone creates and
gives me. I leave it near his name for a few hours, and
then I take it to my studio in Virginia, where I keep*
720   *a collection of those gifts. All year long I work in my
studio, but come summer I go looking for another gift to
give him.*
    Thank you for your gift.

                           Your friend,
                           John Wilson
  P.S. I hope your hand is healing.

Mrs. English stood staring awhile at the letter. She
turned away and touched her eyes. Then she went to a shelf
on the wall behind her, took down a large book, leafed
730 through it quickly, found what she was searching for, and
held it out for Zebra to see.
    Zebra found himself looking at the glistening black wall
of the Vietnam Memorial in Washington, D.C. And at the
names on it, the thousands of names. . . . **PAUSE & REFLECT**

Later, in the schoolyard during recess, Zebra stood alone
at the chain-link fence and gazed down the street toward

PAUSE & REFLECT
Reread lines 713–734. Why
did John Wilson take Zebra's
drawing to the Vietnam
Veterans Memorial? Discuss
with a partner.

Franklin Avenue. He thought how strange it was that all the houses on this street had seemed to turn toward John Wilson that day, the windows and porches and columns and doors, as if saluting him.

740 Had that been only his imagination?

Maybe, Zebra thought, just maybe he could go for a walk to Franklin Avenue on Saturday or Sunday. He had not walked along Franklin Avenue since the accident; had not gone down that steep hill. Yes, he would walk carefully down that hill to the corner and walk back up and past the school and then the four blocks home. **®**

Andrea came over to him.

"We didn't get picked for the story class with Mrs. English," she said. "I won't have to listen to any

750 more of your gloomy stories."

Zebra said nothing.

"You know, I think I'll walk home today instead of taking the school bus," Andrea said.

"Actually, I think I'll walk, too," Zebra said. "I was thinking maybe I could pick up some really neat stuff in the street."

"You are becoming a pleasant life form," Andrea said.

® CHARACTER AND PLOT
Reread lines 742–747. Why is it important for Zebra to walk down the steep hill again?

_____

_____

_____

_____

_____

_____

_____

_____

_____

IN OTHER WORDS In his letter, John Wilson tells Zebra that he brings a gift to the wall for his friend Leon every year. He thanks Zebra for the gift and says he hopes Zebra's hand is healing. Zebra decides he will walk down the hill where he had his accident. Zebra and Andrea walk home together.

▶ Why does Zebra want to pick up some "neat stuff" as he walks home? Discuss your answer with a classmate.

Literary Analysis: Character and Plot

How does Zebra change from the beginning of the story's plot to the end? Complete the chart below with information from the story to show how Zebra and other characters change. Consider changes in their personalities, interests, and attitudes.

READING 6B Analyze the development of plot through the internal and external responses of the characters, including their motivation and conflicts.

Character	Beginning of Story	End of Story
Zebra		
Mr. Wilson		
Andrea		

Why does Zebra change? Briefly explain the reasons for physical and emotional changes that happen over the course of the story's plot.

_____

_____

_____

_____

_____

_____

_____

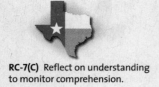

RC-7(C) Reflect on understanding to monitor comprehension.

Reading Strategy: Monitor

Look back at the questions you wrote as you read "Zebra." Rewrite two of your questions below, and then write an answer for each question.

Question 1	My question:
	My answer:
Question 2	My question:
	My answer:

How does asking and answering questions like these help you understand the story?

_____

_____

What has the power to HEAL?

Review the two lists you made on page 46. After reading this story, can you think of other ways in which people can heal? Explain.

_____

_____

_____

Vocabulary Practice

Circle the part of each sentence that answers the question.

1. Is someone who is **gaunt** fat or thin?

2. When you **grimace,** do you frown or smile?

3. Is a **wince** a show of pleasure or pain?

Academic Vocabulary in Speaking

The word **develop** (dih VEL uhp) is a verb that means *to grow in a way that seems natural.*

.The mother watched her child **develop** into a happy, healthy teenager.

TURN AND TALK With a partner, talk about how the relationship between Zebra and Mr. Wilson **develops** in the story. How does it grow and change? Be sure to use the word **develop** in your discussion.

READING 6B Analyze the development of plot through the internal and external responses of the characters, including their motivation and conflicts.

Texas Assessment Practice

DIRECTIONS Use "Zebra" to answer questions 1–6.

1 In lines 132–159, a stranger asks Zebra some questions about his school. What does he want to know?

- **A** When the school day starts
- **B** What sports teams the school has
- **C** Whether students might like an art class
- **D** How many students are in the school

2 How are Zebra's emotions revealed in lines 258–260?

- **F** Through Zebra's actions
- **G** Through a physical description of Zebra
- **H** Through Zebra's words
- **J** Through other characters' reactions to Zebra

3 A characteristic of Zebra's that affects the plot is his —

- **A** joyfulness
- **B** thoughtlessness
- **C** sadness
- **D** selfishness

4 After he comes home from summer camp, what does Zebra learn from his doctors?

- **F** He needs four or five additional operations.
- **G** His hand will never improve.
- **H** He no longer needs a leg brace.
- **J** He can start running immediately.

5 Which character trait do Zebra and John Wilson have in common?

- **A** Nervousness
- **B** Dependability
- **C** Carelessness
- **D** Hopefulness

6 Andrea states directly how she feels about Zebra when she says —

- **F** "Eeewwww, what is *that*?"
- **G** "Mr. Wilson will have a laughing fit over that."
- **H** "I like your zebra."
- **J** "You are becoming a pleasant life form."

The Legacy of the Vietnam War

- Book Excerpt, page 79
- Letter, page 82
- Timeline, page 85

READING 10A Evaluate a summary of the original text for accuracy of main ideas. **RC-7(E)** Summarize texts in ways that maintain meaning and logical order.

Background

To stop the spread of communism (KOM yuh niz uhm), U.S. troops fought in Vietnam from 1965 until 1973. Over 58,000 U.S. men and women lost their lives in the Vietnam War. The Vietnam Veterans Memorial is in Washington, D.C. It is made up of two black granite walls that form a "V" shape. Each wall contains the names of the men and women who were killed during the Vietnam War. Many people visit the memorial each year to remember those who died.

Skill Focus: Summarize

All good informational writing has a main idea. A **main idea** is the most important thing the writer wants you to know. **Supporting details** are facts and examples that help you understand the main idea. Once you find the main idea and supporting details, you can write a summary of a selection. A **summary** briefly retells the main idea and supporting details in your own words. Follow these steps to write a good summary.

- Break down each text into parts, such as paragraphs or sections.

- Record the main idea and supporting details in each part. Think about the text's overall meaning—the writer's message.

- For the summary, write a sentence that explains the overall meaning of the text. Then provide the most important details in additional sentences.

As you read these texts, notes in the side column will ask you to reread main ideas and supporting details. Use a chart like the one below to help you write a summary.

A Wall of Remembrance
Main Idea of Part 1: The items left at the Vietnam Veterans Memorial are unique.
Detail: There are a wide variety of items that are left to honor the dead.
Detail: People also leave personal notes and letters.

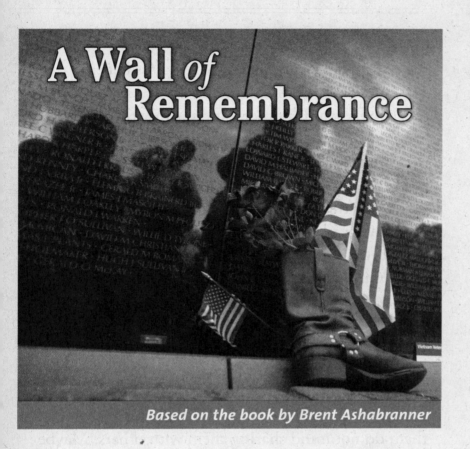

A Wall *of* Remembrance

Based on the book by Brent Ashabranner

**SET A PURPOSE
FOR READING**
Read the following
selection to learn about
the things people leave
at the Vietnam Veterans
Memorial.

Ⓕ OCUS ON FORM
This is based on an
excerpt, or part, of a
nonfiction book about
an important event in
history. The purpose
of a nonfiction book is
to provide interesting
information. Unlike a
news article, a nonfiction
book does not need to
focus on events that are
happening today.

The Vietnam Veterans Memorial is different from
other national memorials. Visitors leave more messages
and personal objects there than at any other memorial.
On special days people leave many things. On rainy
or snowy days visitors sometimes leave only a few.
But I have never been to the memorial when there
were none.

Some of the items puzzle me, and others touch
me deeply. They always make me think of the family
10 and friends who still love and miss those who died
in Vietnam. What is the meaning of the dollar bill

beneath panel 24E? An empty red glass beneath panel 14W? A can of sardines, a teddy bear, Tinker Toys, a soccer ball beneath other panels? Only the person who brought the item knows what it means. And only that person knows what it would have meant to a special name on the wall. **Ⓐ**

The written messages left at the memorial are different. It is easier to understand the feelings
20 behind them. I remember a card a woman left for her husband. His name was on the black granite wall. She left the card for what would have been their twenty-fifth wedding anniversary. It reminded me of how long ago the war ended. It also reminded me of how long important memories are a part of our lives.

I think it is all right to read the messages. They express grief and love, but I think the people who leave them do not mind sharing them with others. Maybe they want to share them. **Ⓑ**

IN OTHER WORDS The writer tells about the many items and messages left at the Vietnam Veterans Memorial. They remind him of the people who love those who died.

▶ Reread lines 8–25. What item causes the writer to remember how long it has been since the war ended? Underline the sentence that tells you.

30 More than 55,000 messages and items have been left at the wall since it was opened. That number does not include the thousands of flowers that have been left. Flowers and plants are not saved. But the

Ⓐ SUMMARIZE
Underline the phrase that states the main idea in lines 1–17. Circle two details that support this main idea.

Ⓑ SUMMARIZE
Reread lines 26–29. Then, in your own words, write the main idea of this paragraph and list the most important details.

_____

_____

_____

_____

_____

National Park Service gathers all other items at the end of each day and sends them to a **warehouse** called the Museum Resource Center. Every item is labeled with a code and is placed in a plastic bag.

David Guynes was the center's director at one time.
40 He told me: "There are so many questions, so many mysteries, in these items. So many stories are in them, so much feeling, emotion, pain. What can be learned about America and Americans from the things people have brought? Altogether, these materials make up a very important part of the story of the Vietnam War. This is the material of history."

Duery Felton is in charge of the National Vietnam Veterans Collection at the Museum Resource Center. He told me that the number of items and messages left on special days is going up. Park rangers once
50 collected 2,300 items during a three-day period around Memorial Day.

In a way, each of the things left at the memorial is different. The person who left it and the person whose name is on the wall had a relationship that was theirs alone. **C**

IN OTHER WORDS The National Park Service collects and stores each item left at the memorial. The number of items and messages left by visitors is growing. Still, each item is special in its own way to the person who left it.

VISUAL VOCABULARY

A **warehouse** (WAIR hows) is a large building used to store many things.

C SUMMARIZE

Reread lines 30–37. For this section, look at the main idea and the details that support it in the chart below. Now, find the main idea and supporting details for lines 38–45.

Main Idea, lines 30–37
The thousands of items left at the wall are carefully stored for safekeeping.

Details
All items (except for flowers) are sent to a warehouse.
These items are labeled, coded, and stored there.

↓

Main Idea, lines 38–45

Details

SET A PURPOSE
FOR READING
Read the following letter to learn more about one item that was left at the Vietnam Veterans Memorial.

❍ SUMMARIZE
Reread lines 2–7. With a partner, discuss the main idea of this paragraph.

A Mother's Words

By Mrs. Eleanor Wimbish

BACKGROUND Mrs. Eleanor Wimbish's son, William (Bill) R. Stocks, died in the Vietnam War. For years she left letters under Bill's name on the Vietnam Veterans Memorial.

Dear Bill,

Today is February 13, 1984. I came to this black wall again to see and touch your name, and as I do I wonder if anyone ever stops to realize that next to your name, on this black wall, is your mother's heart. A heart broken 15 years ago today, when you lost your life in Vietnam. ❍

And as I look at your name, William R. Stocks, I think of how many, many times I used to wonder

10 how scared and homesick you must have been in that strange country called Vietnam. And if and how it might have changed you, for you were the most happy-go-lucky kid in the world, hardly ever sad or unhappy. And until the day I die, I will see you as you laughed at me, even when I was very mad at you, and the next thing I knew, we were laughing together.

IN OTHER WORDS Mrs. Wimbish visits the Vietnam Veterans Memorial, where she sees and touches her son's name on the wall.

▶ What does Mrs. Wimbish say her son Bill was like? Circle the words that tell you this.

But on this past New Year's Day, I had my answer. I talked by phone to a friend of yours from Michigan, who spent your last Christmas and the last four
20 months of your life with you. Jim told me how you died, for he was there and saw the helicopter crash. He told me how you had flown your quota and had not been scheduled to fly that day. How the regular pilot was unable to fly and had been replaced by someone with less experience. How they did not know the exact cause of the crash. . . .

He told me how, after a while over there, instead of a yellow streak, the men got a mean streak down their backs. **❸** Each day the streak got bigger and the
30 men became meaner. Everyone but you, Bill. He said how you stayed the same, happy-go-lucky guy that you were when you arrived in Vietnam. How your warmth and friendliness drew the guys to you. How your lieutenant gave you the nickname of "Spanky," and soon your group, Jim included, were all known as "Spanky's gang." How when you died it made it so much harder on them for you were their moral support. And he said how you of all people should never have been the one to die. **❻**

IN OTHER WORDS Mrs. Wimbish writes that she talked to Jim, a friend of Bill's, who had seen Bill's helicopter crash. Jim said that Bill had been very important to the men in his group. An officer had called him "Spanky."

❸ LANGUAGE COACH
"Yellow streak" and "mean streak" in line 28 are **idioms** (ID ee uhmz). Idioms are expressions that mean something different from the usual meanings of the individual words. The writer defines what a "mean streak" is in lines 29–30. "Yellow" is often used to indicate that someone lacks courage. With a partner, define what "yellow streak" means.

❻ SUMMARIZE
Underline at least two details in lines 27–39 that show you what Bill was like and the influence he had on others.

G SUMMARIZE
Put brackets [ ] around the
most important details in
lines 47–50. Then, in your
own words, restate the main
idea expressed in these lines.

_____

_____

_____

_____

_____

_____

40   How it hurts to write this. But I must face it and then
put it to rest. I know after Jim talked to me, he must
have relived it all over again and suffered so. Before I
hung up the phone I told Jim I loved him. Loved him
for just being your close friend, and for being there with
you when you died. How lucky you were to have him
for a friend, and how lucky he was to have had you. . . .

They tell me the letters I write to you and leave here
at this memorial are waking others up to the fact that
there is still much pain left, after all these years, from
50 the Vietnam War. **G**

But this I know. I would rather have had you for
21 years, and all the pain that goes with losing you, than
never to have had you at all.

IN OTHER WORDS Mrs. Wimbish says that writing the
letter is painful. She says it must have hurt Jim to retell
what happened to Bill.

▶ Mrs. Wimbish knows that other people read the letters
she leaves at the memorial. With a partner, discuss how the
letters affect the people who read them.

Timeline: U.S. Involvement in Vietnam

In 1858, to control the government, France attacked Vietnam. After decades of anger, many Vietnamese supported the Communist movement against the French. Meanwhile, the United States began trying to stop the spread of communism across the world.

USA	VIETNAM
1950s **1950** The United States sends economic aid to the French forces in Vietnam.	**1954** The French are defeated. Vietnam divides into Communist North and non-Communist South. **1957** Communist rebels (the Viet Cong) fight for control of South Vietnam.
1960s **1965** Antiwar ⊕ protests become widespread. **1968** U.S. citizens begin to think the war cannot be won.	**1965** The United States bombs North Vietnam. The first U.S. combat troops arrive in South Vietnam. **1968** The number of U.S. troops in Vietnam reaches its peak. The North Vietnamese and the Viet Cong launch the Tet offensive, a series of surprise attacks.
1970s **1970** Four students are killed at an antiwar demonstration in Ohio. 	**1973** All U.S. troops leave Vietnam. **1975** South Vietnam surrenders to the Communists. The U.S. Embassy in Vietnam is evacuated. **1978** Thousands of refugees flee Vietnam to escape poverty and punishment for aiding the United States during the war.
1980s **1982** The Vietnam Veterans Memorial is dedicated in Washington, D.C.	**1986** The Vietnamese government begins economic restructuring.
1990s **1995** The United States and Vietnam restore full diplomatic relations.	

PAUSE & REFLECT

Read the following timeline to learn how the United States was involved with Vietnam in the past.

⊕ LANGUAGE COACH

Anti- is a **prefix,** or word part, that means "opposed to" or "against." So "antiwar protests" are public demonstrations against the war.

PAUSE & REFLECT

A timeline shows events in the order in which they occurred. How many years were U.S. troops in Vietnam?

_____

_____

_____

_____

_____

READING 10A Evaluate a summary of the original text for accuracy of main ideas. **RC-7(E)** Summarize texts in ways that maintain meaning and logical order.

Practicing Your Skills: Summary

Review the side-column notes you took on main ideas and important details as you read the excerpt from *A Wall of Remembrance*. Then, use them to complete the chart below. Write a summary that explains the overall meaning of the selection.

Main Ideas and Details	Summary
Part 1 Main Idea: _____ _____ _____ _____ Details: _____ _____ _____ _____ Part 2 Main Idea: _____ _____ _____ _____ Details: _____ _____ _____ _____ Part 3 Main Idea: _____ _____ _____ _____ Details: _____ _____ _____ _____	_____ _____

Academic Vocabulary in Speaking

The word **analyze** (AN uh lyz) is a verb that means *to examine something by looking critically or closely at it.*

Tawny took apart her alarm clock because she wanted to **analyze** how it worked.

TURN AND TALK With a partner, discuss how the three selections you've just read **analyze** some of the effects of the Vietnam War. Be sure to use the word **analyze** in your discussion.

Texas Assessment Practice

DIRECTIONS Use the selections on the Vietnam War to answer questions 1–4.

1 The excerpt from *A Wall of Remembrance* is mainly about —

- **A** the importance of the items left at the Vietnam Veterans Memorial
- **B** the writer's feelings about the letters he read
- **C** the National Park Service's efforts to collect items at the wall
- **D** the effect of the Vietnam War on people

2 From lines 27–39 of "A Mother's Words," readers can conclude that Bill Stocks —

- **F** fought bravely in battle
- **G** worried about upsetting Jim
- **H** respected his lieutenant
- **J** was always happy-go-lucky

3. What happened in Vietnam as antiwar protests increased in the United States?

- **A** Vietnam was divided into two nations.
- **B** The first United States troops arrived in South Vietnam.
- **C** South Vietnam surrendered to communists.
- **D** The United States and Vietnam restored diplomatic relations.

4. Which of the following ideas is presented in both *A Wall of Remembrance* and "A Mother's Words"?

- **F** Soldiers formed lasting friendships during the Vietnam War.
- **G** People express feelings in notes left at the memorial.
- **H** The number of items at the memorial varies from day to day.
- **J** Remembrances are stored in the Museum Resource Center.

READING 6C Analyze different forms of point of view, including first-person.

The Scholarship Jacket

Based on the short story by **Marta Salinas**

What stands in the way of your DREAMS?

Your dream might be to become a star football player or a chess champion. You *can* make your dreams come true, but some things can keep you from achieving your dreams, too.

TURN AND TALK With a partner, talk about your dreams. Make a list on the lines at left. Next, think about obstacles, or things that might get in the way of making one of your dreams come true. Finally, write down each obstacle, and one or two ways to overcome it.

Literary Analysis: First-Person Point of View

When people talk, you learn about who they are and what they believe. The same is true in stories told in first-person point of view. **First-person point of view** is being used when a character in the story tells the story. The person telling the story is called a **narrator** (NAIR ay ter).

First-Person Point of View
The Narrator   • is a character in the story   • uses *I* and *me* to refer to himself or herself   • describes his or her own thoughts, feelings, and impressions   • does not know what other characters think and feel

In "The Scholarship Jacket," the narrator is Martha. Notice how the story is told from her point of view. You know what she sees, hears, thinks, and feels.

Dreams

1. become a chess champion

2. _____

3. _____

4. _____

5. _____

Obstacles; ways to overcome them

1. No chess clubs at my school; start a chess club

_____

_____

_____

_____

Reading Skill: Make Inferences

An **inference** (IN fuhr uhns) is a logical guess about something. To make inferences, look at the details in a story and think about what you already know. Record your inferences about this story in a chart like the one below.

RC-7(D) Make complex inferences about texts.

Details from the Story		My Experience		Inference
Martha doesn't play sports because it costs too much.	+	My school team couldn't raise enough money to go to a tournament.	=	Some people can't afford to play sports in school.

Vocabulary in Context

Note: Words are listed in the order in which they appear in the story.

Agile (AJ uhl) is an adjective that means *able to move quickly*.
   Athletes must be **agile** to play sports well.

Eavesdrop (EEVZ drop) is a verb that means *to listen secretly to someone's private conversation*.
   Martha did not mean to **eavesdrop** on her teachers.

Falsify (FAWL suh fy) is a verb that means *to make untrue by adding or changing information*.
   The teacher refused to **falsify** the student's records.

Dismay (dis MAY) is a noun that means *a feeling of worry or alarm*.
   Martha expressed **dismay** at the cost of the jacket.

Vile (vyl) is an adjective that means *very unpleasant or bad*.
   She experienced a **vile** reaction to the bad news.

Vocabulary Practice

Review the words and sample sentences above. Then, use each vocabulary word in a question to a classmate, such as "What is something that is likely to **dismay** you?" After your partner answers your questions, switch roles.

SET A PURPOSE FOR READING
Read "The Scholarship Jacket" to find out if Martha gets the jacket she deserves.

Ⓐ MAKE INFERENCES
An **inference** is a logical conclusion you make based on details in the story. With a partner, discuss what you can tell about how the narrator and her sister feel about school.

VOCABULARY
The word **agile** (AJ uhl) is an adjective that means *able to move quickly*.

The Scholarship Jacket

Based on the short story by
MARTA SALINAS

BACKGROUND Mexican Americans living in Texas, like Martha's family, sometimes face unfair treatment. The scholarship jacket featured in this story is a letter jacket. It is like those given to athletes for taking part in school sports, but this one is awarded for academic achievement.

At eighth-grade graduation every year, my small Texas school awarded a jacket in the school colors—gold and green—to the student with the highest grades over eight years. This scholarship jacket had a big gold S and your name on it.

My oldest sister, Rosie, had won the jacket several years earlier. I fully expected to win it, too. I was fourteen, in the eighth grade, and had been a straight A student since first grade. I looked forward to owning that jacket. Ⓐ

10   My father, a farm worker, didn't earn enough money to feed eight children, so I moved in with my grandparents when I was six. My family didn't play sports at school because it cost too much. We were all quite **agile**, but none of us would ever earn a school sports jacket. The scholarship jacket was our only chance.

IN OTHER WORDS The narrator's school awards a jacket to the student with the best grades from first through eighth grade.

► Why does the narrator want to win the jacket? Put check marks ✔ beside the sentences that tell you this.

In May, close to graduation, everyone was ready for school to end. One day as I was walking to gym class, I remembered I had left my gym shorts in a bag under my desk. I had to walk back to class to get them.

20   I stopped outside my classroom door when I heard angry voices. I didn't mean to <u>eavesdrop</u>, but I didn't know what to do. I needed those shorts. Mr. Schmidt, my history teacher, and Mr. Boone, my math teacher, were arguing about me. I couldn't believe it. **Ⓑ**

IN OTHER WORDS One day the narrator leaves her gym shorts in a bag under her desk. She walks back to class to get the bag. When she gets there, she hears two teachers arguing about her.

"I refuse to do it! I don't care who her father is. Her grades don't even begin to compare to Martha's. I won't lie or <u>falsify</u> records. Martha has top grades and you know it." That was Mr. Schmidt and he sounded very angry. Mr. Boone's voice sounded calm and quiet.

30   "Joann's father is on the School Board; he owns the only store in town. We could say it was a close tie and—"

The pounding in my ears drowned out most of the rest of the words: ". . . Martha is Mexican . . . resign . . . won't do it. . . . " **Ⓒ** Mr. Schmidt walked out of the room and down the hall. Luckily, he didn't see me. I waited a few minutes. Then, I went in and grabbed my bag. Mr. Boone looked at me but didn't say anything. I went home very sad. I cried into my pillow that night. I didn't want Grandmother to hear me. It seemed cruel that I had heard

40 the argument.

VOCABULARY

The word **eavesdrop** (EEVZ drop) is a verb that means *to listen secretly to someone's private conversation.*

Ⓑ FIRST-PERSON POINT OF VIEW

When a story is told in **first-person point of view,** you often get to know the narrator very well. What does the narrator reveal about herself in lines 10–24?

_____

_____

_____

_____

VOCABULARY

The word **falsify** (FAWL suh fy) is a verb that means *to make untrue by adding or changing information.*

Ⓒ. LANGUAGE COACH

To reflect what Martha hears, the writer uses **sentence fragments,** or parts of sentences that are missing information. Fill in the blank to complete this sentence fragment from line 34: "_____ won't do it."

IN OTHER WORDS Martha, the narrator, hears two teachers arguing about who should get the award for having top grades.

► With a partner, discuss the arguments Mr. Schmidt and Mr. Boone give for who should get the award.

The next day the principal called me into his office. He looked unhappy. I decided not to make it any easier for him. I looked right in his eyes. He looked away.

"Martha," he said, "there's a change this year with the scholarship jacket. As you know, it has always been free." He cleared his throat and went on. "This year the Board has decided to charge fifteen dollars for the jacket."

I stared at him in shock. A small sound of **dismay** escaped my throat. He still wouldn't look in my eyes.

50 "If you can't pay the fifteen dollars," he said, "the jacket will be given to the next one in line." ❶

With dignity, I said, "I'll speak to my grandfather, sir, and let you know tomorrow." I cried on the walk home.

IN OTHER WORDS The principal tells Martha that beginning this year, the scholarship jacket will cost fifteen dollars.

► Put brackets [ ] around the sentences that show you how the principal feels about the change. Circle the sentences that tell how Martha reacts.

"Where's Grandpa?" I asked Grandma.

"I think he's out back working in the bean field."

I could see him walking between the rows, hoe in hand. As I walked out to him, I tried to think how to ask him for the money. There was a cool breeze blowing and a sweet smell in the air. I didn't appreciate it. I wanted that jacket 60 so much. It meant eight years of hard work. I knew I had to be honest with Grandpa. It was my only chance.

I cleared my throat nervously. "Grandpa, I have a big favor to ask you." He waited silently. I tried again.

VOCABULARY

The word **dismay** (dis MAY) is a noun that means *a feeling of worry or alarm.*

❶ MAKE INFERENCES

With a partner, discuss why you think the principal won't look in Martha's eyes. Then write your answer below.

_____

_____

_____

_____

_____

_____

_____

_____

_____

"Grandpa, this year the scholarship jacket is not free. It costs fifteen dollars. I have to take the money tomorrow. If I don't, it'll be given to someone else."

Grandpa straightened up slowly and leaned on the hoe. He looked out over the field. I waited, hoping he'd say I could have the money. **E**

70   He asked, "What does a scholarship jacket mean?"

I answered quickly. "It means you've earned the jacket by having the highest grades for eight years." Too late I realized the meaning of my words. Grandpa knew I understood that it was not a matter of money. It wasn't that. Finally he spoke again.

"If you pay for it, Marta, it's not a scholarship jacket, is it? Tell your principal I will not pay the money." **F**

IN OTHER WORDS   When Martha asks her grandfather for the fifteen dollars, he says that paying for the jacket means it is no longer an award. He refuses to give the narrator, whom he calls "Marta," the money.

Back at the house, I locked myself in the bathroom for a long time. I was angry with Grandfather—although I 80 knew he was right. I was angry with the Board, too.

It was a very sad girl who stepped into the principal's office the next day.

"What did your grandfather say?" the principal asked.

"He said to tell you he won't pay the fifteen dollars."

The principal mumbled something and walked to the window.

"Why?" he finally asked. "Your grandfather has the money. He owns a two-hundred acre ranch."

I looked at him, forcing back tears. "I know, sir, but 90 he said if I had to pay for it, it wouldn't be a scholarship jacket." I stood up to leave. "You'll just have to give it to Joann." I was almost to the door when he stopped me.

"Martha—wait."

E FIRST-PERSON POINT OF VIEW

How does the first-person point of view limit your understanding of what Martha's grandfather is thinking?

_____

_____

_____

_____

F MAKE INFERENCES

Marta (line 76) is the Spanish version of "Martha." With a partner, discuss why Martha's grandfather and her teachers might call her by different versions of her name.

VOCABULARY

The word **vile** (vyl) is an adjective that means *very unpleasant or bad*.

(Circle) the words in lines 94–95 that help you understand what *vile* means.

⊙ MAKE INFERENCES

Why do you think the principal changes his mind? Using the chart below, make an inference to answer this question.

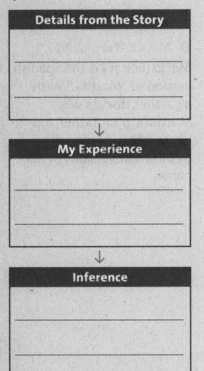

PAUSE & REFLECT

With a partner, discuss how Martha's grandfather helps her overcome obstacles to making her dream come true.

I turned and looked at him. Something bitter and **vile** tasting was coming up in my mouth. I was afraid I was going to be sick. He watched me, biting his lip.

"Okay. We'll make a special case for you. I'll tell the Board. You'll get your jacket." **⊙**

IN OTHER WORDS Martha is upset and angry with her grandfather, although she knows he is right.

▶ How does the principal respond when Martha tells him her grandfather won't pay the money? Underline the sentences that tell you this.

I could hardly believe it. I spoke in a rush. "Oh, thank
100 you, sir!" Suddenly I felt great. I ran into the hall so I could cry where no one would see me.

At the end of the day, Mr. Schmidt winked at me. He said, "I hear you're getting the scholarship jacket this year."

His face looked happy and innocent, but I knew better. I gave him a quick hug and ran to the bus. I cried again on the walk home, but this time because I was so happy. I couldn't wait to tell Grandpa. I ran straight to the field and joined him. Without saying anything, I knelt down and started pulling weeds. Grandpa didn't ask what had
110 happened. After a little while, I stood up and faced him.

"The principal said I'm getting the jacket after all. That's after I told him what you said."

Grandpa didn't say anything; he just patted me on the shoulder and smiled. Then he said, "Better go see if your grandmother needs any help with supper." I gave him a big grin. He didn't fool me. I skipped and ran back to the house whistling some silly tune.

IN OTHER WORDS Martha is happy that she will get the jacket.

▶ With a partner, discuss how Mr. Schmidt and Martha's grandfather react to her good news.

PAUSE & REFLECT

Literary Analysis: First-Person Point of View

First-person point of view is being used when a character in a story is the storyteller, or narrator. Who is the narrator in "The Scholarship Jacket"? Write your answer in the first box below. Then, give three details from the story that show the narrator's thoughts and feelings.

READING 6C Analyze different forms of point of view, including first-person.

Narrator

Narrator's Thoughts and Feelings	Narrator's Thoughts and Feelings	Narrator's Thoughts and Feelings

What stands in the way of your DREAMS?

Look back at the steps you listed on page 88 to overcome obstacles to a dream. What smaller steps can you take to make each step of your dream come true? Write your answer on the lines below.

_____

_____

_____

_____

_____

_____

Reading Skill: Make Inferences

Make an inference, or logical guess, about what each of the following characters in the story is like. Use the quotations provided and your own experience to help you decide how you would describe each character to a friend.

Details from the Story	My Experience	Inference
Martha: "You'll just have to give it to Joann." (lines 91–92)		
Mr. Boone: "We could say it was a close tie and—" (line 31)		
Grandfather: "If you pay for it, Marta, it's not a scholarship jacket, is it?" (lines 76–77)		

Vocabulary Practice

Circle the word or phrase that has the opposite meaning as the boldfaced word.

1. **falsify:** **(a)** make right **(b)** lie about **(c)** explain

2. **dismay:** **(a)** alarm **(b)** sadness **(c)** relief

3. **agile:** **(a)** clumsy **(b)** talented **(c)** lively

4. **eavesdrop:** **(a)** spy on **(b)** respect privacy **(c)** run away

5. **vile:** **(a)** horrible **(b)** good **(c)** cautious

Academic Vocabulary in Speaking

The word **respond** (rih SPOND) means *to answer or reply*

Shawn loves to **respond** to questions on game shows by shouting out the answers.

TURN AND TALK With a partner, discuss how you would **respond** if you'd been told you must pay for an award, such as a scholarship jacket. Be sure to use the word **respond** in your conversation.

Texas Assessment Practice

DIRECTIONS Use "The Scholarship Jacket" to answer questions 1–6.

1 Lines 25–31 are important because they show that Martha —

- A doesn't deserve the jacket
- B might not receive the jacket
- C is not interested in the jacket
- D cannot afford to pay for the jacket

2 In lines 41–53, which sentence tells the reader that Martha is upset with what the principal tells her?

- F *I decided not to make it any easier for him.*
- G *I looked right in his eyes.*
- H *I'll speak to my grandfather, sir.*
- J *I cried on the walk home.*

3 The sentence "I waited, hoping he'd say I could have the money" (lines 68–69) helps the reader understand that Martha —

- A believes the principal's decision is unfair
- B is afraid of her grandfather
- C will pay for the jacket if she has to
- D does not want to work hard

4 Grandpa won't pay for the jacket because he doesn't —

- F have the money
- G believe the jacket should be bought
- H like the principal
- J want Martha to have it

5 How does the principal change at the end of the story?

- A He begins to like Martha's grandfather.
- B He talks to Martha's teachers.
- C He decides to give Martha the jacket.
- D He finds out that Martha is a good student.

6 Because this story is in first-person point of view, the reader better understands the narrator's —

- F desire to win the jacket
- G difficulties in getting good grades
- H wish to leave school
- J inability to play basketball

READING 6C Analyze different forms of point of view, including third-person omniscient.

A Retrieved Reformation
Based on the short story by O. Henry

Who deserves a second CHANCE?

We all make mistakes. Some mistakes are small, and some mistakes can change our lives. Luckily, we sometimes get a second chance, an opportunity to make things right again. Why might someone deserve a second chance after making a big mistake?

TURN AND TALK Think about some of the mistakes you've seen people make. Write down a list of mistakes like the one to the left. Choose one example to discuss with a partner. Did the person who made the mistake deserve a second chance? What did he or she learn from the mistake?

Literary Analysis: Third-Person Point of View

If a story is filled with words like *I*, *me*, and *mine*, it's probably told from the **first-person point of view.** But if the narrator is not a character in the story and the story is told using the words *he*, *she*, or *they*, then that story is probably told from the **third-person point of view.** In many third-person stories the narrator is **omniscient;** that is, he or she knows everything about each character. Look at the following examples.

First-Person Point of View	Third-Person Omniscient Point of View
I walked into the warden's office.	Jimmy walked into the warden's office. He knew what to expect.

Big Mistakes

1. My sister dropped my dad's cell phone in a toilet.

2. _____

3. _____

4. _____

5. _____

Reading Strategy: Predict

When you **predict,** you make a guess about what will happen next in a story based on details the author provides. As you read "A Retrieved Reformation," you will be asked to record predictions and the reasons behind your predictions.

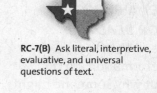

RC-7(B) Ask literal, interpretive, evaluative, and universal questions of text.

Event in the Story	My Prediction	My Reasons
The warden tells Jimmy to stop breaking into safes.	Jimmy will go back to a life of crime.	Jimmy's friends seem a little dishonest.

Vocabulary in Context

Note: Words are listed in the order in which they appear in the story.

Rehabilitate (ree huh BIL ih tayt) is a verb that means *to restore to useful life.*

    The thief wanted to **rehabilitate** himself and live an honest life.

Eminent (EM uh nuhnt) is an adjective that means *famous or respected.*

    Everyone knew and respected the **eminent** banker.

Elusive (ih LOO siv) is an adjective that means *hard to catch.*

    Ben Price spent years trying to catch the **elusive** thief.

Saunter (SAWN tuhr) is a verb that means *to walk in a slow and relaxed way.*

    Ben Price was known to **saunter** confidently when he walked.

Vocabulary Practice

Review the words and sample sentences above. Then, write a narrative paragraph that uses all of the vocabulary words.

_____

_____

_____

_____

**SET A PURPOSE
FOR READING**
Read "A Retrieved
Reformation" to find
out why someone might
take a big risk that could
completely change his life.

**Ⓐ THIRD-PERSON POINT
OF VIEW**
Underline the last sentence
in this paragraph. How
does the narrator know that
Jimmy's friends convinced
the governor to free Jimmy?
What does this fact tell you
about the story's point of
view?

_____

_____

_____

_____

_____

_____

VOCABULARY
The word **rehabilitate** (ree
huh BIL ih tayt) is a verb
that means _to restore to
useful life._

A Retrieved Reformation

Based on the short story by
O. HENRY

BACKGROUND Jimmy Valentine, the main
character in this story, is a safecracker. In
other words, he breaks into safes, locking
steel boxes used to store money and
other valuables. Then, he steals each safe's
contents. Valentine uses special tools,
including drills, to break into the safes he
intends to rob.

A guard walked into the prison shoe shop. One of the
prisoners, Jimmy Valentine, was carefully sewing shoes.
The guard took him to the front office. There the warden,
who ran the prison, handed Jimmy his papers. Jimmy had
been in prison for nearly ten months. Now Jimmy's friends
had convinced the governor to free him. Ⓐ

"Now, Valentine," said the warden. "You're not a bad guy
at heart. Stop breaking into safes, and live a lawful life."

At a quarter past seven on the next morning, Jimmy
10 stood in the warden's outer office. On his way out, he got a
railroad ticket and a five-dollar bill, the state's gift to help
him **rehabilitate** himself and go back to normal life. The

warden gave him a cigar, and they shook hands. Mr. James Valentine walked out into the sunshine.

IN OTHER WORDS Jimmy Valentine has been in prison for breaking into safes. After ten months, the governor sets him free. The warden gives him a railroad ticket, five dollars, and a cigar. He tells Valentine to be good from now on, and Jimmy leaves the prison.

Jimmy went straight to a restaurant. There he used his freedom to enjoy some chicken and a bottle of wine. This was followed by a cigar that was better than the one the warden had given him. From there he took a train to a little town near the state line.

20 Jimmy went to Mike Dolan's café, got his key, and went upstairs. Everything in his room was just as he had left it. Ben Price's collar button still lay on the floor. It had been torn from that <u>eminent</u> detective's shirt when he had fought with Jimmy during Jimmy's arrest.

Jimmy slid back a panel in the wall and dragged out a dusty suitcase. He opened it. The finest set of burglar's tools in the East were inside. Made of special steel, the tools were in the latest designs. Jimmy even had two or three tools that he had invented himself. The set had cost him over nine
30 hundred dollars.

In half an hour Jimmy went downstairs. He was now dressed in good clothes. He carried his suitcase in his hand.

"Got any big jobs planned?" Mike Dolan asked, genially. Dolan was a friendly sort of guy.

"Me?" said Jimmy. He sounded puzzled. "Jobs? I don't understand what you mean. I'm working for the New York Cracker and Wheat Company."

Mike thought this was very funny. **B**

VOCABULARY

The word **eminent** (EM uh nuhnt) is an adjective that means *famous or respected*.

B PREDICT

Reread lines 25–39. Do you think Jimmy will go back to breaking into safes? Record your prediction and reasons below.

My Prediction

↓

My Reasons

IN OTHER WORDS Freed from prison, Jimmy returns to his room above a café and gets his special burglar's tools from their hiding place. His friend Mike Dolan asks him whether he has plans to steal anything. Jimmy jokes with Dolan, saying that he works for a cracker company.

► Reread lines 15–39. <u>Underline</u> the words or phrases that describe what Jimmy does after he leaves prison.

VOCABULARY

The word **elusive** (ih LOO siv) is an adjective that means *hard to catch.*

C PREDICT

Reread lines 40–54. Who do you think is responsible for these crimes? What role do you predict Ben Price will have in this story? Write your predictions and reasons below.

My Predictions
_____
_____
_____
_____

↓

My Reasons
_____
_____
_____
_____
_____

40   A week after Jimmy Valentine's release, a safe was robbed in Richmond, Indiana. There was no clue about who the thief was. Only eight hundred dollars was stolen. Two weeks later another safe in Logansport was opened. Fifteen hundred dollars in cash was stolen. That began to interest the police. Then an old bank safe in Jefferson City was robbed of five thousand dollars. The losses were now high enough to send the case to Ben Price, the detective.

Ben Price said, "Dandy Jim Valentine's stealing again. Yes, I think I'll find Mr. Valentine. The next time I catch
50 him, he'll do his prison sentence without getting out early."

Ben Price knew Jimmy's habits. He had learned them while working on an earlier case. Once people heard that Ben Price was trying to catch the **elusive** thief, people who owned safes felt better. **C**

IN OTHER WORDS Within a few weeks of Jimmy's release from prison, several major burglaries are reported. The police call Ben Price, the famous detective who had arrested Jimmy before.

One afternoon Jimmy Valentine and his suitcase got out of a train in Elmore, Arkansas. Jimmy, who looked like an athletic young man just home from college, went down the sidewalk toward the hotel.

A young lady crossed the street, passed him at the corner,
60 and entered a door with a sign saying "The Elmore Bank." Jimmy Valentine looked into her eyes. He forgot he was a

thief. She blushed slightly. Young men with Jimmy's style and good looks weren't often seen in Elmore.

Jimmy grabbed a boy who was sitting on the steps of the bank. Jimmy asked him questions about the town. Soon the young lady came out. She paid no attention to the young man with the suitcase. She just kept walking.

Jimmy tried to trick the boy. "Isn't that Polly Simpson?" he asked.

70   "Naw," said the boy. "She's Annabel Adams. Her pa owns this bank."

IN OTHER WORDS Jimmy goes to Elmore, Arkansas, where he sees a beautiful woman named Annabel Adams. He tricks a boy into telling him her name. The boy also reveals that Annabel is the banker's daughter.

Jimmy went to the Planters' Hotel. He signed in, pretending to be someone named Ralph D. Spencer, and rented a room. He leaned on the desk and told the clerk that he had come to Elmore to go into business. How was the shoe business, now, in the town? Was there an opening?

The clerk said that there wasn't a real shoe store in town. Other stores sold some shoes. Business in general was fairly good. He hoped Mr. Spencer would decide to locate in 80 Elmore. He would find it a pleasant town to live in, and the people were very friendly.

Mr. Spencer thought he would stop over in the town a few days and think about it. He said he would carry up his suitcase himself. It was rather heavy. **PAUSE & REFLECT**

PAUSE & REFLECT
Why is Ralph's suitcase so heavy? Why does he insist on carrying it himself? Discuss your thoughts with a partner.

Mr. Ralph Spencer was the new identity that replaced Jimmy Valentine's real self. All because of love, Mr. Spencer stayed in Elmore and opened a shoe store. He made many friends. And he met Miss Annabel Adams and became more and more in love with her.

IN OTHER WORDS Jimmy changes his name to Ralph Spencer. Because of Annabel, he moves to town and opens a shoe store. He has fallen in love with the banker's daughter.

---

90   By the end of a year Mr. Ralph Spencer had won the respect of the community. His shoe store was doing well. He and Annabel were engaged to be married in two weeks. Mr. Adams, the country banker, liked Spencer. Annabel loved him and was proud of him. He was as much at home in her family as if he were already part of it.

One day Jimmy sat down in his room and wrote this letter. He mailed it to the safe address of one of his old friends in St. Louis:

Dear Old Pal:

100   I want you to be at Sullivan's place, in Little Rock, next Wednesday night. I want to give you my little kit of tools. I know you'll be glad to get them. You couldn't get one like it for a thousand dollars. I quit the old business a year ago. I've got a nice store. I'm making an honest living. I'm going to marry the finest girl on earth two weeks from now. I wouldn't touch a dollar of another man's money now for a million. After I get married I'm going to sell my store and go West, where there won't be so much danger of being found. I tell you,
110 Billy, she's an angel. She believes in me. I wouldn't do another crime for the whole world. Be there, for I must see you. I'll bring along the tools with me.

Your old friend, **D**

Jimmy

O **LANGUAGE COACH**
Jimmy uses the phases "old pal" and "old friend" in his letter. He's not saying that he or his friend is old. Instead, the adjective *old* in this phrase suggests that they are close, familiar friends. They have been friends for a long time.

IN OTHER WORDS Jimmy leads a new, honest life, still pretending to be named Ralph Spencer. He and Annabel plan to get married. He writes to an old friend, saying that he's now leading an honest life and wants to give the friend his burglary tools.

▶ Reread Jimmy's letter (lines 99–114). Discuss with a partner what the letter tells you about Jimmy. Has he changed?

On the Monday night after Jimmy wrote this letter, Ben Price arrived in Elmore in a **horse-drawn buggy**. He walked around town in his quiet way until he found out what he wanted to know. From across the street, he got a good look at Ralph D. Spencer.

120 "Going to marry the banker's daughter are you, Jimmy?" said Ben to himself, softly. "Well, I don't think so!"

The next morning Jimmy ate breakfast at the Adamses'. He was going to Little Rock that day to order his wedding suit and buy something nice for Annabel. That would be the first time he had left town since he came to Elmore. It had been more than a year now since those last thefts, and he thought he could safely go away. **E**

After breakfast the family went downtown together, including Mr. Adams, Annabel, Jimmy, and Annabel's 130 married sister with her two little girls. The girls were five and nine years old. First they came by the hotel where Jimmy still rented a room. He took his suitcase. Then they went on to the bank. Outside stood Jimmy's horse and buggy with a driver.

IN OTHER WORDS Jimmy doesn't know it, but Ben Price is in town looking for him. Jimmy plans to go to Little Rock to give away his burglar's tools. But before he leaves town, he goes with Annabel's family to visit the bank.

Everyone went inside the banking room. Jimmy set his suitcase down.

The Elmore Bank had just put in a new safe. Mr. Adams was very proud of it and wanted everyone to see it. It had a new kind of door. It fastened with three solid steel bolts that 140 moved together when a single handle was pushed, and it had a time lock. Mr. Adams proudly explained how it worked to Mr. Spencer. The two children, May and Agatha, were delighted by the shining metal and funny clock and knobs.

While they were busy, Ben Price **sauntered** slowly and calmly into the bank. He leaned casually on the counter.

VISUAL VOCABULARY

A **horse-drawn buggy** is a light cart with two or four wheels. It is pulled by a horse.

E **THIRD-PERSON POINT OF VIEW**

What do you know about Ben Price that Jimmy doesn't know? Underline the sentences where you learn about Ben Price's plans for Jimmy.

_____

_____

_____

_____

VOCABULARY

The word **saunter** (SAWN tuhr) is a verb that means *to walk in a slow and relaxed way.*

He told the teller that he didn't want anything; he was just waiting for a man he knew.

IN OTHER WORDS Mr. Adams, Annabel's father, has a new safe at his bank. The safe has a special time lock: the safe can be opened only at certain times. While Adams is showing the safe to everyone, Ben Price walks into the bank. He says he's waiting for someone.

Suddenly there was a scream. May, the older girl, had been playing and had shut Agatha inside the safe. She
150 had then pushed the bolts and turned the knob of the numbered dial to make it lock.

The old banker ran to the handle. He tugged at it for a moment. "The door can't be opened," he groaned.

Agatha's mother screamed again, wildly.

"Hush!" said Mr. Adams, raising his shaking hand. "Agatha!" he called as loudly as he could. "Listen to me." They could just hear the child screaming in the dark safe.

"My darling!" cried the mother. "She will die of fright! Open the door! Oh, break it open! Can't you men do
160 something?"

"There isn't a man nearer than Little Rock who can open that door," said Mr. Adams. "Spencer, what shall we do? That child can't stand it long in there. There isn't enough air, and, besides, she'll go into fits from fright." **F**

IN OTHER WORDS Annabel's young niece, May, accidentally locks her sister Agatha inside the safe. No one knows how to get her out, and she may run out of air. Mr. Adams asks Jimmy what to do.

Agatha's mother was really scared now. She beat the door with her hands. Somebody wildly suggested that they might blow up the safe with dynamite. Annabel turned to Jimmy.

"Can't you do something, Ralph—*try*, won't you?"

He looked at her with an odd smile.
170 "Annabel," he said, "give me that rose you are wearing."

F PREDICT

Jimmy has to make an important choice at this point in the story. What do you think he will do? Record your prediction and reasons below.

My Prediction
_____
_____
_____

↓

My Reasons
_____
_____
_____
_____

Hardly believing that she heard him right, she unpinned the rose from her dress, and placed it in his hand. Jimmy stuffed it into his vest pocket. He threw off his coat and pulled up his shirt sleeves. Ralph D. Spencer went away, and Jimmy Valentine took his place. **PAUSE & REFLECT**

PAUSE & REFLECT

Why does Jimmy ask Annabel to give him the rose she is wearing? Discuss your ideas with a partner.

"Get away from the door, all of you," he ordered.

He set his suitcase on the table, and opened it out flat. From that time on he seemed to be unaware of anyone else. He laid out the shining tools swiftly, whistling softly. The 180 others watched him as if they were under a magical spell.

In a minute Jimmy's **drill** was cutting smoothly into the steel door. In ten minutes he threw back the bolts and opened the door.

Agatha, frightened but safe, was gathered into her mother's arms.

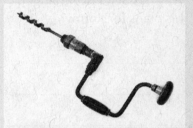

VISUAL VOCABULARY

A **drill** is a tool for making holes in wood or metal. Jimmy is using a hand drill and not an electric drill.

IN OTHER WORDS Annabel asks Ralph, not knowing that he is really Jimmy Valentine, to help Agatha get out of the safe. To everyone's surprise, Jimmy asks Annabel for the rose she is wearing. Then, he uses his burglar's tools to break into the safe. Agatha is free.

► Reread lines 165–185. Underline all of the sentences that describe what Jimmy does after the safe is closed by mistake.

Jimmy Valentine put on his coat, and walked toward the front door. As he walked along, he thought he heard a faraway voice call "Ralph!" But he never paused.

At the door a big man stood somewhat in his way.

190 "Hello, Ben!" said Jimmy, still with his strange smile. "Found me at last, have you? Well, let's go. I don't know that it makes much difference, now."

And then Ben Price acted rather strangely.

G THIRD-PERSON POINT
OF VIEW

G THIRD-PERSON POINT
OF VIEW

Does Jimmy know that Ben
Price was watching him
break into the safe? In what
way has Ben Price changed
his plans for Jimmy?

_____

_____

_____

_____

_____

_____

_____

_____

"Guess you're mistaken, Mr. Spencer," he said.
"Don't believe I recognize you. Your buggy's waiting
for you, ain't it?" **G**

And Ben Price turned and strolled down the street.

IN OTHER WORDS Ben Price watches Jimmy break into the safe
to save Agatha. Afterward, Jimmy leaves, not responding to
Annabel's call. Jimmy sees Price and thinks that Price will arrest
him. Instead, the detective recognizes that Jimmy is no longer
a criminal. He calls Jimmy "Mr. Spencer" and pretends that he
doesn't know who Jimmy is. The detective turns and walks away.

Literary Analysis: Third-Person Point of View

In the final scene, just before Jimmy breaks into the safe to save Annabel's niece, Jimmy and Annabel don't know some important things about the plot. But, since the story is told from the **third-person omniscient point of view,** the narrator has shared extra information with readers. Use the chart below to compare what you knew at this important point in the story with what Jimmy and Annabel knew. Reread lines 135–147 before you fill in the chart.

READING 6C Analyze different forms of point of view, including third-person omniscient.

What I know at this point in the story
_____
_____
_____
_____
_____
_____
_____

What Jimmy knows	What Annabel knows
_____	_____
_____	_____
_____	_____
_____	_____
_____	_____
_____	_____

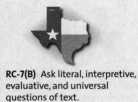

RC-7(B) Ask literal, interpretive, evaluative, and universal questions of text.

Reading Strategy: Predict

Who deserves a second CHANCE?

Do you think Jimmy deserves a second chance? What do you think he will do with his second chance on life?

Use the graphic organizer below to plan your response.

What did Jimmy do after he left prison?

_____

_____

What do you think Jimmy will do after Ben Price gives him a second chance?

_____

_____

What details from the text support your predictions?

_____

_____

Vocabulary Practice

Fill in the correct vocabulary word to complete each sentence.

rehabilitate   eminent   elusive   saunter

1. We searched for hours trying to find our _____ dog.

2. The coach told the player that he would have to _____ his injured knee.

3. The teacher watched Celeste _____ into class, completely unaware of the pop quiz.

4. The crowd really enjoyed the speech by the _____ author.

Academic Vocabulary in Speaking

The word **aware** (uh WAIR) is an adjective that means *realizing or knowing about*.

> I was **aware** that my friends were planning a party for me, but I didn't let them know that.

The word **react** (ree AKT) is a verb that means *to act in response to someone or something*.

> I didn't know how to **react** when they told me that the party was canceled.

TURN AND TALK With a partner, discuss why you think Ben Price decided to let Jimmy Valentine go free. Consider what he was **aware** of and how he **reacted** to it. Be sure to use the words **aware** and **react** in your conversation.

READING 6C Analyze different forms of point of view, including third-person omniscient.
RC-7(B) Ask literal, interpretive, evaluative, and universal questions of text.

Texas Assessment Practice

DIRECTIONS Use "A Retrieved Reformation" to answer questions 1–4.

1 Which passage from the story shows that Jimmy changes once he meets Annabel Adams?

  A Jimmy, who looked like an athletic young man just home from college, went down the sidewalk toward the hotel.

  B Jimmy Valentine looked into her eyes. He forgot he was a thief.

  C Young men of Jimmy's style and good looks weren't often seen in Elmore.

  D Jimmy asked him questions about the town.

2 Jimmy breaks open the safe in lines 177–183 because he —

  F wants to break up with Annabel

  G has decided to turn himself in

  H cannot resist committing crimes

  J needs to rescue a girl trapped inside

3 In lines 194–196, why does Ben say he doesn't recognize Jimmy?

  A He realizes Jimmy is innocent.

  B He wants Jimmy to leave Elmore.

  C He believes Jimmy has changed his ways.

  D He wishes Jimmy would give him his suitcase.

4 By telling this story from the omniscient point of view, the author helps the reader better understand the way —

  F other characters feel about Jimmy

  G criminals are able to crack safes

  H the writer feels about prison

  J Jimmy has changed his behavior

UNIT 3

Lessons to Learn

UNDERSTANDING THEME

Be sure to read the Reader's Workshop on pages 316–321 in *Holt McDougal Literature*.

Academic Vocabulary for Unit 3

You will see these Academic Vocabulary words as you work through this book. You will also be asked to use them as you write and talk about the selections in this unit.

Clause (klawz) is a noun that means *a group of words with a subject and a verb* or *a part of a legal document*.
Sara added a **clause** to her sentence to make her meaning clear.

When might leaving out a **clause** cause a misunderstanding? _____
_____

Context (KON tekst) is a noun that means *the conditions in which an event or idea happens or exists*.
Max didn't recognize his teacher outside of the **context** of school.

Explain how **context** clues can help you understand an unfamiliar

word: _____

Cultural (KUHL chuhr uhl) is an adjective that means *relating to the entire way of life of a group of people*.
The new friends had fun learning about their **cultural** differences by trying each other's traditional foods and music.

Which of your family's **cultural** activities do you enjoy the most? ____
_____

Symbol (SIM buhl) is a noun that means *something chosen to represent or stand for something else, such as a mark or sign*.
People often use a picture of a heart shape as a **symbol** of love.

Draw or describe a **symbol** you might use to represent your school: __
_____

Theme (theem) is a noun that means *the overall message or point of a piece of writing*.
These two stories share the **theme** of standing up for yourself.

If you wrote a story, what **theme** would it express?_____
_____

READING 3 Analyze and make inferences about theme and genre in different cultural and historical contexts. **3C** Analyze how the time and place influence the theme or message of a literary work.

Amigo Brothers
Based on the short story by **Piri Thomas**

What happens when friends COMPETE?

People compete all the time, whether it's to win a game or to see who can get the best grades. Competition can be fun, but it also can be difficult. In "Amigo Brothers," two friends find out if their friendship is stronger than a tough competition.

TURN AND TALK On the lines to the left, list times you competed with a friend. Then, with a partner, discuss how each competition helped or hurt your friendship.

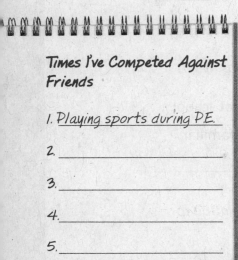

Times I've Competed Against Friends

1. *Playing sports during P.E.*
2. _____
3. _____
4. _____
5. _____

Literary Analysis: Theme and Setting

A story's lesson about life or human nature is its **theme.** For example, if two characters risk their friendship but become even better friends, the **theme** might be: "Big rewards come from taking risks."

Sometimes a character or the narrator will tell you the **theme.** Most often, however, clues help you find the **theme.** Look for clues in lessons that characters learn, in how the story's conflict is resolved, or in the story's **setting.** Use the following questions to help you uncover the **theme** of "Amigo Brothers."

Using Setting to Identify Theme

The **setting,** or place and time, of "Amigo Brothers" can help you identify the story's **theme.** Ask
- Does the setting affect what the characters can do? How?
- Is the setting part of the story's conflict? How?

Reading Skill: Compare and Contrast

When you **compare,** you point out what is the same. When you **contrast,** you point out what is different. As you read "Amigo Brothers," you will be asked to compare and contrast Felix and Antonio, the story's two main characters.

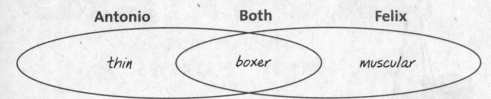

| Antonio | Both | Felix |
| thin | boxer | muscular |

Vocabulary in Context

Note: Words are listed in the order in which they appear in the story.

Unbridled (un BRYD uld) is an adjective that means *without control or restraint.*

> They lost control, bursting into cheers of **unbridled** joy.

Dispel (dih SPEL) is a verb that means *to drive away or get rid of.*

> The boxers fought wildly, helping to **dispel** any worries that the match might be dull.

Bedlam (BED luhm) is a noun that means *noisy confusion.*

> The audience stomped crazily; **bedlam** had broken loose.

Flail (flayl) is a verb that means *to wave wildly.*

> The boxers' arms were so tired that they seemed to **flail** around, flapping uselessly.

Clarity (KLAIR ih tee) is a noun that means *clearness of mind.*

> The punch left him confused, but then **clarity** returned.

Vocabulary Practice

Review the words and sample sentences above. "Amigo Brothers" is about a boxing match between two friends. Based on the Vocabulary words, work with a partner to predict what the friends' match will be like. On the lines below, write down your prediction.

_____

_____

_____

SET A PURPOSE FOR READING
Read "Amigo Brothers" to find out what happens when two boys face a conflict that threatens their friendship.

Ⓐ COMPARE AND CONTRAST
Reread lines 1–13. <u>Underline</u> similarities between the two boys, and put brackets [ ] around differences. Then fill out the diagram below. In the top space, list facts that make Antonio different from Felix. In the bottom space, list facts that make Felix different from Antonio. In the middle where the circles overlap, list facts that are true of both boys.

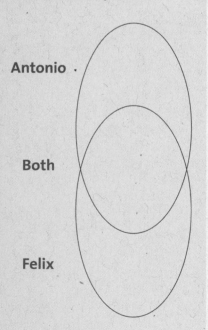

Antonio

Both

Felix

Amigo BROTHERS

Based on the short story by
PIRI THOMAS

BACKGROUND In this story, Felix and Antonio compete to take part in a Golden Gloves boxing tournament. Golden Gloves contests are famous. Amateurs, who are not paid to box, fight in these contests in hopes of becoming known. Past winners include Sugar Ray Robinson, George Foreman, and Muhammad Ali. Each of them later became a professional boxer.

Antonio Cruz and Felix Vargas were seventeen. They had been best friends for so long that they felt like brothers. They lived in the same apartment house on the Lower East Side of Manhattan. Antonio was light skinned, tall, and thin. Felix was dark, short, and muscular.

Both dreamed of becoming the world lightweight boxing champion. They trained together, and in the early mornings they ran along the river.

Both had won four boxing medals. Their styles were
10 different, though. With his long arms, Antonio could hit his opponent from farther away. He was also a better boxer. Felix was a more powerful slugger who could hit very hard. Ⓐ

In just two weeks they would fight each other. The winner would represent their club in the Golden Gloves Tournament.

IN OTHER WORDS Antonio Cruz and Felix Vargas are seventeen-year-old best friends. Both are winning boxers, and in two weeks they will box against each other. The winner of that match will go on to fight in the Golden Gloves boxing competition.

As they ran one morning, Felix said they needed to stop and talk. Their match was less than a week away. They stopped to lean against a railing and looked out at the river.

20   "I don't know how to say this, bro," Felix began.

"It's about the fight, right?" Antonio helped. "I've been worrying about it, too. I don't sleep. I think about pulling punches—holding back so I don't hurt you."

"Me too," said Felix. "I want to win fair and square, but I don't want to hurt you either. Let's make a promise, okay? When we fight, we've gotta be like two strangers who want the same thing." **B**

"*Sí*, I know," Tony smiled.

"Listen, Tony, I think we shouldn't see each other until
30 the fight. I'm going to Aunt Lucy's in the Bronx. I'll train up there."

Felix suggested they split right there. After the fight, he said, they'd be together again, like nothing ever happened. Unashamed to show how they felt, the amigo[1] brothers hugged and went their separate ways. **PAUSE & REFLECT**

IN OTHER WORDS Antonio and Felix are worried about the fight. They both want to win, but they don't want to hurt each other. Still, they agree to fight as if they're two strangers, not two close friends. Then they agree to stay away from each other while they train for the fight.

The night before the fight, Antonio went up to the roof of his apartment building. The only way not to hurt Felix, he thought, was to knock him out quickly. He worried about what the fight would do to their friendship.

---

1. **amigo** (uh MEE goh): Spanish for "friend."

B THEME AND SETTING
The **setting** is where and when a story's events take place. In this part of the story, the two friends stop to talk about a conflict they feel. Underline the words that show the setting for their conversation.

PAUSE & REFLECT
With a partner, discuss why Felix and Antonio agree to stay away from each other until after the fight is over.

VOCABULARY

The word **unbridled** (un BRYD uld) is an adjective that means *without control or restraint*.

ⓒ THEME AND SETTING

Reread lines 44–57. How do you think the boys feel when they enter the boxing ring? On the lines below, explain how the setting affects the way the boys feel.

_____

_____

_____

_____

_____

VISUAL VOCABULARY

A **referee** (ref uh REE) makes sure that players obey the rules of a game.

VOCABULARY

The word **dispel** (dis PEL) is a verb that means *to drive away or get rid of.*

40　　The same night, Felix watched a boxing movie, imagining himself as the hero. It was Felix the Champion against Antonio the Challenger. Like Antonio, he hoped for a quick, clean knockout.

On the day of the tournament, fans filled Tompkins Square Park. Many of them had placed bets on the fight. Antonio's confident fans bet with **unbridled** faith in his boxing skills. Felix's fans bet on the explosive power of his dynamite-packed fists.

In their dressing rooms, Antonio put on white trunks, 50 black socks, and black shoes. Felix wore light blue trunks, red socks and white shoes.

There were six other matches before their fight. Finally, it was time. The crowd roared as they entered the ring.

Bong! Bong! Bong! "Ladies and Gentlemen, *Señores* and *Señoras*. For the main event we have two young Puerto Rican boxers. Felix Vargas at 131 pounds and Antonio Cruz at 133 pounds." ⓒ

IN OTHER WORDS The two friends worry about the fight, each planning to knock the other out quickly. People in the neighborhood are excited. When Felix and Antonio enter the boxing ring, the crowd cheers for them.

The **referee** told them to fight fairly. "Now shake hands and come out fighting."

60　　The bell sounded for round one. Felix punched a hard straight left, but Antonio slipped away. Antonio's three fast lefts snapped Felix's head back. If Felix had any doubt that Antonio would fight to win, that doubt was being **dispelled**. Antonio wasn't pulling any punches. Both would fight to win.

Antonio danced around, moving fast and gracefully, punching again and again. Felix moved in closer so he could reach Antonio. At the end of the round, he trapped

Antonio against the ropes and smashed him in the
70 stomach. Two hard lefts to his head set Felix's ear ringing.

Bong! Both boxers froze mid-punch as round one ended.

Felix's right ear rang as he moved to his corner. Antonio
had red marks on the skin over his ribs. "Remember,"
Antonio's trainer told him, "Felix always goes for the body."

Felix's trainer warned him, too. "You gotta get in close,
or he'll chop you up from way back."

IN OTHER WORDS In the first round, the two friends do not hold
back. They fight hard. Both want to win.

Bong! Bong! Round two. Felix rushed in and landed a
solid right to the head. Hurt, Antonio hit back hard and
fast. Felix returned a left to Antonio's head and a right to
80 the body. ◐

Antonio waited while Felix danced around. Then, Felix
rushed in and slugged Antonio. Antonio hit him hard
on the chin, and lights seemed to explode inside Felix's
head. **Bedlam** broke loose as the screaming fans went
crazy. Felix felt his legs fold under him, but he managed
to fight off Antonio's attack. Felix came back with a
powerful right.

Antonio smashed Felix's right eye, which puffed up right
away. Toe to toe, the boxers battered each other. Right, left,
90 right, left. The crowd stood and roared.

A sudden punch to the chin made Antonio's legs feel
like jelly. His arms **flailed** desperately. Felix hit wildly until
Antonio punched him hard on the nose.

Then Felix landed a fierce blow. Antonio dropped to the
floor, then staggered to his feet. He slugged Felix hard, and
Felix went down flat on his back.

He got up dazed, in a fog. The crowd roared wildly as
the bell sounded to mark the end of round two.

◐ **LANGUAGE COACH**
Onomatopoeia (on uh mat
uh PEE uh) is the use of a
word whose sound imitates
its meaning. For example,
buzz is a word that sounds
like what it means. In lines
71 and 77 the writer uses
onomatopoeia to describe
one of the sounds at the
fight. (Circle) the word each
time you see it.

VOCABULARY
The word **bedlam** (BED
luhm) is a noun that means
noisy confusion.

VOCABULARY
The word **flail** (flayl) is a verb
that means *to wave wildly*.

VOCABULARY

The word **clarity** (KLAIR ih tee) is a noun that means *clearness of mind.*

ⓔ THEME AND SETTING

A story's **theme** is its message about life or human nature. Reread lines 109–120 and note clues about the story's theme. Then fill out the rest of the chart below.

Clues from Setting

Clues from Conflict

Clues from Character
Felix and Antonio realize
how important their
friendship is.

↓

Possible Theme

IN OTHER WORDS In the second round, the boys continue the fight, this time even harder than before. Felix knocks Antonio down, but Antonio stands up and punches Felix. Felix falls flat on his back, but he gets up. The crowd shouts wildly.

Both fighters were hurt, but the doctor said they were
100 okay to keep fighting. The cold-water sponges brought them <u>clarity</u>. They could think clearly, and they were ready to fight again.

Bong!—the last round. So far the fight seemed even, but there could be no tie. There had to be a winner.

Antonio charged, driving Felix against the ropes. They pounded each other fiercely. Felix's eye was closed, and blood poured from Antonio's nose. The crowd watched in silence.

The bell sounded the end of the fight, but the boxers
110 kept on pounding each other. The referee and trainers pulled them apart, and someone poured cold water over them.

Felix and Antonio looked around and hurried toward each other. The audience cried out in alarm. Would they fight to the death? Then the crowd cheered as the amigo brothers hugged.

"Ladies and Gentlemen, *Señores* and *Señoras*. The winner and champion is . . . " The announcer was about to point to the winner, but he was alone in the ring.
120 The champions had already left, arm in arm. **ⓔ**

IN OTHER WORDS In the last round, the fight is even. No one can tell who is winning. When the bell rings to end the fight, the referees pull the boys apart because they're still fighting. Then, Felix and Antonio rush toward each other.

► At first, the crowd is worried; then it begins to cheer. <u>Underline</u> the words that explain why the crowd cheers.

Literary Analysis: Theme and Setting

Remember that authors don't often tell you a story's **theme,** or message about life. Instead they use conflict, characters, and **setting** to provide clues about **theme.** "Amigo Brothers" uses all three types of clues. In the chart below, list clues from the story. Then, state the story's **theme** in a sentence or two.

READING 3 Analyze and make inferences about theme and genre in different cultural and historical contexts. **3C** Analyze how the time and place influence the theme or message of a literary work.

Clues from Setting	Clues from Conflict	Clues from Character
_____	_____	_____
_____	_____	_____
_____	_____	_____
_____	_____	_____
_____	_____	_____

Theme

_____

_____

_____

Review your completed chart. Explain how the **setting** of "Amigo Brothers" helps show its theme. Support your answer with evidence from the story.

_____

_____

_____

_____

_____

Reading Skill: Compare and Contrast

Complete the diagram below to **compare** and **contrast** Felix and Antonio. In the left space, list facts about Antonio that make him different from Felix. In the right space, list facts about Felix that make him different from Antonio. In the middle, where the two circles overlap, list facts that are true of both boys.

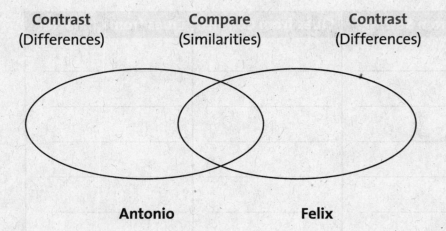

Contrast (Differences)   Compare (Similarities)   Contrast (Differences)

Antonio   Felix

Think about the two boys. Are they more alike than they are different? Or are they are more different than they are alike? Write your answer below.

_____

_____

_____

Vocabulary Practice

Identify each statement as true (T) or false (F).

_____ 1. If **bedlam** erupts in a locker room, the team is nervously quiet.

_____ 2. When things **flail** they remain still.

_____ 3. A person who feels **unbridled** joy is happy.

_____ 4. **Clarity** might give you confidence while taking a test.

_____ 5. Listening to a scary story will **dispel** feelings of fear.

Academic Vocabulary in Speaking

The word **theme** is a noun that means *the overall message or point of a piece of writing.*

The **theme,** or message, of Michelle's story is that friends forgive each other.

TURN AND TALK With a partner, talk about what it means when Felix and Antonio walk out of the ring without finding out who won the fight. Be sure to use the word **theme** in your conversation.

READING 3 Analyze and make inferences about theme and genre in different cultural and historical contexts. **3C** Analyze how the time and place influence the theme or message of a literary work.

Texas Assessment Practice

DIRECTIONS Use "Amigo Brothers" to answer questions 1–6.

1 Which statement shows a difference between Felix and Antonio?

- **A** They were so alike that they felt like brothers.
- **B** Antonio was thin, but Felix was muscular.
- **C** Each of the two dreamed of becoming a boxing champion.
- **D** Whenever they practiced with each other, they fought as though they intended to win.

2 From the way Felix and Antonio act the night before the match, what can you tell about them?

- **F** They don't want to be friends anymore.
- **G** They are nervous about fighting each other.
- **H** They don't care about winning the match.
- **J** They like watching movies together.

3 Which statement from the story shows how much the fight means to Felix and Antonio?

- **A** *Antonio waited while Felix danced around.*
- **B** *There had to be a winner.*
- **C** *They pounded each other fiercely.*
- **D** *The champions had already left, arm in arm.*

4 The boys leave the ring before hearing who won because —

- **F** the referee stops the fight
- **G** they can't hear who won
- **H** they will always be champions to each other
- **J** neither boy wants to defeat his friend

5 Which statement best describes the theme of the story?

- **A** Friendship is very fragile and can be destroyed by conflict.
- **B** A strong friendship can survive even the most extreme tests.
- **C** Competition sometimes brings out the best in friends.
- **D** Friends always grow apart over time.

6 The setting of Tompkins Square Park helps support the theme by —

- **F** showing how important exercise is to the boys
- **G** displaying the excitement around the fight
- **H** pointing out the differences between Felix and Antonio
- **J** providing an excellent place for fans to gather before the fight

READING 3A Describe multiple themes in a work of fiction.

The War of the Wall
Short story by Toni Cade Bambara

What makes a COMMUNITY?

Being part of a community, or larger group of people, helps us understand who we are. In this story, an "outsider" forces a neighborhood to rethink what it means to be a community.

LIST IT Think about a community that you belong to. It could be your neighborhood, your school, or some other group. Then, on the lines at left write down some things you have in common with others in this community.

What do I have in common with other people in my community?

Community: _____

_____

_____

_____

Things in common: _____

_____

_____

_____

Literary Analysis: Multiple Themes

Most stories have one main theme, or message about life. But a story may have **multiple themes.** You can find clues about possible themes in a story's title, setting (where and when it happens), characters, and conflict (the problem the characters face). The chart below shows some possible themes of "Amigo Brothers," a story on page 116.

Finding Themes
Title: "Amigo Brothers"
Setting: a poor inner-city neighborhood
Characters: Antonio and Felix, best friends who both dream of becoming boxing champions.
Conflict: They have to fight each other for the championship. They worry about how the fight will affect their friendship.
Possible Themes
• Friendship is more important than personal goals.
• Strong friendships can survive hard times.

Reading Strategy: Monitor

Good readers **monitor,** or check, their understanding as they read. A good way to check your understanding is to ask yourself questions. Sometimes you'll need to reread a section to find the answer. Other times you may need to read further in the story. As you read "The War of the Wall," write down answers to the questions in the margins, and think about your own questions about what is happening in the story.

RC-7(B) Ask literal, interpretive, evaluative, and universal questions of the text. RC-7(C) Reflect on understanding to monitor comprehension.

My Questions	Answers
Why is the narrator angry at the painter?	The narrator thinks the wall belongs to the people in the neighborhood. The painter is from out of town.

Vocabulary in Context

Note: Words are listed in the order in which they appear in the story.

Aroma (uh ROH muh) is a noun that means *odor* or *smell*.
   The **aroma** coming from the kitchen made me hungry.

Masterpiece (MAS ter pees) is a noun that means *a great work of art*.
   The lady wanted to paint a **masterpiece** on the wall.

Inscription (in SKRIP shuhn) is a noun that means *something written, carved, or engraved on a surface*.
   The **inscription** on the wall said the painting was for our community.

Vocabulary Practice

Review the vocabulary words and sample sentences above. Then, discuss these questions with a partner:

1. What is your favorite aroma?

2. Where could you go to see a masterpiece?

3. What is something important enough to include in an inscription?

**SET A PURPOSE
FOR READING**
Read this story to find out
what happens when a
stranger comes to town.

THE WAR OF THE WALL

Short story by
TONI CADE BAMBARA

BACKGROUND Murals are large pictures
painted on the walls of buildings. In
the 1960s, African American artists
painted murals as symbols of respect
for different groups. They painted
their "walls of respect" in many cities
across the United States, including small
Southern towns like the one in "The
War of the Wall."

Me and Lou had no time for courtesies. We were late
for school. So we just flat out told the painter lady to quit
messing with the wall. It was our wall, and she had no right
coming into our neighborhood painting on it. Stirring in
the paint bucket and not even looking at us, she mumbled
something about Mr. Eubanks, the barber, giving her
permission. That had nothing to do with it as far as we
were concerned. We've been pitching pennies against that
wall since we were little kids. Old folks have been dragging
10 their chairs out to sit in the shade of the wall for years.
Big kids have been playing handball against the wall since
so-called integration[1] when the crazies 'cross town poured
cement in our pool so we couldn't use it. I'd sprained

---

1. **since so-called integration** (in tih GRAY shuhn): since the 1960s, when
separating people of different races was no longer allowed. "So-called"
suggests that the narrator does not believe that integration (bringing people
of different races together as equals) has really happened.

my neck one time boosting my cousin Lou up to chisel Jimmy Lyons's name into the wall when we found out he was never coming home from the war in Vietnam to take us fishing.

"If you lean close," Lou said, leaning hipshot against her beat-up car, "you'll get a whiff of bubble gum and
20 kids' sweat. And that'll tell you something—that this wall belongs to the kids of Taliaferro Street." I thought Lou sounded very convincing. But the painter lady paid us no mind. She just snapped the brim of her straw hat down and hauled her bucket up the ladder. **A**

"You're not even from around here," I hollered up after her. The license plates on her old piece of car said "New York." Lou dragged me away because I was about to grab hold of that ladder and shake it. And then we'd really be late for school.

30 When we came from school, the wall was slick with white. The painter lady was running string across the wall and taping it here and there. Me and Lou leaned against the gumball machine outside the pool hall and watched. She had strings up and down and back and forth. Then she began chalking them with a hunk of blue chalk. **B**

IN OTHER WORDS The narrator and Lou see a lady about to paint a wall in their neighborhood. The wall is special to them partly because they had cut Jimmy Lyons's name into it after he died in the Vietnam War. They tell the lady to leave the wall alone, but she keeps working on it.

The Morris twins crossed the street, hanging back at the curb next to the beat-up car. The twin with the red ribbons was hugging a jug of cloudy lemonade. The one with yellow ribbons was holding a plate of dinner away from her

A MULTIPLE THEMES
Reread lines 1–24. Place brackets [ ] around the story title and the names of main characters. Then, circle the lines that give details about the story's setting (where and when it happens). Next, underline the lines that hint at the story's conflict, or main problem. Finally, on the lines below, write one possible theme of the story.

_____

_____

_____

_____

B MONITOR
Reread lines 25–35. Then, fill out the rest of the chart to check your understanding.

My Questions
1. What is the painter doing to the wall?
2. _____

↓

Answers
1. _____
_____
2. _____
_____

VOCABULARY

The word **aroma** (uh ROH muh) is a noun that means *odor* or *smell*.

(Circle) the items in lines 45–50 that might have an *aroma*.

40 dress. The painter lady began snapping the strings. The blue chalk dust measured off halves and quarters up and down and sideways too. Lou was about to say how hip it all was, but I dropped my book satchel on his toes to remind him we were at war.

Some good <u>aromas</u> were drifting our way from the plate leaking pot likker[2] onto the Morris girl's white socks. I could tell from where I stood that under the tinfoil was baked ham, collard greens, and candied yams.[3] And knowing Mrs. Morris, who sometimes bakes for my mama's 50 restaurant, a slab of buttered cornbread was probably up under there too, sopping up some of the pot likker. Me and Lou rolled our eyes, wishing somebody would send us some dinner. But the painter lady didn't even turn around. She was pulling the strings down and prying bits of tape loose.

Side Pocket came strolling out of the pool hall to see what Lou and me were studying so hard. He gave the painter lady the once-over, checking out her paint-spattered jeans, her chalky T-shirt, her floppy-brimmed straw hat. He hitched up his pants and glided over toward the painter 60 lady, who kept right on with what she was doing.

"Whatcha got there, sweetheart?" he asked the twin with the plate.

"Suppah," she said all soft and countrylike.

"For her," the one with the jug added, jerking her chin toward the painter lady's back.

Still she didn't turn around. She was rearing back on her heels, her hands jammed into her back pockets, her face squinched up like the <u>masterpiece</u> she had in mind was taking shape on the wall by magic. We could have been 70 gophers crawled up into a rotten hollow for all she cared. She didn't even say hello to anybody. Lou was muttering

VOCABULARY

The word **masterpiece** (MAS ter pees) is a noun that means *a great work of art*.

---

2. **pot likker:** the broth or liquid in which meat or vegetables have been cooked.

3. **collard** (KOL uhrd) **greens and candied yams:** collard greens are a vegetable related to cabbage. Candied yams are sweet potatoes cooked in a sugary sauce.

something about how great her concentration was. I butt him with my hip, and his elbow slid off the gum machine.

IN OTHER WORDS The Morris twins bring the painter a plate of food. Meanwhile, the lady continues working. She completely ignores the people watching her.

"Good evening," Side Pocket said in his best ain't-I-fine voice. But the painter lady was moving from the milk crate to the step stool to the ladder, moving up and down fast, scribbling all over the wall like a crazy person. We looked at Side Pocket. He looked at the twins. The twins looked at us. The painter lady was giving a show. It was like those
80 old-timey music movies where the dancer taps on the tabletop and then starts jumping all over the furniture, kicking chairs over and not skipping a beat. She didn't even look where she was stepping. And for a minute there, hanging on the ladder to reach a far spot, she looked like she was going to tip right over. **PAUSE & REFLECT**

"Ahh," Side Pocket cleared his throat and moved fast to catch the ladder. "These young ladies here have brought you some supper."

"Ma'am?" The twins stepped forward. Finally the
90 painter turned around, her eyes "full of sky," as my grandmama would say. Then she stepped down like she was in a trance.[4] She wiped her hands on her jeans as the Morris twins offered up the plate and the jug. She rolled back the tinfoil, then wagged her head as though something terrible was on the plate.

"Thank your mother very much," she said, sounding like her mouth was full of sky too. "I've brought my own

PAUSE & REFLECT
Why do you think the painter is ignoring the people watching her? Discuss your thoughts with a partner.

---

4. **trance** (trans): a condition of daydreaming or being unaware of what is going on.

dinner along." And then, without even excusing herself, she went back up the ladder, drawing on the wall in a wild way. Side Pocket whistled one of those oh-brother breathy whistles and went back into the pool hall. The Morris twins shifted their weight from one foot to the other, then crossed the street and went home. Lou had to drag me away, I was so mad. We couldn't wait to get to the firehouse to tell my daddy all about this rude woman who'd stolen our wall.

IN OTHER WORDS The painter begins drawing on the wall as the children watch. Finally, Side Pocket tells her about the food the twins have brought.

▶ What does the painter do about the food? <u>Underline</u> the words that tell you this.

All the way back to the block to help my mama out at the restaurant, me and Lou kept asking my daddy for ways to run the painter lady out of town. But my daddy was busy talking about the trip to the country and telling Lou he could come too because Grandmama can always use an extra pair of hands on the farm.

Later that night, while me and Lou were in the back doing our chores, we found out that the painter lady was a liar. She came into the restaurant and leaned against the glass of the steam table, talking about how starved she was. I was scrubbing pots and Lou was chopping onions, but we could hear her through the service window. She was asking Mama was that a ham hock in the greens, and was that a neck bone in the pole beans, and were there any vegetables cooked without meat, especially pork.

"I don't care who your spiritual leader is," Mama said in that way of hers. "If you eat in the community, sistuh, you gonna eat pig by-and-by, one way or t'other."

Me and Lou were cracking up in the kitchen, and several customers at the counter were clearing their throats, waiting for Mama to really fix her wagon for not speaking to the elders when she came in. **C** The painter lady took a stool at the counter and went right on with her questions. Was there cheese in the baked macaroni, she wanted to know? Were there eggs in the salad? Was it honey or sugar in the iced tea? Mama was fixing Pop Johnson's plate. And every time the painter lady asked a fool question, Mama would dump another spoonful of rice on the pile. She was tapping her foot and heating up in a dangerous way. But Pop Johnson was happy as he could be. Me and Lou peeked through the service window, wondering what planet the painter lady came from. Who ever heard of baked macaroni without cheese, or potato salad without eggs? **D**

IN OTHER WORDS The painter goes to the restaurant where the narrator's mother works. The painter's attitude and questions about the food confuse the local people and make Mama angry.

"Do you have any bread made with unbleached flour?" the painter lady asked Mama. There was a long pause, as though everybody in the restaurant was holding their breath, wondering if Mama would dump the next spoonful on the painter lady's head. She didn't. But when she set Pop Johnson's plate down, it came down with a bang.

When Mama finally took her order, the starving lady all of a sudden couldn't make up her mind whether she wanted a vegetable plate or fish and a salad. She finally settled on the broiled trout and a tossed salad. But just

The phrase "fix her wagon" (line 128) is an idiom. An **idiom** is a phrase that can't be understood from the ordinary meaning of its words. The idiom "fix her wagon" means "to criticize and scold her."

D MONITOR
Reread lines 126–141. Why is the lady asking all these questions about the food? Discuss your answer with a partner.

when Mama reached for a plate to serve her, the painter lady leaned over the counter with her finger all up in the air.

"Excuse me," she said. "One more thing." Mama was holding the plate like a Frisbee, tapping that foot, one hand on her hip. "Can I get raw beets in that tossed salad?"

"You will get," Mama said, leaning her face close to the painter lady's, "whatever Lou back there tossed. Now sit 160 down." And the painter lady sat back down on her stool and shut right up.

All the way to the country, me and Lou tried to get Mama to open fire on the painter lady. But Mama said that seeing as how she was from the North, you couldn't expect her to have any manners. Then Mama said she was sorry she'd been so impatient with the woman because she seemed like a decent person and was simply trying to stick to a very strict diet. Me and Lou didn't want to hear that. Who did that lady think she was, coming into our 170 neighborhood and taking over our wall? **E**

"Welllll," Mama drawled, pulling into the filling station so Daddy could take the wheel, "it's hard on an artist, ya know. They can't always get people to look at their work. So she's just doing her work in the open, that's all."

IN OTHER WORDS After many more questions from the painter, the narrator's mother serves the lady her food. Then, the narrator's family takes a trip to the countryside.

▶ The children try to get Mama to say something bad about the painter. What does she say instead? Underline the sentences that tell you this.

Me and Lou definitely did not want to hear that. Why couldn't she set up an easel downtown or draw on the

E MULTIPLE THEMES
Identify the story's conflict, or main problem. Then, with a partner, discuss possible themes related to the conflict. Write your answers below.

Conflict

↓

Possible Themes
•
•

sidewalk in her own neighborhood? Mama told us to quit fussing so much; she was tired and wanted to rest. She climbed into the back seat and dropped down into the warm hollow Daddy had made in the pillow.

All weekend long, me and Lou tried to scheme up ways to recapture our wall. Daddy and Mama said they were sick of hearing about it. Grandmama turned up the TV to drown us out. On the late news was a story about the New York **subways**. When a train came roaring into the station all covered from top to bottom, windows too, with writings and drawings done with spray paint, me and Lou slapped five. Mama said it was too bad kids in New York had nothing better to do than spray paint all over the trains. Daddy said that in the cities, even grown-ups wrote all over the trains and buildings too. Daddy called it "graffiti." Grandmama called it a shame.

We couldn't wait to get out of school on Monday. We couldn't find any black spray paint anywhere. But in a junky hardware store downtown we found a can of white epoxy⁵ paint, the kind you touch up old refrigerators with when they get splotchy and peely. We spent our whole allowance on it. And because it was too late to use our bus passes, we had to walk all the way home lugging our book satchels and gym shoes, and the bag with the epoxy.

VISUAL VOCABULARY
A **subway** is an electric railway that runs underground. Subway trains are used in very large cities.

IN OTHER WORDS From a TV news story, the narrator and Lou get the idea of spray painting graffiti on the wall. The next day, they buy the paint and walk home.

When we reached the corner of Taliaferro and Fifth, it looked like a block party or something. Half the neighborhood was gathered on the sidewalk in front of the wall. I looked at Lou, he looked at me. We both looked at

---

5. **epoxy** (ih POK see): a plastic used in glues and paints.

the bag with the epoxy and wondered how we were going to work our scheme. The painter lady's car was nowhere in sight. But there were too many people standing around to do anything. Side Pocket and his buddies were leaning on their cue sticks, hunching each other. Daddy was there with a lineman[6] he catches a ride with on Mondays. Mrs. Morris had her arms flung around the shoulders of the twins on either side of her. Mama was talking with some of her customers, many of them with napkins still at the throat. Mr. Eubanks came out of the barbershop, followed by a man in a striped poncho, half his face shaved, the other half full of foam.

"She really did it, didn't she?" Mr. Eubanks huffed out his chest. Lots of folks answered right quick that she surely did when they saw the straight razor in his hand.

Mama beckoned[7] us over. And then we saw it. The wall. Reds, greens, figures outlined in black. Swirls of purple and orange. Storms of blues and yellows. It was something. I recognized some of the faces right off. There was Martin Luther King, Jr. And there was a man with glasses on and his mouth open like he was laying down a heavy rap. Daddy came up alongside and reminded us that that was Minister Malcolm X. The serious woman with a rifle I knew was Harriet Tubman because my grandmama has pictures of her all over the house. And I knew Mrs. Fannie Lou Hamer 'cause a signed photograph of her hangs in the restaurant next to the calendar.[8] **F**

Then I let my eyes follow what looked like a vine. It trailed past a man with a horn, a woman with a big white flower in her hair, a handsome dude in a tuxedo

F MONITOR
Reread lines 220–231. Why are people standing in front of the wall? Write your answer on the lines below.

_____

_____

_____

_____

_____

---

6. **lineman:** a person who repairs telephone or power lines.

7. **beckon** (BEK uhn): to call using hand signals or a nod.

8. **Martin Luther King, Jr. . . . Minister Malcolm X . . . Harriet Tubman . . . Fannie Lou Hamer:** Martin Luther King, Jr., and Malcolm X were leaders in the movement for civil rights during the 1960s. About 100 years earlier, Harriet Tubman led many enslaved people in the South to freedom in the North. Fannie Lou Hamer worked to get African Americans registered to vote.

seated at a piano, and a man with a goatee holding a book. When I looked more closely, I realized that what had looked like flowers were really faces. One face with yellow petals looked just like Frieda Morris. One with red petals looked just like Hattie Morris. I could hardly believe

240 my eyes.

"Notice," Side Pocket said, stepping close to the wall with his cue stick like a classroom pointer. "These are the flags of liberation," he said in a voice I'd never heard him use before. We all stepped closer while he pointed and spoke. "Red, black and green," he said, his pointer falling on the leaflike flags of the vine. "Our liberation flag.[9] And here Ghana, there Tanzania. Guinea-Bissau, Angola, Mozambique."[10] Side Pocket sounded very tall, as though he'd been waiting all his life to give this lesson.

250 Mama tapped us on the shoulder and pointed to a high section of the wall. There was a fierce-looking man with his arms crossed against his chest guarding a bunch of children. His muscles bulged, and he looked a lot like my daddy. One kid was looking at a row of books. Lou hunched me 'cause the kid looked like me. The one that looked like Lou was spinning a globe on the tip of his finger like a basketball. There were other kids there with microscopes and compasses. And the more I looked, the more it looked like the fierce man was not so much

260 guarding the kids as defending their right to do what they were doing. **G**

Then Lou gasped and dropped the paint bag and ran forward, running his hands over a rainbow. He had to tiptoe and stretch to do it, it was so high. I couldn't breathe

G LANGUAGE COACH
The word *compasses*, in line 258, is a **multiple-meaning word.** It has more than one possible meaning. Here, *compasses* could mean "instruments used to tell directions" or "instruments used to draw arcs or circles." Since the children in the mural have a globe and microscopes, the compasses are probably drawing compasses. Globes, microscopes, and drawing compasses are all used for learning, as in classes at school.

---

9. **Red, black and green . . . liberation** (lib uh RAY shuhn) **flag:** a banner of red, black, and green stripes has been used in the United States as well as Africa to stand for liberation, or freedom.

10. **Ghana** (GAH nuh) . . . **Tanzania** (tan zuh NEE uh) . . . **Guinea-Bissau** (gin ee bih SOW) **Angola** (ang GOH luh) **Mozambique** (moh zuhm BEEK): countries in southern and western Africa.

VOCABULARY

The word **inscription** (in SKRIP shuhn) is a noun that means *something written, carved, or engraved on a surface.*

either. The painter lady had found the chisel marks and had painted Jimmy Lyons's name in a rainbow.

"Read the <u>inscription</u>, honey," Mrs. Morris said, urging little Frieda forward. She didn't have to urge much. Frieda marched right up, bent down, and in a loud voice
270 that made everybody quit oohing and ahhing and listen, she read,

> *To the People of Taliaferro Street*
> *I Dedicate This Wall of Respect*
> *Painted in Memory of My Cousin*
> *Jimmy Lyons*

IN OTHER WORDS The narrator and Lou head to the wall to spray paint it. But when they get to the wall, people are looking at it.

▶ Reread lines 250–261. What do the boys see on the wall? With a partner, discuss the painting the lady has made for the community.

Literary Analysis: Multiple Themes

Some stories have more than one theme. You can find themes in many ways. You might find a theme by thinking about how a problem is solved. You might find a theme by thinking about the lesson a character learns. Or, you might find a theme by thinking about the setting or title of the story. Look back at your answers to notes A and E. In the chart below, write down details about the title, setting, characters, and conflict. Use these details to find the story's themes.

READING 3A Describe multiple themes in a work of fiction.

Title: The War of the Wall	What the title means: The narrator wanted to fight about the wall with the painter.	Possible theme: You should only fight about things that are really important.
Setting: _____ _____	Why the setting matters: _____ _____	Possible theme: _____ _____
Characters: _____ _____	What the main character learns: _____ _____	Possible theme: _____ _____
Conflict: _____ _____	How the problem is resolved: _____ _____	Possible theme: _____ _____

Now explain which theme you think is the most important in the story and why.

_____

_____

_____

_____

RC-7(B) Ask literal, interpretive, evaluative, and universal questions of the text. **RC-7(C)** Reflect on understanding to monitor comprehension.

Reading Strategy: Monitor

The example below shows how monitoring can help you understand a story.

Question	Answer	Why Monitoring Helped
Why is the lady painting the wall?	Her cousin, who died in Vietnam, lived in the neighborhood.	It helped me understand that she was painting the wall in his memory.

Now look at the questions in notes B, D, and F and think about your answers to them. How did answering each question help you understand "The War of the Wall"?

_____

_____

_____

What makes a COMMUNITY?

How does the lady's painting bring the people in the community together?

_____

_____

_____

Vocabulary Practice

Circle the answer that is most closely related to each boldface vocabulary word.

1. **aroma: (a)** arguing with a friend **(b)** writing a letter
   (c) smelling a rose

2. **masterpiece: (a)** a game of catch **(b)** a prize-winning play
   (c) a stormy day

3. **inscription: (a)** military service **(b)** words on a trophy
   (c) parts of a car

Academic Vocabulary in Speaking

The word **cultural** (KUHL chuhr uhl) is an adjective that means *relating to the entire way of life of a group of people*.

At the **cultural** arts show, we saw pottery, sculptures, and paintings from Kenya.

The word **symbol** (SIM buhl) is a noun that means *something chosen to represent or stand for something else, such as a mark or sign*.

The painting is a **symbol** of respect for our community.

TURN AND TALK With a partner, talk about the importance of what the lady painted on the wall. Be sure to use the words **cultural** and **symbol** in your discussion.

READING 3A Describe multiple themes in a work of fiction.

Texas Assessment Practice

DIRECTIONS Use "The War of the Wall" to answer questions 1–4.

1 The narrator thinks the painter is a liar because she says she —

- (A) is from the neighborhood
- (B) brought her own dinner
- (C) is painting for the community
- (D) is related to Jimmy Lyons

2 How does the narrator's view of the painting change?

- (F) He realizes that the painting honors people he cares about.
- (G) He understands that the painter lady is trying her best to fit in.
- (H) He decides that the wall isn't important to him after all.
- (J) He notices that everyone else likes it, so he thinks he should like it too.

3 Which answer best describes one of the story's themes?

- (A) Public art is for all to enjoy.
- (B) Don't break the law to get your way.
- (C) Trusting people you don't know can get you in trouble.
- (D) There are different ways to be connected in a community.

4 The setting affects the theme of the story because it —

- (F) includes a restaurant
- (G) is a small Southern town with its own culture and customs
- (H) is located near farms, far away from a city
- (J) has a playground where all the local kids get together

READING 9 Analyze the author's purpose in cultural and contemporary contexts.

Homeless
Problem-Solution Essay

Background

The bus station in the following selection is in New York City. The station is huge and draws in many homeless people. The station has programs to help the homeless. Even with the efforts of government and volunteer organizations, homelessness is a difficult problem to solve.

Skill Focus: Identify Author's Purpose

An **author's purpose** is the reason he or she writes a piece. An author may write to

- give readers information about a topic
- share his or her feelings with readers
- entertain readers
- persuade, or convince, readers to share his or her opinion

Authors often write with more than one of these purposes, but one is usually the most important. Authors don't usually state their purposes for writing. However, you can uncover the purpose for yourself by following these steps:

1. Note which parts of the topic get the most attention or emphasis.

2. Write down key details, words, and phrases the author uses. What is the author trying to say? Why is this important?

3. Decide which purpose (or purposes) this information seems to fit. Does it inform, express feelings, entertain, or persuade?

As you read, you will use a chart like the one below to gather evidence that will help you identify the **author's purpose.**

Key Details, Words, and Phrases	Why This Is Important	Purpose(s)
We walk around people "lying on the sidewalk."	We ignore people instead of helping them.	to persuade

**SET A PURPOSE
FOR READING**
Read "Homeless" to
discover the writer's
insights into the problem
of homelessness and the
solution she suggests.

FOCUS ON FORM
"Homeless" is a problem-
solution essay. In this
type of nonfiction
writing, a writer explains
a problem and offers a
possible solution.

HOMELESS

by Anna Quindlen
from *The New York Times*

Her name was Ann, and we met in the Port Authority
Bus Terminal several Januarys ago. I was doing a story
on homeless people. She said I was wasting my time
talking to her; she was just passing through, although
she'd been passing through for more than two weeks.
To prove to me that this was true, she rummaged
through a tote bag and a manila envelope and finally

unfolded a sheet of typing paper and brought out her photographs.

10   They were not pictures of family, or friends, or even a dog or cat, its eyes brown-red in the flashbulb's light. They were pictures of a house. It was like a thousand houses in a hundred towns, not suburb, not city, but somewhere in between, with aluminum siding and a chainlink fence, a narrow driveway running up to a one-car garage and a patch of backyard. The house was yellow. I looked on the back for a date or a name, but neither was there. There was no need for discussion. I knew what she was trying to tell me, for it was
20 something I had often felt. She was not adrift, alone, anonymous, although her bags and her raincoat with the grime shadowing its creases had made me believe she was. She had a house, or at least once upon a time had had one. Inside were curtains, a couch, a stove, potholders. You are where you live. She was somebody. **Ⓐ**

Ⓐ LANGUAGE COACH

"You are where you live" is a **metaphor** (MET uh fawr), a figure of speech that compares two different things. The author is saying that people think of who they are based on where and how they live.

IN OTHER WORDS The author tells about a homeless woman she met. Because the woman has a picture of a house she once lived in, she does not consider herself homeless. The author connects having a place to live with a person's feeling that he or she is someone who matters.

I've never been very good at looking at the big picture, taking the global view, and I've always been a person with an overactive sense of place, the legacy[1]

---

1. **legacy** (LEG uh see): something handed down from an ancestor or from the past.

of an Irish grandfather. So it is natural that the thing
30 that seems most wrong with the world to me right now
is that there are so many people with no homes. I'm
not simply talking about shelter from the elements, or
three square meals a day or a mailing address to which
the welfare[2] people can send the check—although
I know that all these are important for survival. I'm
talking about a home, about precisely those kinds of
feelings that have wound up in cross-stitch and French
knots on samplers[3] over the years.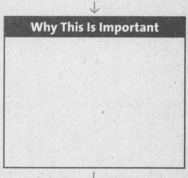

Home is where the heart is. There's no place
40 like it. I love my home with a ferocity totally out of
proportion to its appearance or location. I love dumb
things about it: the hot-water heater, the plastic rack
you drain dishes in, the roof over my head, which
occasionally leaks. And yet it is precisely those dumb
things that make it what it is—a place of certainty,
stability,[4] predictability, privacy, for me and for my
family. It is where I live. What more can you say about
a place than that? That is everything.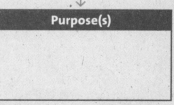

Yet it is something that we have been edging away
50 from gradually during my lifetime and the lifetimes
of my parents and grandparents. There was a time
when where you lived often was where you worked and
where you grew the food you ate and even where you
were buried. When that era passed, where you lived
at least was where your parents had lived and where

---

2. **welfare:** a program of financial aid provided by the government
   to people in need.
3. **in cross-stitch and French knots on samplers:** spelled out in fancy
   stitching on decorations.
4. **stability** (stuh BIL ih tee): a state of being lasting and reliable.

B AUTHOR'S PURPOSE
Reread lines 29–38. With a partner, underline words and phrases that tell you what problem the writer is identifying. Next, fill in the first two boxes of the chart below. Finally, fill in which purpose or purposes this idea best fits—to inform, to entertain, to express feelings, or to persuade.

Key Words and Phrases

↓

Why This Is Important

↓

Purpose(s)

C AUTHOR'S PURPOSE
Statements that reveal the author's feelings can help you identify her purpose. Reread lines 39–48. Bracket [ ] the words that tell you the writer's feelings about the idea of home.

you would live with your children when you became enfeebled.[5] Then, suddenly, where you lived was where you lived for three years, until you could move on to something else and something else again.

60 And so we have come to something else again, to children who do not understand what it means to go to their rooms because they have never had a room, to men and women whose fantasy is a wall they can paint a color of their own choosing, to old people reduced to sitting on molded plastic chairs, their skin blue-white in the lights of a bus station, who pull pictures of houses out of their bags. Homes have stopped being homes. Now they are real estate.

IN OTHER WORDS The author points out the importance of having a home for a person's emotional well-being and sense of comfort.

► Reread lines 49–68. With a partner, discuss how the expectation of having a home has changed over the years.

People find it curious that those without homes
70 would rather sleep sitting up on benches or huddled in doorways than go to shelters. Certainly some prefer to do so because they are emotionally ill, because they have been locked in before and they are damned if they will be locked in again. Others are afraid of the violence and trouble they may find there. But some seem to want something that is not available in shelters, and they will not compromise, not for a **cot**, or oatmeal,

VISUAL VOCABULARY
A **cot** is a small bed that can be folded up and carried easily.

5. **enfeebled** (en FEE buhld): lacking strength; made weak.

or a shower with special soap that kills the bugs. "One room," a woman with a baby who was sleeping on her
80 sister's floor, once told me, "painted blue." That was the crux[6] of it; not size or location, but pride of ownership. Painted blue. **D**

This is a difficult problem, and some wise and compassionate people are working hard at it. But in the main I think we work around it, just as we walk around it when it is lying on the sidewalk or sitting in the bus terminal—the problem, that is. It has been customary to take people's pain and lessen our own participation in it by turning it into an issue, not a
90 collection of human beings. We turn an adjective into a noun: the poor, not poor people; the homeless, not Ann or the man who lives in the box or the woman who sleeps on the subway grate. **PAUSE & REFLECT**

Sometimes I think we would be better off if we forgot about the broad strokes and concentrated on the details. Here is a woman without a bureau. There is a man with no mirror, no wall to hang it on. They are not the homeless. They are people who have no homes. No drawer that holds the spoons. No window to look
100 out upon the world. My God. That is everything. **E**

IN OTHER WORDS The author ends the essay by pointing out the needs of several homeless people. She emphasizes homeless people as individuals and the importance of having a place to call home—something readers may take for granted.

6. **crux:** the most important point.

D AUTHOR'S PURPOSE
The author repeats the words "painted blue" in lines 80 and 82. How does the idea of being able to paint a room fit the **author's purpose** in writing this essay?

_____
_____
_____
_____
_____

PAUSE & REFLECT
With a partner, discuss how thinking of homelessness in terms of people instead of problems might change people's attitudes.

E AUTHOR'S PURPOSE
Reread lines 94–100. What action does the writer want readers to take?

_____
_____
_____
_____
_____
_____

READING 9 Analyze the author's purpose in cultural and contemporary contexts.

Practicing Your Skills: Identify Author's Purpose

Why do you think Anna Quindlen wrote this essay—to provide information, express feelings, entertain, or persuade? Use the chart below to help you decide. First, look at the example in the first row. Then write down two more sets of words, phrases, and details from the essay that seem important. Then, fill out the second column—why the details you choose are important. Finally, fill out the third column by saying which purpose you think the details support.

Key Details, Words, and Phrases	Why This Is Important	Purpose(s)
We walk around people "lying on the sidewalk."	We ignore people instead of helping them.	to persuade

Based on your completed chart, (circle) Anna Quindlen's purpose (or purposes) for writing "Homeless" in the list below. Then complete the sentence starter that follows the list.

• to give readers information

• to share feelings with readers

• to entertain readers

• to persuade, or convince, readers to share her opinion

I think the author wrote the essay for this purpose (or these purposes) because

_____

_____

_____

Academic Vocabulary in Speaking

The word **context** (KON tekst) is a noun that means *the conditions in which an event or idea happens or exists*.

Shouting might be necessary in a bus station, but in the **context** of a library it seems rude.

A **clause** (klawz) is a noun that means *a group of words with a subject and verb* or *a part of a legal document*.

A **clause** in his contract kept the star player from appearing in ads.

TURN AND TALK With a partner, discuss why the author chooses groups of words that emphasize details about her own home. Be sure to use the words **clause** and **context** in your discussion.

READING 9 Analyze the author's purpose in cultural and contemporary contexts.

Texas Assessment Practice

DIRECTIONS Use "Homeless" to answer questions 1–4.

1 Based on lines 1–25, you can guess that Ann —

- **A** will be going home soon
- **B** is proud of the home she lived in
- **C** wants to help the writer with her story
- **D** misses her family

2 From the information in lines 39–48, you can tell that the writer —

- **F** dislikes her house because of its problems
- **G** hopes her children will live in the same house
- **H** takes a lot of pride in the house she lives in
- **J** sees her house differently than most people do

3 In lines 94–96, the author writes, "Sometimes I think we would be better off if we forgot about the broad strokes and concentrated on the details." This statement shows that she thinks homeless people —

- **A** should be thought of as individual people
- **B** would rather not go to shelters
- **C** all used to have homes of their own
- **D** need more help than they have gotten

4 The author probably wrote this essay to —

- **F** persuade readers to think differently about homelessness
- **G** compare the different ways people live today
- **H** entertain readers with a story about her home
- **J** explain why people become homeless

UNIT 4

Finding a Voice
MOOD, TONE, AND STYLE

Be sure to read the Reader's Workshop on pp. 454–459 in *Holt McDougal Literature*.

Academic Vocabulary for Unit 4

You will see these Academic Vocabulary words as you work through this book. You will also be asked to use them as you write and talk about the selections in this unit.

Communicate (kuh MYOO nih kayt) is a verb that means *to tell ideas or information to others.*
Jason will **communicate** the assignment to students who missed class.

What are the different ways you **communicate** with friends? _____

_____

Describe (dih SKRYB) is a verb that means *to tell or write about in detail.*
Elena likes to read books that **describe** foreign countries.

Describe your favorite weekend activities: _____

_____

Illustrate (IL uh strayt) is a verb that means *to explain or make clear by using examples.*
A writing assignment should **illustrate** main points with examples.

How would you **illustrate** a new cover for your favorite book? _____

_____

Interpret (in TER prit) is a verb that means *to explain or make clear.*
A guide at the science museum will **interpret** the exhibits.

How would you **interpret** a friend's laugh after you told a joke? _____

_____

Style (styl) is a noun that means *the way in which something is said or done.*
This author uses a **style** of short, simple sentences.

Describe your **style** of dress when you go to school: _____

_____

READING 3C Analyze how place and time influence the theme or message in a literary work.
8 Analyze how an author's use of language suggests mood.

Dark They Were, and Golden-Eyed

Short story by **Ray Bradbury**

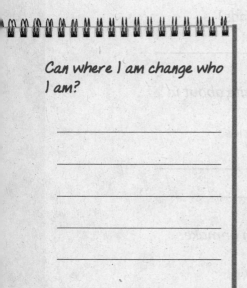

Can where I am change who I am?

_____

_____

_____

_____

_____

Can where you are CHANGE who you are?

If you had to move away from everything you know, how much would you change, and how much would you stay the same? In "Dark They Were, and Golden-Eyed," you'll see how a family changes after moving to a very different place.

TURN AND TALK With a partner, discuss whether the place where you live can affect your personality. Then, write your responses on the lines at left.

Literary Analysis: Mood

The feeling you get from a story is called its **mood**. Writers create mood by using descriptive words and by showing what characters think and how they talk. Mood can also be expressed through **imagery**—words and phrases that appeal to a reader's senses of sight, sound, touch, smell, and taste.

IDENTIFYING MOOD	
Descriptive Words	**Imagery**
• cheerful	• foggy
• somber	• gritty
• wondrous	• perfumed
• eerie	• sour
• terrifying	• screeching
• peaceful	
• silly	

Reading Strategy: Reading Science Fiction

In **science fiction,** writers often explore the future while making a comment about problems of today's world. As you read this story, notes in the side column will ask you to look for characteristics of science fiction like those shown below.

READING 3 Analyze genre in different cultural and contemporary contexts. **3C** Analyze how place and time influence the theme or message in a literary work.

Characteristics	Examples in the Story
Scientific information based on known facts	*Mars once had water.*
Elements of life today familiar to most readers	*the morning paper*
Imaginary elements that are not real in our own time and place	*family travels by rocket*

Vocabulary in Context

NOTE: Words are listed in the order in which they appear in the story.

Convivial (kuhn VIV ee uhl) is an adjective that means *enjoying the company of others.*

He didn't feel like talking, but he tried to be **convivial.**

Subtly (SUHT lee) is an adverb that means *not obviously or in a way that is hard to notice.*

He noticed that the food had **subtly** changed.

Recede (ree SEED) is a verb that means *to become fainter or more distant.*

After it lifted off, we watched the rocket **recede** into the sky.

Dwindle (DWIN duhl) is a verb that means *to become less, until little remains.*

The rocket's roar will **dwindle** as it recedes into the sky.

Pendulum (PEN joo luhm) is a noun that means *a weight hung so that it can swing freely, as used in certain clocks.*

The **pendulum** in the grandfather clock kept a steady beat.

Vocabulary Practice

Review the words and sample sentences above. Based on these words, what do you think the story will be about? Discuss your thoughts with a partner.

SET A PURPOSE
FOR READING
Read "Dark They Were, and Golden-Eyed" to learn how a family changes when they move to a strange new place.

DARK THEY WERE, AND GOLDEN-EYED

Short story by
RAY BRADBURY

BACKGROUND The planet Mars has long been a popular setting for science fiction stories and movies. "Martians" in these stories and movies are often shown as little green people with big heads. In this science fiction story, Ray Bradbury provides a very different look at what it could mean to be a "Martian."

The rocket metal cooled in the meadow winds. Its lid gave a bulging *pop*. From its clock interior stepped a man, a woman, and three children. The other passengers whispered away across the Martian meadow, leaving the man alone among his family.

The man felt his hair flutter and the tissues of his body draw tight as if he were standing at the center of a vacuum. His wife, before him, seemed almost to whirl away in smoke. The children, small seeds, might at any instant be
10 sown to all the Martian climes.

The children looked up at him, as people look to the sun to tell what time of their life it is. His face was cold.

"What's wrong?" asked his wife.

"Let's get back on the rocket."

"Go back to Earth?"

"Yes! Listen!"

The wind blew as if to flake away their identities. At any moment the Martian air might draw his soul from him, as marrow comes from a white bone. He felt

20 submerged in a chemical that could dissolve his intellect and burn away his past. Ⓐ

They looked at Martian hills that time had worn with a crushing pressure of years. They saw the old cities, lost in their meadows, lying like children's delicate bones among the blowing lakes of grass.

"Chin up, Harry," said his wife. "It's too late. We've come over sixty million miles."

The children with their yellow hair hollered at the deep dome of Martian sky. There was no answer but the racing

30 hiss of wind through the stiff grass. Ⓑ

He picked up the luggage in his cold hands. "Here we go," he said—a man standing on the edge of a sea, ready to wade in and be drowned.

They walked into town.

IN OTHER WORDS A man, woman, and three children step out of a spaceship that has just traveled from Earth to Mars. The man wants to return to Earth, but they decide to stay. Nearby, they see the remains of old cities. Together, they walk to town.

Their name was Bittering. Harry and his wife Cora; Dan, Laura, and David. They built a small white cottage and ate good breakfasts there, but the fear was never gone. It lay with Mr. Bittering and Mrs. Bittering, a third unbidden partner at every midnight talk, at every dawn

40 awakening.

"I feel like a salt crystal," he said, "in a mountain stream, being washed away. We don't belong here. We're Earth

Ⓐ **MOOD**
Reread lines 1–21. Circle the words in those lines that describe how the man feels after landing on Mars.

Ⓑ **MOOD**
Reread lines 22–30. Then, Underline words that describe how Mars looks. With a partner, discuss how you would describe the mood of the story so far.

◉ READING SCIENCE FICTION

Reread lines 56–72. Then, in the chart below, list an example of how Bradbury uses elements of life today in this imaginary setting.

Elements of Life Today

people. This is Mars. It was meant for Martians. For heaven's sake, Cora, let's buy tickets for home!"

But she only shook her head. "One day the atom bomb will fix Earth. Then we'll be safe here."

"Safe and insane!"

Tick-tock, seven o'clock sang the voice-clock; *time to get up.* And they did.

50 Something made him check everything each morning— warm hearth, potted blood-geraniums—precisely as if he expected something to be amiss. The morning paper was toast-warm from the 6 A.M. Earth rocket. He broke its seal and tilted it at his breakfast place. He forced himself to be **convivial**.

"Colonial days all over again," he declared. "Why, in ten years there'll be a million Earthmen on Mars. Big cities, everything! They said we'd fail. Said the Martians would resent our invasion. But did we find any Martians? 60 Not a living soul! Oh, we found their empty cities, but no one in them. Right?"

A river of wind submerged the house. When the windows ceased rattling Mr. Bittering swallowed and looked at the children.

"I don't know," said David. "Maybe there're Martians around we don't see. Sometimes nights I think I hear 'em. I hear the wind. The sand hits my window. I get scared. And I see those towns way up in the mountains where the Martians lived a long time ago. And I think I see things 70 moving around those towns, Papa. And I wonder if those Martians *mind* us living here. I wonder if they won't do something to us for coming here." ◉

"Nonsense!" Mr. Bittering looked out the windows. "We're clean, decent people." He looked at his children. "All dead cities have some kind of ghosts in them.

Memories, I mean." He stared at the hills. "You see a staircase and you wonder what Martians looked like climbing it. You see Martian paintings and you wonder what the painter was like. You make a little ghost in your
80 mind, a memory. It's quite natural. Imagination." He stopped. "You haven't been prowling up in those ruins, have you?"

"No, Papa." David looked at his shoes.

"See that you stay away from them. Pass the jam."

"Just the same," said little David, "I bet something happens." **PAUSE & REFLECT**

IN OTHER WORDS The family has left Earth because they are afraid the Earth will be destroyed by war and atomic bombs. Although they have not seen any Martians, they fear that the Martians may still be on the planet and may not like people from Earth taking over.

Something happened that afternoon. Laura stumbled through the settlement, crying. She dashed blindly onto the porch.
90 "Mother, Father—the war, Earth!" she sobbed. "A radio flash just came. Atom bombs hit New York! All the space rockets blown up. No more rockets to Mars, ever!"

"Oh, Harry!" The mother held onto her husband and daughter.

"Are you sure, Laura?" asked the father quietly.

Laura wept. "We're stranded on Mars, forever and ever!"

For a long time there was only the sound of the wind in the late afternoon.

Alone, thought Bittering. Only a thousand of us here.
100 No way back. No way. No way. ❶ Sweat poured from his face and his hands and his body; he was drenched in the

PAUSE & REFLECT
Bradbury's descriptions of the Martian ruins create a very tense mood. Reread lines 84–86. Then, with a partner, discuss what you think might happen to the Bittering family.

❶ LANGUAGE COACH
Sentence fragments are incomplete sentences. They are often used in dialogue to show how people really talk. In lines 99–100, sentence fragments help express Bittering's fearful thoughts.

hotness of his fear. He wanted to strike Laura, cry, "No, you're lying! The rockets will come back!" Instead, he stroked Laura's head against him and said, "The rockets will get through someday."

"Father, what will we do?"

"Go about our business, of course. Raise crops and children. Wait. Keep things going until the war ends and the rockets come again."

110 The two boys stepped out onto the porch.

"Children," he said, sitting there, looking beyond them, "I've something to tell you."

"We know," they said.

In the following days, Bittering wandered often through the garden to stand alone in his fear. As long as the rockets had spun a silver web across space, he had been able to accept Mars. For he had always told himself: Tomorrow, if I want, I can buy a ticket and go back to Earth. **E**

But now: The web gone, the rockets lying in jigsaw

120 heaps of molten girder and unsnaked wire. Earth people left to the strangeness of Mars, the cinnamon dusts and wine airs, to be baked like gingerbread shapes in Martian summers, put into harvested storage by Martian winters. What would happen to him, the others? This was the moment Mars had waited for. Now it would eat them.

IN OTHER WORDS Laura receives a disturbing message on the radio.

▶ Reread lines 90–98. <u>Underline</u> what has happened on Earth. What does this event mean for the people on Mars?

He got down on his knees in the flower bed, a spade in his nervous hands. Work, he thought, work and forget.

E **READING SCIENCE FICTION**

Reread lines 114–118. What imaginary elements, or things that are not real in our own time and place, help characterize this passage as science fiction? Write your answers on the lines below.

Imaginary Elements

He glanced up from the garden to the Martian
mountains. He thought of the proud old Martian names

130 that had once been on those peaks. Earthmen, dropping
from the sky, had gazed upon hills, rivers, Martian seas left
nameless in spite of names. Once Martians had built cities,
named cities; climbed mountains, named mountains; sailed
seas, named seas. Mountains melted, seas drained, cities
tumbled. In spite of this, the Earthmen had felt a silent guilt
at putting new names to these ancient hills and valleys. **F**

Nevertheless, man lives by symbol and label. The names
were given.

Mr. Bittering felt very alone in his garden under the

140 Martian sun, anachronism[1] bent here, planting Earth
flowers in a wild soil.

Think. Keep thinking. Different things. Keep your
mind free of Earth, the atom war, the lost rockets.

He perspired. He glanced about. No one watching. He
removed his tie. Pretty bold, he thought. First your coat
off, now your tie. He hung it neatly on a peach tree he had
imported as a sapling from Massachusetts.

He returned to his philosophy of names and mountains.
The Earthmen had changed names. Now there were Hormel

150 Valleys, Roosevelt Seas, Ford Hills, Vanderbilt Plateaus,
Rockefeller Rivers, on Mars. It wasn't right. The American
settlers had shown wisdom, using old Indian prairie names:
Wisconsin, Minnesota, Idaho, Ohio, Utah, Milwaukee,
Waukegan, Osseo. The old names, the old meanings.

Staring at the mountains wildly, he thought: Are you up
there? All the dead ones, you Martians? Well, here we are,
alone, cut off! Come down, move us out! We're helpless!

The wind blew a shower of peach blossoms.

He put out his sun-browned hand and gave a small cry.

160 He touched the blossoms and picked them up. He turned

F READING SCIENCE
FICTION
Reread lines 132–136.
Here, Bradbury makes
a connection between
Martians and elements of
human life today. What did
Martians do that humans
have done? With a partner,
discuss what happened to
what the Martians did.

---

1. **anachronism** (uh NAK ruh niz uhm): something placed outside of its proper
   time period; examples might include a dinosaur appearing in a story that
   takes place today or a polar bear living in a jungle.

them, he touched them again and again. Then he shouted for his wife.

"Cora!"

She appeared at a window. He ran to her.

"Cora, these blossoms!"

She handled them.

"Do you see? They're different. They've changed! They're not peach blossoms any more!"

"Look all right to me," she said.

170   "They're not. They're wrong! I can't tell how. An extra petal, a leaf, something, the color, the smell!"

The children ran out in time to see their father hurrying about the garden, pulling up radishes, onions, and carrots from their beds.

"Cora, come look!"

They handled the onions, the radishes, the carrots among them.

"Do they look like carrots?"

"Yes . . . no." She hesitated. "I don't know."

180   "They're changed."

"Perhaps."

"You know they have! Onions but not onions, carrots but not carrots. Taste: the same but different. Smell: not like it used to be." He felt his heart pounding, and he was afraid. He dug his fingers into the earth. "Cora, what's happening? What is it? We've got to get away from this." He ran across the garden. Each tree felt his touch. "The roses. The roses. They're turning green!"

And they stood looking at the green roses.

190   And two days later Dan came running. "Come see the cow. I was milking her and I saw it. Come on!"

They stood in the shed and looked at their one cow.

It was growing a third horn. **G**

And the lawn in front of their house very quietly and slowly was coloring itself like spring violets. Seed from Earth but growing up a soft purple.

G MOOD
Reread lines 165–193. Then, underline the words and phrases that appeal to a reader's senses of sight, sound, touch, smell, or taste. How do these images make you feel, or what mood do they create in the story?

_____

_____

_____

_____

_____

_____

_____

_____

_____

_____

"We must get away," said Bittering. "We'll eat this stuff and then we'll change—who knows to what? I can't let it happen. There's only one thing to do. Burn this food!"

200 "It's not poisoned."

"But it is. **Subtly**, very subtly. A little bit. A very little bit. We mustn't touch it."

He looked with dismay at their house. "Even the house. The wind's done something to it. The air's burned it. The fog at night. The boards, all warped out of shape. It's not an Earthman's house any more."

"Oh, your imagination!"

He put on his coat and tie. "I'm going into town. We've 210 got to do something now. I'll be back."

"Wait, Harry!" his wife cried. But he was gone.

IN OTHER WORDS The family notices that everything they have brought from Earth is changing.

▶ In lines 189–196, mark brackets [ ] around three changes they notice.

In town, on the shadowy step of the grocery store, the men sat with their hands on their knees, conversing with great leisure and ease.

Mr. Bittering wanted to fire a pistol in the air.

What are you doing, you fools! he thought. Sitting here! You've heard the news—we're stranded on this planet. ❿ Well, move! Aren't you frightened? Aren't you afraid? What are you going to do?

220 "Hello, Harry," said everyone.

"Look," he said to them. "You did hear the news, the other day, didn't you?"

They nodded and laughed. "Sure. Sure, Harry."

"What are you going to do about it?"

"Do, Harry, do? What *can* we do?"

"Build a rocket, that's what!"

VOCABULARY

The word **subtly** (SUHT lee) is an adverb that means *not obviously* or *in a way that is hard to notice*.

❿ **READING SCIENCE FICTION**

In lines 212–214, Bradbury describes a scene that you might see in a small town today. Underline the imaginary element in line 217—the thing that would be out of place if the scene were in our own place and time.

"A rocket, Harry? To go back to all that trouble? Oh, Harry!"

"But you *must* want to go back. Have you noticed the
230 peach blossoms, the onions, the grass?"

"Why, yes, Harry, seems we did," said one of the men.

"Doesn't it scare you?"

"Can't recall that it did much, Harry."

"Idiots!"

"Now, Harry."

Bittering wanted to cry. "You've got to work with me. If
we stay here, we'll all change. The air. Don't you smell it?
Something in the air. A Martian virus, maybe; some seed,
or a pollen. Listen to me!"
240 They stared at him.

"Sam," he said to one of them.

"Yes, Harry?"

"Will you help me build a rocket?"

"Harry, I got a whole load of metal and some blueprints.
You want to work in my metal shop on a rocket, you're
welcome. I'll sell you that metal for five hundred dollars.
You should be able to construct a right pretty rocket, if you
work alone, in about thirty years."

Everyone laughed. ❶
250 "Don't laugh."

Sam looked at him with quiet good humor.

"Sam," Bittering said. "Your eyes—"

"What about them, Harry?"

"Didn't they used to be gray?"

"Well now, I don't remember."

"They were, weren't they?"

"Why do you ask, Harry?"

"Because now they're kind of yellow-colored."

"Is that so, Harry?" Sam said, casually.
260 "And you're taller and thinner—"

"You might be right, Harry."

❶ **MOOD**
Reread lines 229–249. How
is Harry's mood different
from the mood shared
by the other men? Which
mood—Harry's or the other
men's—seems to be the
mood of the story?

_____

_____

_____

_____

_____

_____

_____

_____

"Sam, you shouldn't have yellow eyes."

"Harry, what color eyes have *you* got?" Sam said.

"My eyes? They're blue, of course."

"Here you are, Harry." Sam handed him a pocket mirror. "Take a look at yourself."

Mr. Bittering hesitated, and then raised the mirror to his face.

270 There were little, very dim flecks of new gold captured in the blue of his eyes. **J**

"Now look what you've done," said Sam a moment later. "You've broken my mirror."

IN OTHER WORDS Harry goes into town to talk with other men about the changes he has noticed. He wants to build a rocket to return to Earth.

▶ With a partner, discuss how the other men react to Harry's plan.

Harry Bittering moved into the metal shop and began to build the rocket. Men stood in the open door and talked and joked without raising their voices. Once in a while they gave him a hand on lifting something. But mostly they just idled and watched him with their yellowing eyes.

"It's suppertime, Harry," they said.

His wife appeared with his supper in a wicker basket.

280 "I won't touch it," he said. "I'll eat only food from our Deepfreeze. Food that came from Earth. Nothing from our garden."

His wife stood watching him. "You can't build a rocket."

"I worked in a shop once, when I was twenty. I know metal. Once I get it started, the others will help," he said, not looking at her, laying out the blueprints.

"Harry, Harry," she said, helplessly.

"We've *got* to get away, Cora. We've got to!"

J **READING SCIENCE FICTION**

Reread lines 262–270. With a partner, discuss whether the changes in the men's eyes are imaginary elements or scientific information.

The nights were full of wind that blew down the empty
290 moonlit sea meadows past the little white chess cities lying for their twelve-thousandth year in the shallows. In the Earthmen's settlement, the Bittering house shook with a feeling of change. **Ⓚ**

Lying abed, Mr. Bittering felt his bones shifted, shaped, melted like gold. His wife, lying beside him, was dark from many sunny afternoons. Dark she was, and golden-eyed, burnt almost black by the sun, sleeping, and the children metallic in their beds, and the wind roaring forlorn and changing through the old peach trees, the violet grass,
300 shaking out green rose petals.

The fear would not be stopped. It had his throat and heart. It dripped in a wetness of the arm and the temple and the trembling palm.

A green star rose in the east.

A strange word emerged from Mr. Bittering's lips.

"Iorrt. Iorrt." He repeated it.

It was a Martian word. He knew no Martian.

In the middle of the night he arose and dialed a call through to Simpson, the archaeologist.
310 "Simpson, what does the word *Iorrt* mean?"

"Why that's the old Martian word for our planet Earth. Why?"

"No special reason."

The telephone slipped from his hand.

"Hello, hello, hello, hello," it kept saying while he sat gazing out at the green star. "Bittering? Harry, are you there?" **Ⓛ**

The days were full of metal sound. He laid the frame of the rocket with the reluctant help of three indifferent men. He grew very tired in an hour or so and had to sit down.
320 "The altitude," laughed a man.

Ⓚ LANGUAGE COACH
Reread lines 289–291. The phrases "sea meadows" and "chess cities" are figures of speech called **metaphors**. Here, Bradbury compares the Martian meadows to a sea and the Martian cities to the white game pieces on a chess board.

Ⓛ MOOD
Reread lines 310–316. What does Harry realize that causes him to drop the telephone? How does this event affect the story's mood?

"Are you *eating*, Harry?" asked another.

"I'm eating," he said, angrily.

"From your Deepfreeze?"

"Yes!"

"You're getting thinner, Harry."

"I'm not!"

"And taller."

"Liar!"

IN OTHER WORDS Harry begins to change.

▶ Reread lines 305–307. Draw brackets [ ] around details that show Harry becoming more Martian.

His wife took him aside a few days later. "Harry, I've
330 used up all the food in the Deepfreeze. There's nothing left.
I'll have to make sandwiches using food grown on Mars."

He sat down heavily.

"You must eat," she said. "You're weak."

"Yes," he said.

He took a sandwich, opened it, looked at it, and began
to nibble at it.

"And take the rest of the day off," she said. "It's hot.
The children want to swim in the canals and hike. Please
come along."

340 "I can't waste time. This is a crisis!"

"Just for an hour," she urged. "A swim'll do you good."

He rose, sweating. "All right, all right. Leave me alone.
I'll come." Ⓜ

"Good for you, Harry."

The sun was hot, the day quiet. There was only an
immense staring burn upon the land. They moved along
the canal, the father, the mother, the racing children in
their swimsuits. They stopped and ate meat sandwiches.
He saw their skin baking brown. And he saw the yellow

Ⓜ **MOOD**
Reread lines 333–343. The members of the Bittering family have started to change physically. What other way is Harry changing now? Put a check mark ✔ next to the sentences that show how Harry is changing.

350 eyes of his wife and his children, their eyes that were never yellow before. A few tremblings shook him, but were carried off in waves of pleasant heat as he lay in the sun. He was too tired to be afraid.

"Cora, how long have your eyes been yellow?"

She was bewildered. "Always, I guess."

"They didn't change from brown in the last three months?"

She bit her lips. "No. Why do you ask?"

"Never mind."

360 They sat there.

"The children's eyes," he said. "They're yellow, too."

"Sometimes growing children's eyes change color."

"Maybe *we're* children, too. At least to Mars. That's a thought." He laughed. "Think I'll swim." **N**

N READING SCIENCE FICTION

In lines 349–364, Harry talks with his wife about how they are all changing physically. What familiar element of life today does Bradbury use in line 364 to show that Harry isn't as worried as he once was?

IN OTHER WORDS All of the food brought from Earth is gone, and Harry begins to eat food grown on Mars. The family goes swimming, and Harry again notices how his wife and children are changing. Their skin is brown, and their eyes are yellow.

They leaped into the canal water, and he let himself sink down and down to the bottom like a golden statue and lie there in green silence. All was water-quiet and deep, all was peace. He felt the steady, slow current drift him easily.

370 If I lie here long enough, he thought, the water will work and eat away my flesh until the bones show like coral. Just my skeleton left. And then the water can build on that skeleton—green things, deep water things, red things, yellow things. Change. Change. Slow, deep, silent change. And isn't that what it is up *there*?

He saw the sky submerged above him, the sun made Martian by atmosphere and time and space.

Up there, a big river, he thought, a Martian river; all of us lying deep in it, in our pebble houses, in our sunken boulder houses, like **crayfish** hidden, and the water washing away our old bodies and lengthening the bones and—

He let himself drift up through the soft light.

Dan sat on the edge of the canal, regarding his father seriously.

"*Utha,*" he said.

"What?" asked his father.

The boy smiled. "You know. *Utha's* the Martian word for 'father.'"

"Where did you learn it?"

"I don't know. Around. *Utha!*"

"What do you want?"

The boy hesitated. "I—I want to change my name."

"Change it?"

"Yes."

His mother swam over. "What's wrong with Dan for a name?"

Dan fidgeted. "The other day you called Dan, Dan, Dan. I didn't even hear. I said to myself, That's not my name. I've a new name I want to use." PAUSE & REFLECT

Mr. Bittering held to the side of the canal, his body cold and his heart pounding slowly. "What is this new name?"

"Linnl. Isn't that a good name? Can I use it? Can't I, please?"

Mr. Bittering put his hand to his head. He thought of the silly rocket, himself working alone, himself alone even among his family, so alone.

He heard his wife say, "Why not?"

He heard himself say, "Yes, you can use it."

"Yaaa!" screamed the boy. "I'm Linnl, Linnl!"

Racing down the meadowlands, he danced and shouted.

VISUAL VOCABULARY

A **crayfish** is a freshwater animal that looks like a small lobster.

PAUSE & REFLECT

Reread lines 383–399. With a partner, discuss why Dan wants to change his name.

VISUAL VOCABULARY

A **mosaic** (moh ZAY ik) is a design made from pieces of stone or glass set into a pattern.

◎ MOOD

Reread lines 413–421. Circle the descriptive words Bradbury uses to create a certain mood. Then, with a partner, discuss how the mood of the story has changed.

VOCABULARY

The word **recede** (ree SEED) is a verb that means *to become fainter or more distant.*

The word **dwindle** (DWIN duhl) is a verb that means *to become less, until little remains.*

Mr. Bittering looked at his wife. "Why did we do that?"

"I don't know," she said. "It just seemed like a good idea."

They walked into the hills. They strolled on old **mosaic** paths, beside still pumping fountains. The paths were covered with a thin film of cool water all summer long. You kept your bare feet cool all the day, splashing as in a creek, wading.

They came to a small deserted Martian villa with a good view of the valley. It was on top of a hill. Blue marble halls, 420 large murals, a swimming pool. It was refreshing in this hot summertime. The Martians hadn't believed in large cities. ◎

"How nice," said Mrs. Bittering, "if we could move up here to this villa for the summer."

"Come on," he said. "We're going back to town. There's work to be done on the rocket."

IN OTHER WORDS The family begins to adopt Martian ways. However, Harry hasn't completely given up the idea of leaving.

But as he worked that night, the thought of the cool blue marble villa entered his mind. As the hours passed, the rocket seemed less important.

In the flow of days and weeks, the rocket **receded** and 430 **dwindled**. The old fever was gone. It frightened him to think he had let it slip this way. But somehow the heat, the air, the working conditions—

He heard the men murmuring on the porch of his metal shop.

"Everyone's going. You heard?"

"All going. That's right."

Bittering came out. "Going where?" He saw a couple of trucks, loaded with children and furniture, drive down the dusty street.

440 "Up to the villas," said the man.

"Yeah, Harry. I'm going. So is Sam. Aren't you Sam?"

"That's right, Harry. What about you?"

"I've got work to do here."

"Work! You can finish that rocket in the autumn, when it's cooler."

He took a breath. "I got the frame all set up."

"In the autumn is better." Their voices were lazy in the heat.

"Got to work," he said.

450 "Autumn," they reasoned. And they sounded so sensible, so right.

"Autumn would be best," he thought. "Plenty of time, then."

No! cried part of himself, deep down, put away, locked tight, suffocating. No! No!

"In the autumn," he said.

"Come on, Harry," they all said.

"Yes," he said, feeling his flesh melt in the hot liquid air. "Yes, in the autumn. I'll begin work again then."

PAUSE & REFLECT

460 "I got a villa near the Tirra Canal," said someone.

"You mean the Roosevelt Canal, don't you?"

"Tirra. The old Martian name."

"But on the map—"

"Forget the map. It's Tirra now. Now I found a place in the Pillan Mountains—"

"You mean the Rockefeller Range," said Bittering.

"I mean the Pillan Mountains," said Sam.

"Yes," said Bittering, buried in the hot, swarming air. "The Pillan Mountains."

PAUSE & REFLECT

Reread lines 452–459. With a partner, discuss why the rocket is becoming less important to Harry.

Ⓟ READING SCIENCE FICTION
What elements of life today are the Bitterings giving up in lines 475–489? List the items on the lines below.

_____

_____

_____

_____

_____

_____

_____

_____

_____

_____

_____

_____

_____

_____

_____

_____

_____

_____

470   Everyone worked at loading the truck in the hot, still afternoon of the next day.

Laura, Dan, and David carried packages. Or, as they preferred to be known, Ttil, Linnl, and Werr carried packages.

The furniture was abandoned in the little white cottage.

"It looked just fine in Boston," said the mother. "And here in the cottage. But up at the villa? No. We'll get it when we come back in the autumn."

Bittering himself was quiet.

480   "I've some ideas on furniture for the villa," he said after a time. "Big, lazy furniture."

"What about your encyclopedia? You're taking it along, surely?"

Mr. Bittering glanced away. "I'll come and get it next week."

They turned to their daughter. "What about your New York dresses?"

The bewildered girl stared. "Why, I don't want them any more." Ⓟ

490   They shut off the gas, the water, they locked the doors and walked away. Father peered into the truck.

"Gosh, we're not taking much," he said. "Considering all we brought to Mars, this is only a handful!"

He started the truck.

Looking at the small white cottage for a long moment, he was filled with a desire to rush to it, touch it, say good-bye to it, for he felt as if he were going away on a long journey, leaving something to which he could never quite return, never understand again.

500   Just then Sam and his family drove by in another truck.

"Hi, Bittering! Here we go!"

The truck swung down the ancient highway out of town. There were sixty others traveling in the same direction. The town filled with a silent, heavy dust from their passage. The canal waters lay blue in the sun, and a quiet wind moved in the strange trees. **Q**

"Good-bye, town!" said Mr. Bittering.

"Good-bye, good-bye," said the family, waving to it.

They did not look back again.

IN OTHER WORDS The settlers from Earth move to the old Martian houses. Harry thinks about staying behind to finish his rocket, but he decides to join everyone else and move to the mountains. The children have changed their names, and the settlers now use the Martian names of mountains and rivers.

---

510 Summer burned the canals dry. Summer moved like flame upon the meadows. In the empty Earth settlement, the painted houses flaked and peeled. Rubber tires upon which children had swung in back yards hung suspended like stopped clock **pendulums** in the blazing air.

At the metal shop, the rocket frame began to rust.

In the quiet autumn Mr. Bittering stood, very dark now, very golden-eyed, upon the slope above his villa, looking at the valley.

"It's time to go back," said Cora.

520 "Yes, but we're not going," he said quietly. "There's nothing there any more."

"Your books," she said. "Your fine clothes."

"Your *llles* and your fine *ior uele rre*," she said.

"The town's empty. No one's going back," he said. "There's no reason to, none at all."

The daughter wove tapestries and the sons played songs on ancient flutes and pipes, their laughter echoing in the marble villa.

Q MOOD
Reread lines 502–506. What mood is created by the descriptive words *silent, heavy, quiet,* and *strange*? Discuss your answer with a partner.

VOCABULARY
The word **pendulum** (PEN joo luhm) is a noun that means *a weight hung so that it can swing freely, as used in certain clocks.*

Mr. Bittering gazed at the Earth settlement far away in
530 the low valley. "Such odd, such ridiculous houses the Earth
people built."

"They didn't know any better," his wife mused. "Such
ugly people. I'm glad they've gone."

They both looked at each other, startled by all they had
just finished saying. They laughed.

"Where did they go?" he wondered. He glanced at
his wife. She was golden and slender as his daughter. She
looked at him, and he seemed almost as young as their
eldest son.

540 "I don't know," she said. ®

"We'll go back to town maybe next year, or the year
after, or the year after that," he said, calmly. "Now—I'm
warm. How about taking a swim?"

They turned their backs to the valley. Arm in arm
they walked silently down a path of clear-running spring
water.

IN OTHER WORDS The family realizes that they no longer want to
return to town.

▶ Reread lines 529–540. With a partner, discuss what has
happened to Harry and his family.

Five years later a rocket fell out of the sky. It lay
steaming in the valley. Men leaped out of it, shouting.

"We won the war on Earth! We're here to rescue
550 you! Hey!"

But the American-built town of cottages, peach trees,
and theaters was silent. They found a flimsy rocket frame
rusting in an empty shop.

**® READING SCIENCE
FICTION**

Are the startling changes
in lines 526–540 examples
of scientific information
or imaginary elements?
Explain.

The rocket men searched the hills. The captain established headquarters in an abandoned bar. His lieutenant came back to report.

"The town's empty, but we found native life in the hills, sir. Dark people. Yellow eyes. Martians. Very friendly. We talked a bit, not much. They learn English fast. I'm sure
560 our relations will be most friendly with them, sir."

"Dark, eh?" mused the captain. "How many?"

"Six, eight hundred, I'd say, living in those marble ruins in the hills, sir. Tall, healthy. Beautiful women."

"Did they tell you what became of the men and women who built this Earth settlement, Lieutenant?"

"They hadn't the foggiest notion of what happened to this town or its people."

"Strange. You think those Martians killed them?"

"They look surprisingly peaceful. Chances are a plague
570 did this town in, sir."

"Perhaps. I suppose this is one of those mysteries we'll never solve. One of those mysteries you read about."

PAUSE & REFLECT

The captain looked at the room, the dusty windows, the blue mountains rising beyond, the canals moving in the light, and he heard the soft wind in the air. He shivered. Then, recovering, he tapped a large fresh map he had thumbtacked to the top of an empty table.

"Lots to be done, Lieutenant." His voice droned on and quietly on as the sun sank behind the blue hills.
580 "New settlements. Mining sites, minerals to be looked for. Bacteriological specimens[2] taken. The work, all the work. And the old records were lost. We'll have a job of

PAUSE & REFLECT

Pause at line 572. How would you explain the mystery of the town and its people? Discuss your answer with a partner.

---

2. **bacteriological specimens** (bak teer ee uh LAH jih kuhl SPEH suh muhnz): samples of different kinds of living things that each have only one cell.

remapping to do, renaming the mountains and rivers and such. Calls for a little imagination.

"What do you think of naming those mountains the Lincoln Mountains, this canal the Washington Canal, those hills—we can name those hills for you, Lieutenant. Diplomacy. And you, for a favor, might name a town for me. Polishing the apple.[3] And why not make
590 this the Einstein Valley, and farther over . . . are you *listening,* Lieutenant?"

The lieutenant snapped his gaze from the blue color and the quiet mist of the hills far beyond the town.

"What? Oh, *yes,* sir!" ⑤

IN OTHER WORDS Years later, people from Earth land on Mars to rescue the settlers. They find the town empty. Martians living nearby tell them that they don't know what happened to the settlers. The men from Earth discuss building a new settlement. One of the men is distracted by the Martian landscape.

⑤ **MOOD**
Reread from line 578 to the end. What is the mood at the end of the story? How does Bradbury create this mood?

_____

_____

_____

_____

_____

_____

_____

_____

_____

_____

_____

_____

_____

_____

_____

3. **polishing the apple:** acting in such a way as to get another person's approval.

Literary Analysis: Mood

In "Dark They Were, and Golden-Eyed," Bradbury uses descriptive words and imagery to give the story a certain mood. Look back at any notes you took as you read. Then, in the chart below, write down examples of Bradbury's use of descriptive words and imagery. Some examples are provided for you. Finally, write a paragraph describing the overall mood of the story.

READING 8 Analyze how an author's use of language suggests mood.

IDENTIFYING MOOD	
Descriptive Words	**Imagery**
alone	a bulging pop
cold	tissues of his body draw tight
submerged	whirl away in smoke
worn	racing hiss of wind

Overall mood of the story:

_____

_____

_____

_____

_____

_____

_____

_____

_____

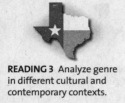

READING 3 Analyze genre in different cultural and contemporary contexts.

Reading Strategy: Reading Science Fiction

Think about the characteristics of science fiction, and look back at the examples you noted as you read the story. Then, list more examples in the chart below.

Characteristics	Examples in the Story
Scientific information based on known facts	*water on Mars*
Elements of life today familiar to most readers	*the morning paper*
Imaginary elements that are not real in our own time and place	*family travels by rocket*

Can where you are CHANGE who you are?

Now that you know what happened to the Bittering family, have you changed your mind about how a place might change you? Explain.

_____

_____

Vocabulary Practice

Circle the letter of the phrase that has a connection to each vocabulary word.

1. **pendulum:** (a) a grandfather clock (b) a racing motorcycle

2. **dwindle:** (a) your supply of money (b) your age

3. **subtly:** (a) a fireworks show (b) a gradually dimming light

4. **convivial:** (a) a dog and a squirrel (b) a friendly crowd

5. **recede:** (a) a plane flying away (b) a plane arriving to land

Academic Vocabulary in Speaking

The word **describe** (dih SKRYB) means *to tell or write about in detail*.
Jana had never seen a bulldog, so I had to **describe** it to her.

The word **illustrate** (IL uh strayt) means *to explain or make clear by using examples*.
The coach threw several pitches to **illustrate** how to throw a curve ball.

READING 3 Analyze genre in different cultural and contemporary contexts.
8 Analyze how an author's use of language suggests mood.

TURN AND TALK With a partner, talk about the changes Harry Bittering begins to notice as his family spends more time on Mars. Be sure to use the words **describe** and **illustrate** in your discussion.

Texas Assessment Practice

DIRECTIONS Use "Dark They Were, and Golden-Eyed" to answer questions 1–4.

1 Which event below could happen only in a science fiction story?

- **A** Humans build space rockets.
- **B** Atom bombs cause destruction on Earth.
- **C** Food can be stored in a deep freeze.
- **D** Humans learn the Martian language.

2 Which of the following is NOT a science fiction element that appears in this story?

- **F** using factual, scientific information
- **G** including background information about the topic from several sources
- **H** using made-up elements that could not happen in our own time and place
- **J** including familiar, everyday things

3 Which word best describes the overall mood created by the characters' speech and feelings in lines 35–44?

- **A** peaceful
- **B** lively
- **C** nervous
- **D** tired

4 Which pair of words *best* describes the mood created in lines 62–72?

- **F** pleasant, happy
- **G** eerie, fearful
- **H** bitter, angry
- **J** sad, lonely

READING 4 Understand the structure and elements of poetry. Analyze the importance of graphical elements (e.g., capital letters, line length, word position) on the meaning of a poem.

maggie and milly and molly and may
who are you,little i
old age sticks

Poems by E. E. Cummings

Are all things CONNECTED?

An octopus always has eight arms, and a spider always has eight legs. When you look at the night sky, you see the same moon that someone in China would see. Connections like these help us understand our world. In these poems, you'll see how connections can help us understand each other, too.

TURN AND TALK Think of a plant or animal, an object, and a person that you share a connection with. Discuss each of these connections with a partner. What makes each living thing, object, or person special to you? What do you have in common with each?

Literary Analysis: Style in Poetry

E. E. Cummings has one of the most original **styles** in literature. As you read these three poems, look for examples of the stylistic elements shown below.

Elements of Cummings's Style	
Word Choice	Uses made-up words and uses words in new ways
Form	Breaks lines at surprising places, sometimes even in the middle of a word
Punctuation, Capitalization, Word Position	Breaks the "rules" of punctuation, capitalization, and word position

Reading Strategy: Monitor

To get the most out of your reading, it is a good idea to **monitor,** or check, your understanding while you are reading. One way to monitor your reading is to **clarify** what you have read so far. To clarify your reading,

RC-7(C) Reflect on understanding to monitor comprehension.

- stop and think about what you know so far
- use clues in the selection to make guesses about meaning
- rephrase lines or ideas in your own words to make the meaning more clear

As you read each poem, use the steps below to rephrase difficult lines in your own words.

Poet's Words
"milly befriended a stranded star"

+

Information from Context
At the beach, a starfish might be stranded.

=

My Words
Milly found a starfish.

SET A PURPOSE FOR READING
Read this poem to discover what four girls find at the beach.

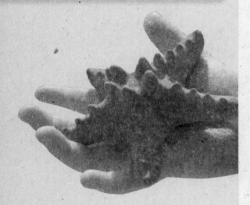

ⓐ STYLE IN POETRY

Reread lines 3–4. Then, in the chart below, list an example of each stylistic element.

Punctuation	
Capitalization	
Word Position	

maggie and milly and molly and may

Poem by
E. E. CUMMINGS

BACKGROUND E. E. Cummings wrote his poems at a time when writers and artists were trying new forms and breaking with tradition. Notice how he breaks the standard rules of both poetry and prose writing.

maggie and milly and molly and may
went down to the beach(to play one day)

and maggie discovered a shell that sang
so sweetly she couldn't remember her troubles,and ⓐ

5 milly befriended a stranded star
whose rays five languid[1] fingers were;

and molly was chased by a horrible thing
which raced sideways while blowing bubbles:and

may came home with a smooth round stone
10 as small as a world and as large as alone.

For whatever we lose(like a you or a me)
it's always ourselves we find in the sea

1. **languid** (LANG gwid): lacking energy; drooping.

IN OTHER WORDS Four characters, possibly children, go to the beach and discover a seashell, a starfish, a crab, and a smooth stone. The speaker suggests that discovering objects from the sea is also a way of discovering something about yourself.

who are you,little i

Poem by
E. E. CUMMINGS

Monitor Your Comprehension

**SET A PURPOSE
FOR READING**
Read this poem to discover
who "little i" is.

who are you,little i

(five or six years old)
peering from some high

window;at the gold **B**

5 of November sunset

(and feeling:that if day
has to become night

this is a beautiful way) **PAUSE & REFLECT**

B MONITOR
Reread lines 1–4. Then,
identify what you know
about the situation or
context. Finally, rephrase
the poet's words in your
own words.

Information from Context:

My Words:

PAUSE & REFLECT
Reread the poem. Then,
with a partner, discuss
the speaker's attitude or
mood. What feeling about
childhood does the poem
express?

IN OTHER WORDS The speaker describes a child's feelings about
a sunset. The speaker's use of "little i" suggests that the speaker
may be remembering a personal childhood experience.

❻ LANGUAGE COACH

You have seen how Cummings breaks the rules of language. Notice the symbol at the end of line 4. This symbol, called an **ampersand,** represents the word *and.* Cummings uses the ampersand two more times in this poem. Do you see the line in which the ampersand doesn't make sense?

❼ STYLE IN POETRY

Reread lines 8–11. Here, Cummings breaks apart the words and syllables of a familiar sign. Circle the four parts of this sign.

old age sticks

Poem by

E. E. CUMMINGS

BACKGROUND This poem may at first look like a jumble of unrelated words run together. However, Cummings uses the odd line breaks and lack of punctuation to help express the poem's meaning.

old age sticks
up Keep
Off
signs)& ❻

5 youth yanks them
down(old
age
cries No

Tres)&(pas)
10 youth laughs
(sing
old age ❼

scolds Forbid

den Stop

15 Must

n't Don't

&)youth goes

right on

gr

20 owing old

● MONITOR

Reread lines 13–20. Put a check mark √ next to the group of lines that hints at how "youth" will change.

IN OTHER WORDS The speaker suggests that older people like to make rules, while younger people like to break them.

► Cummings breaks the rules of standard punctuation in this poem. Can you tell where one complete thought ends and the next one begins? Reread the poem, and draw a vertical line after each complete thought.

READING 4 Understand the structure and elements of poetry. Analyze the importance of graphical elements (e.g., capital letters, line length, word position) on the meaning of a poem. **RC-7(C)** Reflect on understanding to monitor comprehension.

Literary Analysis: Style in Poetry

Cummings uses word choice and form as well as punctuation, capitalization, and word position to help define his style. Reread the poems, and identify two elements of style that the poems share. Write your examples in the chart below, as shown.

Style	Examples
Does not use capital letters	Titles of all three poems: "maggie and milly and molly and may"; "who are you, little i"; "old age sticks"

Reading Strategy: Monitor

Review the poems, and list any lines that at first confused you in the chart below. For each line, write how you rephrased the information in your own words and then explain how rephrasing helped clarify the poem's meaning for you.

Line or Lines	My Rephrasing	How It Clarified Meaning
line 5: "milly befriended a stranded star"	Milly found a starfish.	Made the meaning literal, or really true.

Are all things CONNECTED?

What subject connects these three poems? What else do they have in common?

_____

Academic Vocabulary in Speaking

The word **communicate** (kuh MYOO nih kayt) is a verb that means *to tell ideas or information to others.*

The director of our school play taught us to **communicate** with body movements.

The word **interpret** (in TER prit) is a verb that means *to explain or make clear.*

I can't understand Spanish, so Sabrina had to **interpret** the song's words for me.

The word **style** (styl) is a noun that means *the way in which something is said or done.*

The pitcher's **style** of throwing is very unusual.

TURN AND TALK Read one of Cummings's poems out loud. With a partner, discuss how Cummings's style, including punctuation and line breaks, affects his message. Use at least two of the Academic Vocabulary words above in your discussion.

RC-7(B) Ask literal, interpretive, evaluative, and universal questions of the text.
RC-7(C) Reflect on understanding to monitor comprehension.

Texas Assessment Practice

DIRECTIONS Use the three poems to answer questions 1–4.

1 In lines 1–2 of "maggie and milly and molly and may" Cummings uses unusual —

   A capitalization and punctuation
   B punctuation and word position
   C capitalization and word position
   D punctuation and word choice

2 Where does Cummings ignore the rules of capitalization in "who are you, little i"?

   F in the title
   G in line 4
   H in line 5
   J in line 8

3 In "old age sticks," the attitude of old age toward youth is best described as —

   A friendly
   B angry
   C understanding
   D uninterested

4 The most accurate way to rephrase lines 12–16 of "old age sticks" is —

   F older people try to prevent younger people from doing many things
   G older people have trouble expressing themselves to younger people
   H younger people usually obey older people
   J older people like to share what they know

Included in this unit: TEKS 3, 4, 8, 9, 10, 10D, RC-7(A), RC-7(B)

UNIT 5

Picture the Moment
APPRECIATING POETRY

Be sure to read the Reader's Workshop on pp. 554–559 in *Holt McDougal Literature*.

Academic Vocabulary for Unit 5

You will see these Academic Vocabulary words as you work through this book. You will also be asked to use them as you write and talk about the selections in this unit.

Encounter (en KOWN tuhr) is a noun that means *a meeting, especially one that is not expected.*
Ana had a surprise **encounter** with a snake in her yard.

Would you expect to **encounter** a nature preserve in a city? Explain:

_____

Integrity (in TEG rih tee) is a noun that means *being honest and true to oneself.* It also can mean *the condition of being complete, whole, or undivided.*
The man who returned my wallet had a lot of **integrity**.

Would a person with **integrity** steal or tell a lie? _____

_____

Specific (spih SIF ik) is an adjective that means *definite, exact.* It describes *a certain thing and no other.*
Give **specific** examples of words that rhyme in the poem.

Name **specific** movies or television shows you have seen recently:

_____

Tradition (truh DISH uhn) is a noun that means *a custom, belief, or practice that is passed down from one generation to the next.*
Some cultures have a storytelling **tradition** that is still practiced.

What are your favorite holiday **traditions**? _____

_____

Vary (VAIR ee) is a verb that means *to change or become different in some way.*
The stories have the same subject, but they **vary** in length.

Do you like to **vary** the music you listen to? Explain: _____

_____

The Names
Poem by **Billy Collins**

READING 4 Draw conclusions about the structure and elements of poetry.

Why do we need MEMORIALS?

When something tragic happens, people are often unsure how to handle it. Many people find it helpful to create a memorial, or something to remember and honor the people who died. This poem by Billy Collins is a memorial that tries to help people deal with their loss.

TURN AND TALK How can remembering a sad event help someone heal? Discuss your answer with a partner. Then, list some advantages, or good points, at left.

Poetic Form: Free Verse

Free verse is a type of poetry that does not follow a set of rules. Here are some characteristics of free verse poetry.

Characteristics of Free Verse	Example	Explanation
Does not include a set pattern of **rhyme** (rym). An example of rhyming words is *mean* and *screen*.	*Yesterday, I lay awake in the palm of the* **night.** */ A soft rain stole in, unhelped by any* **breeze,**	Notice that the bold words at the ends of lines do not rhyme.
Often each line of poetry is a different length.	*Names silent in stone / Or cried out behind a door.*	Note that the first line is shorter than the second line.
Free verse does not have a clear rhythm (RITH uhm) or a musical quality. Instead, it sounds like everyday speaking.	*In the morning, I walked out barefoot / Among thousands of flowers*	When read aloud, these lines sound like everyday speech.

As you read "The Names," look for characteristics of free verse poetry.

Good points about remembering sad events:

1. *Remembering helps people express their hurt.*

2. _____

_____

3. _____

_____

4. _____

_____

Literary Analysis: Imagery

Imagery is language that appeals to your senses of sight, hearing, smell, taste, and touch. Poets use imagery to describe things in a vivid way. Look at these lines from "The Names":

Yesterday, I lay awake in the palm of the night.

A soft rain stole in, unhelped by any breeze,

The image "palm of the night" appeals to the sense of sight. The words "soft rain" appeal to the sense of touch. As you read "The Names," you may use a word web to identify examples of imagery.

READING 3 Analyze theme and genre in historical and contemporary contexts.
8 Understand how an author's use of sensory language creates imagery.

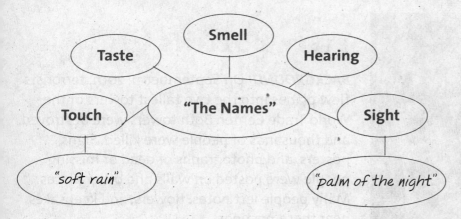

Reading Skill: Understand Historical Context

Sometimes literature focuses on events that happened in the past. Knowing this **historical context** can help you better understand a selection. "The Names" is written about the victims of the attacks of September 11, 2001. To learn more about the poem's historical context, read the **Background** on the next page.

The NAMES

Poem by
BILLY COLLINS

BACKGROUND On September 11, 2001, terrorists flew planes into the two tallest towers of the World Trade Center. Both towers were destroyed, and thousands of people were killed. Signs, posters, and photographs of dead or missing people were posted on walls and other places. Many people left notes, flowers, and keepsakes near these postings.

Yesterday, I lay awake in the palm of the night.
A soft rain stole in, unhelped by any breeze,
And when I saw the silver glaze on the windows,
I started with A, with Ackerman, as it happened,
5 Then Baxter and Calabro,
Davis and Eberling, names falling into place
As droplets fell through the dark.

Names printed on the ceiling of the night.
Names slipping around a watery bend.
10 Twenty-six willows on the banks of a stream. Ⓐ

IN OTHER WORDS The speaker of the poem is lying awake on a rainy night, thinking about all the names on memorials to people who have died or are missing. The speaker begins listing the names, starting with names that begin with the first letters of the alphabet.

In the morning, I walked out barefoot
Among thousands of flowers
Heavy with dew like the eyes of tears,
And each had a name—
15 Fiori inscribed on a yellow petal
Then Gonzalez and Han, Ishikawa and Jenkins.

Names written in the air
And stitched into the cloth of the day.
A name under a photograph taped to a mailbox.
20 Monogram[1] on a torn shirt,
I see you spelled out on storefront windows
And on the bright unfurled **awnings** of this city.
I say the syllables as I turn a corner—
Kelly and Lee,
25 Medina, Nardella, and O'Connor. **B**

IN OTHER WORDS The speaker sees the names of the missing and dead everywhere.

▶ Underline three places the speaker sees the names.

When I peer into the woods,
I see a thick tangle where letters are hidden
As in a puzzle concocted for children. **C**
Parker and Quigley in the twigs of an ash,
30 Rizzo, Schubert, Torres, and Upton,
Secrets in the boughs of an ancient maple.

---

1. **monogram:** the initials of one's name combined into a design.

VISUAL VOCABULARY

Awnings are coverings placed above windows to protect them from the weather.

B **UNDERSTAND HISTORICAL CONTEXT**
Reread lines 17–25. Then, look back at the **Background** on page 188. Based on this information, why do you think the speaker sees names everywhere? Discuss your answer with a partner.

C **FREE VERSE**
Reread lines 26–28. What is one characteristic of a **free verse** poem found in these lines?

_____

_____

_____

⊙ LANGUAGE COACH

In lines 32–36, Collins repeats the word *names* four times. Poets often repeat important words to draw attention to them. From this **repetition** of the word *names* (which is also in the title), you can guess that names are very important in this poem.

Names written in the pale sky.
Names rising in the updraft[2] amid buildings.
Names silent in stone
35 Or cried out behind a door.
Names blown over the earth and out to sea. **⊙**

IN OTHER WORDS The speaker imagines the names of the dead hidden in trees, written in the sky, and rising in the wind. He says that some of the names of the dead have been written in stone, some mourned behind the privacy of doors, and some lost.

In the evening—weakening light, the last swallows.
A boy on a lake lifts his oars.
A woman by a window puts a match to a candle,
40 And the names are outlined on the rose clouds—
Vanacore and Wallace,
(let X stand, if it can, for the ones unfound)
Then Young and Ziminsky, the final jolt of Z.
Names etched on the head of a pin
45 One name spanning a bridge, another undergoing a
   tunnel.
A blue name needled into the skin.

⊕ IMAGERY

Reread lines 45–46. <u>Underline</u> one image that appeals to your sense of touch. Then, reread lines 49–50. Put brackets [ ] around an image that appeals to your sense of sight. Record these images in the web below.

Names of citizens, workers, mothers and fathers,
The bright-eyed daughter, the quick son.
Alphabet of names in green rows in a field.
50 Names in the small tracks of birds. **⊕**
Names lifted from a hat
Or balanced on the tip of the tongue.
Names wheeled into the dim warehouse of memory.
So many names, there is barely room on the walls of
   the heart.

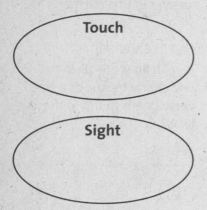

Touch

Sight

---

2. **updraft:** an upward movement of air.

IN OTHER WORDS The speaker imagines the names written in the clouds and on something as tiny as a pin's head, and on bridges and tunnels. The victims include people who were mothers, fathers, daughters, and sons.

► Re-read the last line of the poem. With a partner, discuss what the speaker means by saying that names are "on the walls of the heart."

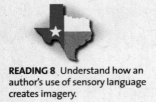

READING 8 Understand how an author's use of sensory language creates imagery.

Literary Analysis: Imagery

Imagery includes words and phrases that appeal to the five senses. Writers use imagery to make something seem real to the reader.

Look back at the poem. Choose three images, and copy them into the chart below. Tell what sense each image appeals to. Then, explain what the image helps you imagine.

IMAGERY		
Image	What sense does it appeal to?	What does it help me imagine?

Reading Skill: Historical Context

"The Names" honors those who died on September 11, 2001. Before reading this poem, what did you already know about the event and how it affected people? What new information did you learn from the poem itself? Complete the chart below, citing details from the poem to support your answer. Examples are given.

What I Knew: *Airplanes flew into the twin towers.*
Detail from Poem: *"I see you spelled out on storefront windows / And on the bright unfurled awnings of this city." (lines 21 22)* **What I Learned:** *People posted photos and names all over the city.*
Detail from Poem: **What I Learned:**

Why do we need MEMORIALS?

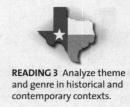

READING 3 Analyze theme and genre in historical and contemporary contexts.

TURN AND TALK Many memorials, such as sculptures, have been built to honor those who died September 11, 2001. Why do you think people have wanted a permanent memorial? Discuss your answer with a partner.

Academic Vocabulary in Speaking

The word **vary** (VAIR ee) is a verb that means *to change or become different in some way.*

> I like to **vary** my diet, sometimes eating only vegetables and other times eating meat.

TURN AND TALK With a partner, discuss some of the imagery you found in "The Names." How do these images help you understand that the speaker's feelings **vary** with each new name? Be sure to use the word **vary** in your discussion.

Texas Assessment Practice

DIRECTIONS Use "The Names" to answer questions 1–6.

1 The image "Names written in the air" appeals to the sense of —

- (A) hearing
- (B) smell
- (C) sight
- (D) taste

2 What does the poet mean by saying "Names silent in stone" in line 34?

- (F) The people do not speak.
- (G) The names are written on gravestones.
- (H) The families gather near the destroyed towers.
- (J) The names are hard to see.

3 The events in history that a writer bases a work on are called the work's —

- (A) imagery
- (B) free verse
- (C) sensory details
- (D) historical context

4 What does the letter *X* stand for in the poem?

- (F) People who were never found
- (G) Firefighters who worked that day
- (H) Names beginning with that letter
- (J) Children missing their lost parents

5 This is a free verse poem because —

- (A) every line rhymes
- (B) the poem has a definite rhythm
- (C) lengths of lines are not predictable
- (D) it is about a serious subject

6 This poem is a memorial to —

- (F) people who have lost loved ones
- (G) those who died on September 11, 2001
- (H) people the poet knew personally
- (J) those who tried to save the victims

READING 4 Draw conclusions about the structure and elements of poetry.

The Charge of the Light Brigade
Poem by Alfred, Lord Tennyson

The Highwayman
Poem by Alfred Noyes

What is HONOR?

What does it mean when someone acts with honor? In "The Charge of the Light Brigade" and "The Highwayman," characters give up their lives for very different reasons. Are these reasons truly honorable?

TURN AND TALK In the chart at the left, list people who you believe have acted honorably. Choose the person from your list you think is most honorable. Compare your chart with a partner's. Discuss how each of you defines what it means to be honorable.

Literary Analysis: Rhythm and Meter

Rhythm is the pattern of stressed and unstressed syllables in a line of poetry that creates the poem's music, how the poem sounds when read aloud. Rhythm that follows the same pattern from line to line is called **meter**. When you "scan" a line of poetry, you identify its rhythm by marking the syllables—part of words with a vowel sound—that are stressed (´) and unstressed (˘).

Stressed syllables are pronounced more strongly than unstressed syllables. In the first line below, the first syllable of *honor*, *hon–*, is pronounced more strongly than its second syllable, *–or*. You would mark *hon–* as stressed and *–or* as unstressed. Reading the poem aloud will help you hear which syllables are stressed or unstressed in each word.

The first line below is marked for you. Mark each syllable in the second line as stressed or unstressed.

Hónŏr thĕ chárge thĕy máde!

Honor the Light Brigade!

As you read the following selections, notice each poem's rhythm and meter and the effect they create.

Honorable People

People I know:

Why they are honorable:

People from history or other famous figures:

Why they are honorable:

Reading Strategy: Reading a Narrative Poem

"The Charge of the Light Brigade" and "The Highwayman" are **narrative poems,** which means each poem tells a story. Like novels and short stories, narrative poems have characters, a setting, and a plot based on a **conflict,** a struggle or problem. As you read each poem, you will keep track of these elements in a story map for each poem.

READING 4 Draw conclusions about the structure and elements of poetry.

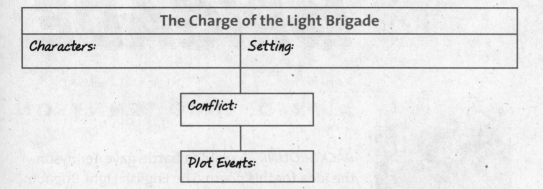

The Charge of the Light Brigade	
Characters:	Setting:

Conflict:

Plot Events:

Vocabulary in Context

Note: Words are listed in the order in which they appear in the poem "The Highwayman."

Claret (KLAR uht) is an adjective that means *dark red.*
   The bleeding wound left a **claret** stain on his shirt.

Cascade (kas KAYD) is a noun that means a *waterfall or something that pours down like a waterfall.*
   Her hair fell in a great **cascade** down her back.

Writhe (ryth) is a verb that means to *twist in pain.*
   She **writhed,** trying to free her wrists from the tight rope.

Vocabulary Practice

Use the vocabulary word in your answer to each question.

1. What could **claret** have to do with wine?

_____

2. What is something that forms a **cascade?**

_____

3. Why might a snake **writhe?**

_____

SET A PURPOSE FOR READING
Read this poem to find out what happens when a group of soldiers face a powerful enemy.

THE CHARGE OF THE LIGHT BRIGADE

Poem by
ALFRED, LORD TENNYSON

BACKGROUND A real-life battle gave Tennyson the idea for this poem. The English Light Brigade was a group of 600 soldiers riding horses. Their commanders sent the Light Brigade into battle against Russian troops, but there were many more Russian soldiers than English. The members of the Light Brigade knew they were sure to lose the battle and probably their lives. What they decided to do next made them world famous.

Ⓐ RHYTHM AND METER
Reread lines 1–4 aloud, tapping your desk with each stressed syllable. How many stressed syllables are in each line?

Line 1: _____

Line 2: _____

Line 3: _____

Line 4: _____

Half a league,[1] half a league,
Half a league onward,
All in the valley of Death
     Rode the six hundred. Ⓐ
5 "Forward, the Light Brigade!
Charge for the guns!" he said:
Into the valley of Death
     Rode the six hundred.

IN OTHER WORDS Six hundred British soldiers of the Light Brigade ride into battle.

---

1. **league** (leeg): a distance of about three miles; "half a league" is about one and a half miles.

"Forward, the Light Brigade!"
10 Was there a man dismay'd?
Not tho' the soldier knew
    Some one had blunder'd:[2]
Theirs not to make reply,
Theirs not to reason why,
15 Theirs but to do and die:
Into the valley of Death
    Rode the six hundred. ⓑ

IN OTHER WORDS The soldiers know that their leaders have
made a mistake and that many of them may die. They ride into
battle anyway.

▶ Reread lines 13–15. Discuss with a partner why the soldiers
choose to go forward into battle.

Cannon to right of them,
Cannon to left of them,
20 Cannon in front of them
    Volley'd[3] and thunder'd;
Storm'd at with shot and shell,
Boldly they rode and well,
Into the jaws of Death,
25 Into the mouth of Hell
    Rode the six hundred.

Flash'd all their **sabers** bare,
Flash'd as they turn'd in air
Sabring the gunners there,
30 Charging an army, while
    All the world wonder'd:
Plunged in the battery[4] smoke,
Right thro' the line they broke;

---

2. **blunder'd** (BLUHN durd): made a mistake.
3. **volley'd** (VOL eed): fired many weapons at the same time.
4. **battery** (BAT uh ree): a group of guns and cannons used together.

ⓑ **READING A NARRATIVE POEM**
Begin filling out your story map with what you know so far.

Characters:	Setting:

Conflict:

VISUAL VOCABULARY

A **saber** (SAY buhr) is a heavy sword with a curved blade.

Cossack[5] and Russian
35 Reel'd from the saber-stroke,
    Shatter'd and sunder'd.
Then they rode back, but not,
    Not the six hundred.

IN OTHER WORDS With their swords held out, the soldiers ride directly into the enemy army and fight bravely. Cannons and guns fire around them, filling the air with smoke. Enemy troops fall back from the attack but then return to battle. Many of the English are killed.

C RHYTHM AND METER
Reread lines 39–41 aloud. With a partner, mark the stressed and unstressed syllables in each line. How does the meter of these lines sound like what is happening to the soldiers of the Light Brigade in this battle?

Cannon to right of them,
40 Cannon to left of them,
Cannon behind them **C**
    Volley'd and thunder'd;
Storm'd at with shot and shell,
While horse and hero fell,
45 They that had fought so well
Came thro' the jaws of Death.
Back from the mouth of Hell,
All that was left of them,
    Left of six hundred.

IN OTHER WORDS The members of the brigade who were still alive return to camp after the fight.

---

50 When can their glory fade?
O, the wild charge they made!
    All the world wonder'd.
Honor the charge they made!
Honor the Light Brigade,
55   Noble six hundred! **PAUSE & REFLECT**

PAUSE & REFLECT
With a partner, discuss whether you think the Light Brigade should have gone into battle when they knew they could not win.

IN OTHER WORDS The courage of the soldiers in the Light Brigade impressed the world.

▶ Underline what the speaker thinks about what the Light Brigade did.

---

5. **Cossack** (KOS ak): a member of a group of people living in southwestern Russia.

The Highwayman

Poem by

ALFRED NOYES

BACKGROUND Traveling in the 1700s in England was dangerous. Highwaymen, or robbers, used to stop stagecoaches (closed wagons pulled by horses) to rob rich passengers. Some of these robbers were thought of as exciting people who wore beautiful clothes and had great adventures. Others were thought of as heroes because they shared stolen money with the poor. This poem tells the story of a highwayman, his romance with the daughter of an innkeeper (someone who runs a small hotel), and an attempt to capture him.

Part One

The wind was a torrent[1] of darkness among the gusty
 trees.
The moon was a ghostly galleon[2] tossed upon cloudy
 seas.
The road was a ribbon of moonlight over the purple
 moor,[3]

---

1. **torrent** (TAWR uhnt): a fast, heavy rush of wind or water.
2. **galleon** (GAL ee uhn): a large sailing ship.
3. **moor**: a wide, rolling open area, usually covered with low-growing shrubs.

VOCABULARY

The word **claret** (KLAIR uht) is an adjective that means *dark red*.

D. RHYTHM AND METER

Reread lines 10–12. Their rhythm sounds very similar to the rhythm of three lines in the first stanza. Underline the lines in the first stanza they sound like.

E READING A NARRATIVE POEM

Bracket [ ] words or phrases in the first three stanzas that describe the poem's setting. Circle the characters that are introduced in these stanzas. Record the information in your story map.

Characters:	Setting:

And the highwayman came riding—
5   Riding—riding—
The highwayman came riding, up to the old
   inn-door.

He'd a French cocked-hat on his forehead, a bunch
   of lace at his chin,
A coat of the **claret** velvet, and breeches of brown
   doeskin.[4]
They fitted with never a wrinkle. His boots were up
   to the thigh.
10 And he rode with a jeweled twinkle,
   His pistol butts a-twinkle.
His rapier hilt[5] a-twinkle, under the jeweled sky. **D**

IN OTHER WORDS On a moonlit night, a highwayman rides his horse through the dark countryside. He comes to an old country inn, or small hotel. The highwayman wears fine clothes that fit him well. His weapons have jewels on them.

Over the cobbles[6] he clattered and clashed in the
   dark inn-yard.
He tapped with his whip on the shutters, but all was
   locked and barred.
15 He whistled a tune to the window, and who should
   be waiting there
But the landlord's black-eyed daughter,
   Bess, the landlord's daughter,
Plaiting[7] a dark red love-knot into her long black
   hair. **E**

---

4. **French cocked-hat . . . coat of claret velvet . . . breeches of brown doeskin:** stylish clothing, including a hat turned up on both sides, a deep red velvet coat, and soft pants made of female deer skin.
5. **rapier hilt** (RAY pee uhr hilt): a sword handle.
6. **cobbles:** rounded stones used for paving roads.
7. **plaiting:** braiding.

IN OTHER WORDS The highwayman rides up to the inn and knocks, but the inn is locked. He whistles and Bess, the inn-keeper's beautiful daughter, comes to the window. She braids a ribbon through her hair, making a special kind of knot that shows her love for him.

And dark in the dark old inn-yard a stable wicket[8]
    creaked
20 Where Tim the ostler[9] listened. His face was white
    and peaked.
His eyes were hollows of madness, his hair like
    moldy hay,
But he loved the landlord's daughter,
The landlord's red-lipped daughter.
Dumb as a dog he listened, and he heard the robber
    say—

25 "One kiss, my bonny sweetheart, I'm after a prize
    tonight,
But I shall be back with the yellow gold before the
    morning light;
Yet, if they press me sharply, and harry me through
    the day,
Then look for me by moonlight,
Watch for me by moonlight,
30 I'll come to thee by moonlight, though hell should
    bar the way." **PAUSE & REFLECT**

PAUSE & REFLECT
With a partner, discuss what Tim hears the highwayman tell Bess. What do you think Tim might do next?

IN OTHER WORDS Tim, a man who cares for horses at the inn, looks pale and sickly. Tim loves Bess, but Bess loves the highwayman, so Tim is jealous of him. Tim hears the highwayman tell Bess that he is going to rob a stagecoach and return with gold before the sun rises, if he can. If soldiers harry, or chase, him, the highwayman will return the next night instead.

8. **wicket:** a small door or gate.
9. **ostler** (AHS lur): a worker who takes care of horses at an inn.

He rose upright in the stirrups. He scarce could reach
    her hand,
But she loosened her hair in the casement. His face
    burnt like a brand[10]
As the black <u>cascade</u> of perfume came tumbling
    over his breast;
And he kissed its waves in the moonlight,
35   (O, sweet black waves in the moonlight!)
Then he tugged at his rein in the moonlight, and
    galloped away to the west.

IN OTHER WORDS The highwayman cannot reach up far enough to kiss Bess's face as she stands at the casement, or window. She lets her hair down for him so he can kiss it. He rides off to the west.

Part Two

He did not come in the dawning. He did not come at
    noon;
And out of the tawny[11] sunset, before the rise of the
    moon,
When the road was a gypsy's ribbon, looping the
    purple moor,
40 A redcoat troop came marching—
    Marching—marching—
King George's men came marching, up to the old
    inn-door.

They said no word to the landlord. They drank his
    ale instead.
But they gagged his daughter, and bound her, to the
    foot of her narrow bed.
45 Two of them knelt at her casement, with muskets at their
    side!

---

10. **brand:** a mark made by burning the skin with a hot iron to show ownership.
11. **tawny** (TAW nee): having a golden brown color.

There was death at every window;
    And hell at one dark window;
For Bess could see, through her casement, the road
    that *he* would ride. **F**

IN OTHER WORDS The highwayman does not return that day.
Soldiers come to the inn. The soldiers say nothing to Bess's father,
the innkeeper. They drink his beer. Then they tie Bess to the foot
of her bed. Two soldiers with muskets, or guns, watch out her
window for the highwayman to arrive.

F **READING A NARRATIVE POEM**
With a partner, discuss how the soldiers may have learned when the highwayman would visit Bess.

They had tied her up to attention, with many a
    sniggering jest.[12]
50 They had bound a musket beside her, with the
    muzzle beneath her breast!
"Now, keep good watch!" and they kissed her. She
    heard the doomed man say—
Look for me by moonlight;
    Watch for me by moonlight;
I'll come to thee by moonlight, though hell should bar the way!

IN OTHER WORDS The soldiers tie Bess so that the musket's
muzzle, or end of the gun, points at her heart. They tell her to
watch for the highwayman. She knows they will kill him when he
arrives.

▶ With a partner, discuss why the soldiers tie Bess to a gun in
this stanza.

---

55 She twisted her hands behind her; but all the knots
    held good!
She <u>writhed</u> her hands till her fingers were wet with
    sweat or blood!
They stretched and strained in the darkness, and the
    hours crawled by like years,

VOCABULARY
The word **writhe** (ryth) is a verb that means *to twist in pain.*

---

12. **sniggering jest:** a mocking joke.

Till, now, on the stroke of midnight,
  Cold, on the stroke of midnight,
60 The tip of one finger touched it! The trigger at least
    was hers!

The tip of one finger touched it. She strove no more
    for the rest.
Up, she stood up to attention, with the muzzle
    beneath her breast.
She would not risk their hearing; she would not
    strive again;
For the road lay bare in the moonlight;
65   Blank and bare in the moonlight;
And the blood of her veins, in the moonlight,
    throbbed to her love's refrain. **G**

G **READING A NARRATIVE POEM**

Reread lines 61–66. With a partner, discuss what you think Bess is getting ready to do.

IN OTHER WORDS Bess struggles for hours trying to loosen the ropes. She finally frees one of her fingers and puts it on the trigger of the gun. It is midnight. Bess does not want the soldiers to hear her. She watches the road for the highwayman.

Tlot-tlot; tlot-tlot! Had they heard it? The horse hoofs
    ringing clear;
Tlot-tlot, tlot-tlot, in the distance? Were they deaf that
    they did not hear?
Down the ribbon of moonlight, over the brow of the
    hill,
70 The highwayman came riding—
    Riding—riding—
The redcoats looked to their priming![13] She stood up,
    straight and still. **H**

H **RHYTHM AND METER**

With a partner, mark the stressed and unstressed syllables in lines 67–68. What action that takes place in this stanza does the meter of these lines sound like?

---

13. **looked to their priming:** prepared their muskets by pouring in the gunpowder used to fire them.

Tlot-tlot, in the frosty silence! *Tlot-tlot,* in the echoing
    night!
Nearer he came and nearer. Her face was like a light.
75 Her eyes grew wide for a moment; she drew one last
    deep breath,
Then her finger moved in the moonlight,
    Her musket shattered the moonlight,
Shattered her breast in the moonlight and warned
    him—with her death. ❶

IN OTHER WORDS Bess hears the sound of the highwayman's
horse. The soldiers get ready to fire their guns at him. Bess takes
a deep breath and pulls the trigger. The shot kills her. As she
planned, the sound of the shot warns the highwayman that he is
in danger.

---

❶ **READING A
NARRATIVE POEM**
With a partner, discuss why
Bess kills herself to warn
the highwayman about the
soldiers.

He turned. He spurred to the west; he did not know
    who stood
80 Bowed, with her head o'er the musket, drenched
    with her own blood!
Not till the dawn he heard it, his face grew grey to
    hear
How Bess, the landlord's daughter,
    The landlord's black-eyed daughter,
Had watched for her love in the moonlight, and died
    in the darkness there.

IN OTHER WORDS The highwayman quickly turns around and
rides away. At dawn he learns that Bess has killed herself to
warn him about the soldiers.

---

85 Back, he spurred like a madman, shouting a curse to
    the sky,

With the white road smoking behind him and his
　　　rapier brandished high.
Blood-red were his spurs[14] in the golden noon;
　　　wine-red was his velvet coat;
When they shot him down on the highway,
　　Down like a dog on the highway,
90 And he lay in his blood on the highway, with a
　　　bunch of lace at his throat. **PAUSE & REFLECT**

PAUSE & REFLECT
With a partner, discuss why the highwayman goes back to the inn after he hears about Bess's death.

And still of a winter's night, they say, when the wind is in the
　　　trees,
When the moon is a ghostly galleon tossed upon cloudy seas,
When the road is a ribbon of moonlight over the purple moor,
A highwayman comes riding—
95　　*Riding—riding—*
A highwayman comes riding, up to the old inn-door.

Over the cobbles he clatters and clangs in the dark inn-yard.
He taps with his whip on the shutters, but all is locked and
　　　barred.
He whistles a tune to the window, and who should be waiting
　　　there
100 *But the landlord's black-eyed daughter,*
　　　Bess, the landlord's daughter,
Plaiting a dark red love-knot into her long black hair.

IN OTHER WORDS When he hears that Bess is dead, the highwayman rides back to the inn. The soldiers shoot him on the road. He lies there bleeding to death in his fine clothes. Later, people tell a legend, or story, in which the ghosts of the highwayman and Bess meet at the inn.

▶ Discuss with a partner what happens when the highwayman goes back to the inn.

---

14. **spurs:** a small spiked wheel attached to each of a rider's boots and used to make a horse go faster.

Literary Analysis: Rhythm and Meter

Read lines 13–15 of "The Charge of the Light Brigade" aloud. Mark the stressed and the unstressed syllables in each line to show what its **meter** is.

READING 4 Draw conclusions about the structure and elements of poetry.

Theirs not to make reply,

Theirs not to reason why,

Theirs but to do and die . . .

Do the same for lines 34–36 from "The Highwayman" below.

And he kissed the waves in the moonlight,

> *(Oh, the sweet black waves in the moonlight!)*

Then he tugged at his rein in the moonlight, and galloped
> *away to the west.*

How does the repeated rhythm affect the way you read the two sets of lines?

_____

_____

_____

_____

_____

_____

_____

_____

_____

_____

_____

_____

_____

READING 4 Draw conclusions about the structure and elements of poetry.

Reading Strategy: Reading a Narrative Poem

Now that you have read both poems, choose one and complete the story map below for it. Be sure to choose only the most important plot events to include in your map.

Poem I Chose:	
Characters:	Setting:

Conflict:

Plot Event 1:	Plot Event 2:	Plot Event 3:

What is HONOR?

Review the poems. Who do you think behaved the most honorably—the soldiers in "The Charge of the Light Brigade," the highwayman, or Bess? Why?

_____

_____

_____

_____

_____

Vocabulary Practice

Choose the word from the list that best fits each sentence.

1. He tripped and fell, which made him _____ in pain.

2. A thin, _____ colored stream of blood trickled down his face.

3. The _____ of cool water from the shower felt refreshing.

WORD LIST

claret

cascade

writhe

Academic Vocabulary in Speaking

The word **tradition** (truh DISH uhn) is a noun that means *a custom, belief, or practice that is passed down from one generation to the next.*

Our family **tradition** is to have an annual New Year's party.

TURN AND TALK People often tell tales of those who have died heroically. What are some reasons for this **tradition**? Be sure to use the word **tradition** in your conversation.

Texas Assessment Practice

DIRECTIONS Use "The Charge of the Light Brigade" and "The Highwayman" to answer questions 1–4.

1 What is the outcome of the Light Brigade's charge?
- (A) The Light Brigade suffers heavy losses.
- (B) The Russian soldiers surrender.
- (C) The Light Brigade become prisoners.
- (D) The two armies sign a truce.

2 The pattern of stressed and unstressed syllables in one line of poetry is called —
- (F) a narrative
- (G) meter
- (H) rhyme
- (J) rhythm

3 What kind of poem tells a story, with characters, a setting, and a plot?
- (A) Haiku
- (B) Sonnet
- (C) Lyric poem
- (D) Narrative poem

4 Why do the soldiers want to catch the highwayman?
- (F) He is a robber.
- (G) He harmed Tim.
- (H) He deserted the army.
- (J) He threatened the landlord's daughter.

READING 4 Draw conclusions about the structure and elements of poetry.

Two Haiku
Poems by Matsuo Bashō

Fireflies
Poem by Paul Fleischman

Fireflies in the Garden
Poem by Robert Frost

How do the SEASONS affect you?

When we spend much of our time indoors, we may not notice changes happening in nature. However, the seasons still affect our lives. The poems you're about to read show how the changing seasons can even affect our emotions.

TURN AND TALK Choose your favorite season of the year. With a partner, take turns talking about words or phrases that make you think of that season. Write down your answers in the chart to the left.

Poetic Form: Haiku

Haiku is a kind of poetry that poets in Japan began to write hundreds of years ago. Poets use only a few words to write haiku.

Key points about haiku:

• Each poem has 17 syllables. (A **syllable** (SIL uh buhl) is a part of a word. *Spring* is a word with one syllable; *haiku* has two syllables.)

• Each poem is three lines long.

• The first and third lines each contain 5 syllables. The second line has 7 syllables.

• In each haiku, one or more images remind readers of a season.

Read the haiku below by Bashō. Notice that it has 17 syllables in three lines.

On sweet plum blossoms   ← The first line contains 5 syllables.

The sun rises suddenly.   ← The second line has 7 syllables.

Look, a mountain path.   ← The third line has 5 syllables.

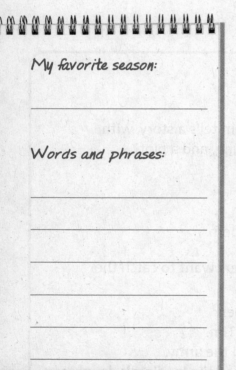

My favorite season:

_____

Words and phrases:

_____

_____

_____

_____

_____

Literary Analysis: Symbol and Theme

A **symbol** is a person, place, object, or activity that stands for something beyond itself.

READING 3 Analyze theme and genre in cultural and historical contexts. **RC-7(B)** Ask interpretive and evaluative questions of text.

 = United States   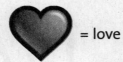 = love

By using symbols, poets can share their ideas with us by using only a few words. As you read the poems, identify the symbols in them. After you find the symbols in each poem, think about the ideas behind each symbol.

TURN AND TALK What are some other symbols you are familiar with? In the space below, draw or write down two symbols. Tell what they represent.

Symbol	What the Symbol Means

Remember that **theme** is a message about life that the writer shares with the reader. Often, the symbols a writer chooses give readers hints about the message the writer wants to share.

Reading Strategy: Ask Questions

Poets make images, or word pictures, by using sensory details. These details are words and phrases that appeal to your senses of sight, touch, taste, smell, and hearing. To help you interpret—or understand the meaning of—sensory details, ask yourself questions such as these:

• What image do the details help me "see" or imagine?

• What ideas do the details make me think of?

As you read these poems, you will note details and what they help you "see."

What sensory details seem important?	What do they make me think of?
1. sun rising	1. a new day
2.	2.

SET A PURPOSE FOR READING

Read these haiku to see what the speaker "sees" in nature.

Ⓐ SYMBOL AND THEME
What do you think the mountain path symbolizes, or represents? Discuss your ideas with a partner.

Ⓑ ASK QUESTIONS
Reread the second haiku. Then choose one image, or sensory detail, that helps you imagine or "see" what the poet is talking about. Write your answer in the chart below.

What sensory details seem important?
_____
_____
_____

↓

What do they make me think of?
_____
_____
_____
_____

TWO HAIKU

Poems by
MATSUO BASHŌ

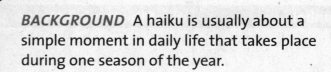

BACKGROUND A haiku is usually about a simple moment in daily life that takes place during one season of the year.

On sweet plum blossoms
The sun rises suddenly.
Look, a mountain path! Ⓐ

A crow
has settled on a bare branch—
autumn evening.[1] Ⓑ

---

1. When a haiku is translated from the original Japanese into English, the number of syllables per line sometimes changes.

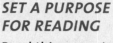

Fireflies

Poem by
PAUL FLEISCHMAN

BACKGROUND "Fireflies" is written as if two people are reading the poem aloud. Read this poem aloud with a partner. Both of you will read line 1, "Light," at the same time. Reader 2 will read line 2, "is the ink we use," alone. Continue reading the poem in this way.

SET A PURPOSE FOR READING
Read this poem to picture fireflies on a June night.

READER 1	READER 2
Light	Light
	is the ink we use
Night	Night
is our parchment[1]	
5	We're
	fireflies
fireflies	flickering
flitting	
	flashing
10 fireflies	
glimmering	fireflies
	gleaming
glowing	
Insect calligraphers[2]	Insect calligraphers

ASK QUESTIONS
Reread lines 5–13. What words or details help you see the fireflies in your mind? Circle them.

---

1. **parchment**: fine-quality paper, usually made from the skin of goats or sheep.
2. **calligraphers** (kuh LIG ruh fers): creators of beautiful handwriting.

¹⁵ practicing penmanship

copying sentences

Six-legged scribblers   Six-legged scribblers
of vanishing messages,

fleeting³ graffiti
²⁰ Fine artists in flight   Fine artists in flight
adding dabs of light

bright brush strokes
Signing the June nights   Signing the June nights
as if they were paintings   as if they were paintings
²⁵   We're
flickering   fireflies
fireflies   flickering
fireflies.   fireflies. **PAUSE & REFLECT**

IN OTHER WORDS The speakers in the poems are fireflies.
Fireflies are compared to artists, or calligraphers, who write in the
night sky with their glowing bodies.

PAUSE & REFLECT
Reread lines 20–24. Notice
that the fireflies are
described as artists here.
With a partner, talk about
which details help you "see"
these artists.

---

3. **fleeting:** passing swiftly; soon gone.

Fireflies in the Garden

Poem by

ROBERT FROST

**SET A PURPOSE
FOR READING**

Read this poem to consider a comparison between fireflies and stars.

BACKGROUND This poem takes place in the countryside at the end of the day. The stars and fireflies have just come out and are twinkling in the night sky. Fireflies *emulate*, or try to look like, the stars. Though the fireflies sometimes look like stars, they cannot *sustain*, or keep up, the way stars continue to shine in the sky.

Here come real stars to fill the upper skies,
And here on earth come emulating flies, **D**
That though they never equal stars in size,
(And they were never really stars at heart)
5 Achieve at times a very star-like start.
Only of course they can't sustain the part. **E**

IN OTHER WORDS The speaker compares stars with fireflies. The fireflies try to act like stars, but they fall short.

D ASK QUESTIONS

What fills the skies? What is "here on earth"? Reread lines 1–2. Then underline your answers.

E SYMBOL AND THEME

Reread the poem. On the lines below, explain what you think the fireflies symbolize, or stand for. What other creatures try for greatness but often fail?

_____

_____

_____

_____

_____

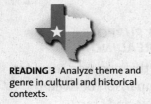

READING 3 Analyze theme and genre in cultural and historical contexts.

Literary Analysis: Theme and Symbol

Poets often try to share a message through their poems. This message, or **theme**, is an observation about life that the writer is making. In poems, a theme may be revealed by sensory details, by symbols, or in other ways.

CHART IT Fill in the Theme Chart below. First, write down one or two sensory details from each poem. Then, write down one symbol you find in each poem. Finally, review the details and symbol for each poem. Use those two elements to help you find the theme, or message, for each poem. The first poem has been done for you.

THEME CHART	
Haiku #1	Sensory Details: *sun rising; mountain path* Symbol: *Mountain path; a new beginning or journey* Theme: *hope for the future*
Haiku #2	Sensory Details: Symbol: Theme:
"Fireflies"	Sensory Details: Symbol: Theme:
"Fireflies in the Garden"	Sensory Details: Symbol: Theme:

How do the SEASONS affect you?

Which season do you like best? Look back at the words and phrases you collected in your chart on page 210. Then, write a short description that tells what you like about that season.

READING 3 Analyze theme and genre in cultural and historical contexts. **4** Draw conclusions about the structure and elements of poetry.

_____

_____

_____

Academic Vocabulary in Speaking

The word **specific** (spih SIF ik) means *definite, exact*. It describes *a certain thing and no other*.

> Each piece of wood had to be a **specific** length for my woodworking project.

TURN AND TALK With a partner, talk about the sensory details in one of the poems you have read. Be sure to use the word **specific** in your conversation.

Texas Assessment Practice

DIRECTIONS Use the two haiku, "Fireflies," and "Fireflies in the Garden" to answer questions 1–4.

1 A haiku is always —

- **A** very short and structured
- **B** written by a Japanese poet
- **C** about what the poet can see
- **D** written in rhyme

2 In "Fireflies," the image in "Fine artists in flight/adding dabs of light" appeals to the sense of —

- **F** hearing
- **G** smell
- **H** touch
- **J** sight

3 What might the fireflies symbolize in "Fireflies in the Garden"?

- **A** Other insects
- **B** People
- **C** Stars
- **D** Summertime

4 A message about nature found in all the poems is that —

- **F** people celebrate the renewal of life in spring
- **G** people always live in harmony with nature
- **H** small moments in nature can inspire us
- **J** nature deserves respect

READING 9 Explain the difference between the theme of a literary work and the author's purpose in an expository text. **10** Draw conclusions about expository text. **10D** Make logical connections between ideas within a text and across two or three texts representing different genres.

Stars with Wings

Based on the science article by Therese Ciesinski

Background

Have you ever seen a firefly flashing at night—or captured one in a jar? What makes fireflies light up? Learn the answer to that and other questions by reading the science article "Stars with Wings."

Skill Focus: Connect Ideas in Text

Whether you are reading poems about fireflies or the back of a cereal box, you are learning something new. To find out more about a new topic, you gather facts, details, and ideas from books, articles, websites, and so on. Sources of information like these are called **texts.** You **connect ideas** in texts to bring together information and understand the topic better.

When you read a text for information, you can use **text features** to make connections. Text features help you see how an article is organized, and they tell you the important ideas. For example, a title tells what an article is about. The writer's main idea is usually in the first paragraph. Headings and subheadings signal the start of new ideas and identify them. Special treatments such as **boldface** or *italics* help you identify important words.

As you read the science article that follows, you will make connections by watching for scientific facts about fireflies and text features that help you identify important details.

Text Features	Scientific Facts
"Stars with Wings"	The article will be about fireflies.
Introductory question and paragraph:	Fireflies eat bugs that eat vegetable gardens.
Subheadings: 1. A Beetle, Actually 2.	1. Fireflies are not bugs or flies. They are beetles. 2.
Italicized words:	glowworms

STARS with WINGS

Based on the science article by Therese Ciesinski

Who needs summer fireworks when you have a backyard display of lightning bugs?

There are many wonderful sights in nature, but few are as magical as the bright wanderings of **fireflies**. On hot July evenings, children run around trying to catch the glow of these lightning bugs in glass jars. "I wonder how many amateur entomologists[1] first became interested in science and insects by collecting fireflies," wonders Greg Hoover, a scientist who studies

10 insects. Hoover is one of the folks who helped have a type of firefly named the state insect of Pennsylvania. He remembers watching fireflies in the woods and plants along the water's edge while he was fishing. "It was really neat. It looked like the New York City skyline at night," he remembers. Fireflies, also called lightning bugs, are more than just pretty. They're also good for the garden: they eat other insects that want to eat your vegetables. Ⓐ

---

1. **amateur entomologists** (AM uh chur ehn tuh MOL uh jists): people who study insects as a hobby.

• A Beetle, Actually

20 A firefly isn't a bug or fly. It's really a soft-bodied beetle. It belongs to a family of insects whose Latin name means "shining fire." There are 124 kinds of fireflies in North America, mostly in the east. They're usually brown or black with light-colored markings, and they grow to be about an inch long.

• Light My Fire

A firefly lights up because of *bioluminescence*,[2] a natural glow caused when oxygen mixes with chemicals in the firefly's abdomen, or stomach. Cells inside the abdomen 30 reflect the light, making it brighter. Some frogs love the taste of lightning bugs. They eat so many that they begin to glow themselves. **B**

• Cool Light

If you hold a glowing firefly in your hand, it won't burn you because its light is "cold." Bioluminescence is 100 percent efficient: it wastes no energy and gives off no heat. It differs from a typical light bulb, which gives off 10 percent of its energy as light and 90 percent as heat. . . .

40 ▶ Hungry for Slugs

Young lightning bugs are useful to humans. The larvae[3] eat snails, slugs, and aphids[4]. . . . The adults of some species don't eat at all; others eat only pollen and nectar from flowers. **C**

---

2. **bioluminescence** (by oh loo muh NES uhns): the production of light by living things.
3. **larvae** (LAHR vee): newly hatched, often wormlike, insects.
4. **slugs:** snails with no shells that often damage plants; and **aphids** (AY fids): tiny insect pests that feed on sap from plants.

B CONNECT IDEAS

Why is the word *bioluminescence* in italics in this section? How does making this word different from the surrounding words help readers?

_____

_____

_____

_____

_____

C CONNECT IDEAS

Place a star next to the subheading that tells you about what fireflies eat.

• Grounded

A firefly is able to glow for only 3 to 8 weeks—a small part of its life. Its life cycle begins when females lay eggs on wet and muddy ground. The larvae—nicknamed *glowworms* because they give off a faint light—hatch
50 in late summer. After feeding for a few weeks, they go underground to escape the winter cold. The glowworms come out again in spring to eat. Later, they seal themselves inside a tiny chamber of soil. After 2 weeks they reappear as adult lightning bugs that can fly. **D**

• Time to Shine

Lightning bugs are most active in July and August. You can usually see them glow between sundown and midnight. During the day, fireflies hang onto tree trunks and branches. "Most people see them in the day
60 but don't realize what they are," says Hoover. "Fireflies like to hang out in crevices in tree bark." **E**

• Water Lovers

Drought, or a serious lack of water, strongly affects firefly populations. They need soggy places with low-growing plants to breed and thrive. Hoover says that the soil's wetness determines how many fireflies appear in any given year. Gardeners may notice fewer fireflies after a drought. **PAUSE & REFLECT**

IN OTHER WORDS A firefly is a beetle. Oxygen and chemicals mix together in the firefly's body, causing it to glow. Fireflies give off light, but not heat. A firefly glows for only a short part of its life. The larvae hatch in summer and go underground in winter, to become adults in spring. During the day, they rest. Fireflies need wet environments to survive.

D LANGUAGE COACH
Many English words are **compound words,** the combination of two other words. For example, *firefly* comes from combining *fire + fly*. What other words can you find in this section that are formed from two other words?

E CONNECT IDEAS
Reread lines 55–61. What do you think is the most important scientific fact in this section? Underline it.

PAUSE & REFLECT
What do you think was the author's purpose for writing this article? Discuss your response with a partner.

_____

_____

_____

_____

_____

_____

READING 10D Make logical connections between ideas within a text and across two or three texts representing different genres.

Practicing Your Skills: Connect Ideas

Take time to connect the ideas you read about. First, review the scientific facts you learned about fireflies from this article. Write three facts in the first three boxes, giving special attention to facts emphasized by text features. Then, use the facts to write a short description of fireflies.

CONNECT IDEAS

Fact:

+

Fact:

+

Fact:

=

Description:

_____

_____

_____

_____

_____

_____

_____

Academic Vocabulary in Writing

The word **encounter** (en KOWN tuhr) is a noun that means *a meeting, especially one that is not expected.*

> After his surprise **encounter** with the skunk, Jake decided he shouldn't go to the party.

WRITE IT What would it be like to walk out at night and suddenly find dozens of glowing, flashing, flying insects all around you? Write a paragraph to describe this **encounter**. Be sure to use the word **encounter** in your writing.

_____

_____

_____

_____

_____

_____

Texas Assessment Practice

DIRECTIONS Use "Stars with Wings" to answer questions 1–4.

1 What causes fireflies to light up?
- **A** Eating slugs
- **B** Larvae
- **C** Sealing themselves in soil
- **D** Bioluminescence

2 Which of the following statements is a scientific fact?
- **F** Fireflies are unable to fly.
- **G** A firefly is a soft-bodied beetle.
- **H** A firefly's light will burn if you touch it.
- **J** Fireflies are most active during the winter.

3 Which of the following is NOT a text feature?
- **A** The title
- **B** Headings
- **C** A sentence
- **D** Boldface type

4 When you connect ideas, you —
- **F** bring together information
- **G** write a personal response
- **H** discuss differences
- **J** summarize main ideas and details

READING 8 Determine the figurative meaning of phrases and analyze how an author's use of language suggests mood.

The Delight Song of Tsoai-Talee

Poem by N. Scott Momaday

Four Skinny Trees

Vignette by Sandra Cisneros

How would you DESCRIBE yourself?

If you had to describe yourself, what would you say? You might describe yourself by comparing yourself to something or someone else. In the selections you are about to read, people compare themselves to one or more elements of nature.

LIST IT Comparing yourself to an element of nature, such as a blooming sunflower or a powerful tiger, can give a clear idea of who you are: "I am like a tiger, because I am powerful and proud." In the notepad at left, compare yourself to something found in nature. Use adjectives—describing words— to show how you and this element of nature are alike.

Literary Analysis: Mood and Figurative Language

Have you ever described a story by using words like *creepy* or *fun*? These words describe the **mood,** or the feeling that a writer creates for the reader. One way writers create mood is with **figurative language,** language that makes imaginative comparisons by expressing ideas that are not really true. Two types of figurative language are **metaphor** and **personification.**

- **Metaphor:** a comparison between two things that are not alike; does not use the words *like* or *as.*

    Example: I am an antelope as I run down the trail.

- **Personification:** a comparison that treats an object, animal, or idea as if it were human.

    Example: My shoes punished the pavement as I ran.

Notepad (left margin):

I am like a _____

because I am _____

_____

_____

I am _____

_____

_____

and I am _____

_____

_____

As you read the following selections, you will fill in a chart like the one below to note how the comparisons the writers make add to the mood of each piece.

READING 8 Determine the figurative meaning of phrases and analyze how an author's use of language suggests mood. **RC-7(A)** Establish purposes for reading selected texts to enhance comprehension.

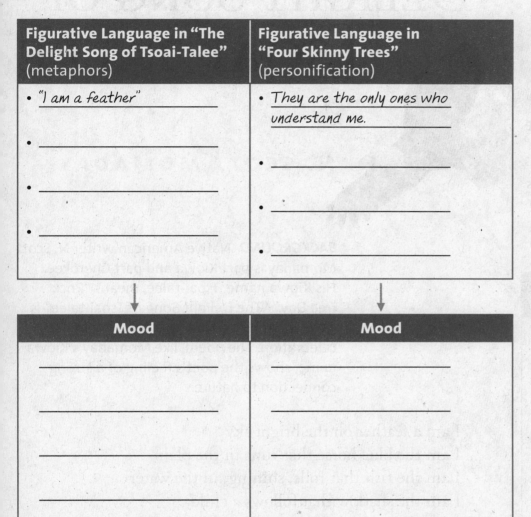

Figurative Language in "The Delight Song of Tsoai-Talee" (metaphors)	Figurative Language in "Four Skinny Trees" (personification)
• "I am a feather"	• They are the only ones who understand me.
• _____	• _____
• _____	• _____
• _____	• _____

Mood	Mood
_____	_____
_____	_____
_____	_____
_____	_____

Reading Strategy: Set a Purpose for Reading

Every time you read, you read with a purpose. That purpose might be to have fun, or it might be to learn information. In this lesson, one **purpose for reading** is to compare the moods of two pieces. As you read, think about other reasons why you want to read each piece. These additional purposes will keep you involved in what you are reading and help you make connections with other ideas and experiences. Questions in the margins will help you identify these additional purposes as you read the two selections.

SET A PURPOSE FOR READING

Read this poem to see how Momaday uses metaphors to set a mood.

Ⓐ MOOD AND FIGURATIVE LANGUAGE

Reread lines 1–6. Circle each element of nature to which the speaker compares himself. Add each metaphor to the chart. Then tell what mood these metaphors create.

Figurative Language in "The Delight Song of Tsoai-Talee" (metaphors)
• I am a feather
• I am the blue horse
• _____
• _____
• _____
• _____

↓

Mood
_____
_____
_____
_____
_____
_____

THE DELIGHT SONG OF TSOAI-TALEE

Poem by

N. SCOTT MOMADAY

BACKGROUND Native American writer N. Scott Momaday is part Kiowa and part Cherokee. His Kiowa name, Tsoai-talee, means "Rock Tree Boy." "The Delight Song of Tsoai-talee" is a Native American chant, a song or poem of celebration. The poem, like Momaday's Kiowa name, shows the poet's feeling of a strong connection to nature.

I am a feather on the bright sky
I am the blue horse that runs in the plain
I am the fish that rolls, shining, in the water
I am the shadow that follows a child
5 I am the evening light, the lustre[1] of meadows
I am an eagle playing with the wind Ⓐ
I am a cluster of bright beads
I am the farthest star
I am the cold of the dawn
10 I am the roaring of the rain
I am the glitter on the crust of the snow
I am the long track of the moon in a lake
I am a flame of four colors
I am a deer standing away in the dusk

---

1. **lustre** (LUHS tuhr): brightness or shininess.

15 I am a field of sumac² and the pomme blanche³
I am an angle of geese in the winter sky
I am the hunger of a young wolf
I am the whole dream of these things **B**

IN OTHER WORDS The speaker lists objects, animals, and events found in nature. He compares himself to several animals, including a deer and a horse.

▶ Reread lines 7–17. With a partner, Underline at least four objects or events to which the speaker compares himself.

You see, I am alive, I am alive
20 I stand in good relation to the earth
I stand in good relation to the gods
I stand in good relation to all that is beautiful
I stand in good relation to the daughter of *Tsen-tainte*⁴
You see, I am alive, I am alive **PAUSE & REFLECT**

IN OTHER WORDS The speaker celebrates his harmony and unity with the earth, the gods, and figures from Native American history.

B **SET A PURPOSE FOR READING**

What connections can you make between the speaker's feelings about his place in the world and your own feelings about your place in the world? Discuss your response with a partner.

PAUSE & REFLECT

Why does the speaker repeat the words in line 19: "You see, I am alive, I am alive"? Discuss your thoughts with a partner.

---

2. **sumac** (SOO mak): a shrub or small tree with small red fruits that are sometimes poisonous.
3. **pomme blanche** (pawm blansh): a plant with heavy roots that can be eaten.
4. **Tsen-tainte:** a heroic and respected 19th-century Kiowa chief known for his bold raids on both white and Native American settlements.

SET A PURPOSE FOR READING
Read this selection to find out how the narrator is like four skinny trees.

ⓒ SET A PURPOSE FOR READING
Why might you want to read about how a child on the verge of becoming a teenager feels about herself? Discuss your response with a partner.

ⓓ MOOD AND FIGURATIVE LANGUAGE
Personification gives human qualities to something that isn't human. Reread lines 1–6. Underline words or phrases that show personification of the trees. Note them in your chart. Then tell what mood this personification creates.

Figurative Language in "Four Skinny Trees" (personification)
• trees "understand" the speaker
• _____
• _____
• _____

↓

Mood
_____
_____
_____

Four Skinny Trees

Vignette by
SANDRA CISNEROS

BACKGROUND "Four Skinny Trees" is from *The House on Mango Street*, a book based on Sandra Cisneros's childhood as a young Mexican American girl growing up in Chicago. In this vignette (vihn YET), or short scene, four trees planted in her city neighborhood help the speaker find strength when she feels powerless. ⓒ

They are the only ones who understand me. I am the only one who understands them. Four skinny trees with skinny necks and pointy elbows like mine. Four who do not belong here but are here. Four raggedy excuses planted by
5 the city. From our room we can hear them, but Nenny just sleeps and doesn't appreciate these things. ⓓ

IN OTHER WORDS The speaker believes she shares a special understanding with four shabby, skinny trees planted in her city neighborhood. She thinks they are awkward and out of place, like her. Her sister, Nenny, does not understand their importance.

Their strength is secret. They send ferocious roots beneath the ground. They grow up and they grow down

and grab the earth between their hairy toes and bite the
10 sky with violent teeth and never quit their anger. This is
how they keep.

Let one forget his reason for being, they'd all droop like
tulips in a glass, each with their arms around the other.
Keep, keep, keep, trees say when I sleep. They teach. **E**

IN OTHER WORDS The trees' hidden strength, their anger and
intensity, helps them grow. If one tree forgets why it is alive,
the other trees will suffer. The trees help the speaker learn to
persist—to keep going.

---

15 When I am too sad and too skinny to keep keeping,
when I am a tiny thing against so many bricks, then it is I
look at trees. When there is nothing left to look at on this
street. Four who grew despite concrete. Four who reach and
do not forget to reach. Four whose only reason is to be and
be. **PAUSE & REFLECT**

IN OTHER WORDS When the speaker feels sad and powerless,
she thinks of the trees. They continue to grow even when it's
hard to grow.

► In the final paragraph, put an arrow → next to the sentence
that tells you it's hard for trees to survive in the city.

E **MOOD AND
FIGURATIVE
LANGUAGE**

Reread lines 7–14. What
words and phrases stand out
to you? Circle them. What
mood do these words create?

_____

_____

_____

_____

_____

PAUSE & REFLECT

Reread lines 18–20. With a
partner, discuss how the
words that describe the trees
can also be said to describe
the speaker.

Literary Analysis: Mood and Figurative Language

You've learned that writers use figurative language, such as metaphors and personification, to express ideas and create a mood. In the chart below, identify each quotation as a metaphor or as an example of personification. Then describe how you think the figurative language adds to the overall mood or feeling of the selection.

READING 8 Determine the figurative meaning of phrases and analyze how an author's use of language suggests mood.

"The Delight Song of Tsoai-Talee"		
Line from Poem	Figure of Speech	Mood/Feeling
"I am a cluster of bright beads"		
"I am the hunger of a young wolf"		
"Four Skinny Trees"		
"They are the only ones who understand me."		
"Four skinny trees with skinny necks and pointy elbows like mine."		

How would you DESCRIBE yourself?

Look at the element of nature you chose in the activity on page 224. Write a metaphor and an example of personification in which you compare yourself to that element of nature.

Metaphor: _____

Personification: _____

Reading Strategy: Set a Purpose for Reading

Look back at the two selections, and list your purposes for reading:

_____

_____

Which purpose kept you the most involved in your reading? Why?

_____

READING 8 Determine the figurative meaning of phrases and analyze how an author's use of language suggests mood. **RC-7(A)** Establish purposes for reading selected texts to enhance comprehension.

Academic Vocabulary in Speaking

The word **integrity** (in TEG rih tee) is a noun that means *being honest and true to oneself*.

> The doctor's **integrity** kept him from overcharging patients.

TURN AND TALK Do you believe that the speaker in "Four Skinny Trees" is honest and true to herself? With a partner, discuss whether her words show **integrity**.

Texas Assessment Practice

DIRECTIONS Use "The Delight Song of Tsoai-Talee" and "Four Skinny Trees" to answer questions 1–4.

1 A comparison that gives human qualities to an object, animal, or idea is called —
   - (A) mood
   - (B) repetition
   - (C) metaphor
   - (D) personification

2 The overall mood of "The Delight Song of Tsoai-Talee" is —
   - (F) serious
   - (G) joyful
   - (H) angry
   - (J) relaxed

3 The speaker in "Four Skinny Trees" is like the trees because —
   - (A) she is sad
   - (B) she is graceful
   - (C) she doesn't belong
   - (D) she is skinny and weak

4 The overall mood of "Four Skinny Trees" is —
   - (F) determined
   - (G) cheerful
   - (H) annoyed
   - (J) silly

Included in this unit: TEKS 3, 3B, 6, RC-7(B), RC-7(C), RC-7(E)

UNIT

6

Sharing Our Stories

MYTHS, LEGENDS, AND TALES

Be sure to read the Reader's Workshop on pp. 640–645 in *Holt McDougal Literature*.

Academic Vocabulary for Unit 6

You will see these Academic Vocabulary words as you work through this book. You will also be asked to use them as you write and talk about the selections in this unit.

Attribute (AT ruh byoot) is a noun that means *an element or characteristic that is a natural part of someone or something.*
Heroes from different cultures often share the same **attributes**.

Describe one **attribute** that most of your friends share: _____

_____

Conduct (kuhn DUKT) is a verb that means *to manage, direct, or control.*
School officials will **conduct** the fire drill in a calm, orderly way.

How would you **conduct** yourself at a formal dinner? _____

_____

Physical (FIZ ih kuhl) is an adjective that means *having to do with the body or material things.*
Many heroes are famous for their **physical** strength or size.

What **physical** activities do you enjoy the most? _____

_____

Status (STAT uhs) is a noun that means *the position or rank of someone or something compared with others.*
Doctors and lawyers have a high **status** in American society.

How could a student improve his or her academic **status**? _____

_____

Task (task) is a noun that means *a job or piece of work to be done.*
Ana helps her mother with at least one **task** each evening.

What is one **task** you complete during the school day? _____

_____

READING 3 Analyze genre in different cultural and historical contexts. **3B** Describe conventions in myths. **6** Understand the structure and elements of fiction.

Prometheus
Based on the Greek myth retold by Bernard Evslin

Orpheus and Eurydice
Based on the Greek myth retold by Olivia Coolidge

Do you THINK before you act?

Did you ever make a decision you wished you could take back? If so, then you know that your actions sometimes have consequences, or effects, that you didn't expect. You're not alone. As you'll see in the Greek myths you're about to read, people have been acting without thinking since ancient times.

LIST IT List some risky decisions you might make, such as trying out for a sport you haven't played before. Then choose one decision and list the possible **consequences,** both good and bad.

Literary Analysis: Characteristics of Myths

Since ancient times, people have passed down **myths**—stories that explain mysteries of the universe. Most myths share the characteristics, or qualities, shown below.

Characteristics of a Myth
• often explains how something connected with humans or nature came to be
• shows consequences of good and bad behavior
• includes gods or other beings with special powers and certain flaws, or weaknesses

As you read the myths, note what they explain and how the gods act in each one.

Decisions I might make

1. _Trying out for a new sport_

2. _____

3. _____

Consequences

Good: I might play well and make new friends

_____

Bad: _____

_____

Reading Strategy: Ask Questions

Myths from other cultures feature unfamiliar characters, places, and situations. As you read, ask questions to check your understanding. If you can't answer your questions, read more slowly, reread a section, or read on for more information.

RC-7(B) Ask literal and interpretive questions of text.
RC-7(C) Reflect on understanding to monitor comprehension.

Question: Why doesn't Zeus want humans to have fire?

→

Answer: Zeus thinks humans won't appreciate the gods if they have the power of fire.

Vocabulary in Context

NOTE: Words are listed in the order in which they appear in the selections.

Aptitude (AP tih tood) is a noun that means *ability*.
   Prometheus has a special **aptitude** for bothering Zeus.

Infinitely (IN fuh nit lee) is an adverb that means *greatly* or *without limits*.
   Compared to humans, the gods are **infinitely** powerful.

Vengeance (VEN juhns) is a noun that means *punishment in return for being angered or wronged*.
   Zeus wants **vengeance** after his orders are not obeyed.

Inconsolable (in kuhn SOH luh buhl) is an adjective that means *unable to be comforted*.
   Eurydice is **inconsolable** after the loss of a loved one.

Ascend (uh SEND) is a verb that means *to go up*.
   The gods do not want humans to **ascend** their mountain.

Vocabulary Practice

Answer the following questions with a partner.

1. What **aptitude** would help you **ascend** a mountain?

2. When someone is **inconsolable**, will the feeling go on **infinitely**?

3. What is a situation in which **vengeance** should be avoided?

**SET A PURPOSE
FOR READING**
Read this myth to discover
what Prometheus does to
show that he is a friend to
humankind.

PROMETHEUS

Based on the Greek myth retold by
BERNARD EVSLIN

BACKGROUND In Greek myths there
were a large number of gods. Not all
of these gods were equal in power and
rank. Prometheus (pruh MEE thee uhs)
was a giant, one of the Titans (TY tuhnz).
The Greek god Zeus (zoos) defeated
the Titans and became ruler over the
other gods. According to one myth, Zeus
ordered Prometheus to create humans.

Prometheus was a young Titan who did not like the
god Zeus. Prometheus always asked Zeus questions, which
often angered Zeus.

One morning Prometheus told Zeus, "I don't understand
your plans. You keep humans from knowing anything, and
you keep them in darkness."

"Perhaps you had better leave humans to me," said Zeus.
"Man is happy without knowing too much and without
fire. Let us not speak of this again."

10   But Prometheus said, "Look at man. Look below. He
lives in caves. He is a helpless, weak creature, at the mercy
of animals and weather. He eats his meat raw. If you mean
something by this, tell me. Why do you refuse to give man
the gift of fire?" Ⓐ

Zeus answered, "Do you not know that every gift has a
cost? This is the way gods must act. It's true that man does
not have fire. On the other hand, he does not have sickness,

Ⓐ **GREEK MYTHS**
You have been introduced
to two Greek gods and what
each thinks of human beings.
Underline Zeus' opinion
of how humans live. Then
place brackets [ ] around
Prometheus' opinion.

war, old age, or worry either. He is happy without fire. And he'll stay that way." **B**

IN OTHER WORDS Prometheus doesn't like Zeus and often bothers him by asking him questions. One day Prometheus asks Zeus why he refuses to give people more knowledge or fire. Zeus points out that the more people know the more difficult life becomes.

---

20   "Happy as animals are happy," said Prometheus. "What use is it to make humans if they must live like animals? Why separate them from the animals at all?"

"Man has another trait," said Zeus, "the ability to love us. Humans have an **aptitude** for admiring our power. They are puzzled by our riddles and amazed by our unpredictability. That is why they were made."

"Would not giving humans the gift of fire make them more interesting?"

"More interesting, perhaps, but **infinitely** more dangerous.
30 For man is very proud. If we improve man's life, he will forget what makes him pleasing to us. He will come to consider himself a god. Then he will attack us. Enough, Prometheus! Go now and trouble me no more with your questions."

IN OTHER WORDS Prometheus says that humans are only as happy as animals. Zeus points out that humans have another valuable trait—they worship the gods.

► What reason does Zeus give for not teaching men about fire? Underline the answer in the story.

All that night Prometheus lay awake making plans. The next morning, he stretched his arm up to the flames of the sun. He captured a spark and carried it down to the people.

At first men were afraid of the fire. It was so hot; it hurt when touched. It made strange shadows on the wall. They

B GREEK MYTHS
Based on the conversation between the two gods in lines 1–19, what part of the natural world do you think this myth will explain? Make a **prediction**—an educated guess.

I think this myth might

explain

VOCABULARY
The word **aptitude** (AP tih tood) is a noun that means *ability*.

VOCABULARY
The word **infinitely** (IN fuh nit lee) is an adverb that means *greatly* or *without limits*.

⊙ ASK QUESTIONS

Make sure you understand what Prometheus has done. What **questions** do you have about his actions and their possible effects? Record your questions in a chart. Reread lines 34–48, and then answer any of your questions that you can at this point.

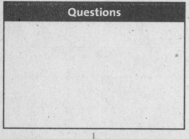

Questions

↓

Answers

Once you've finished reading the myth, go back to your unanswered questions and try again to answer them.

VOCABULARY

The word **vengeance** (VEN juhns) is a noun that means *punishment in return for being angered or wronged.*

Why does Zeus want **vengeance** against Prometheus?

_____

_____

_____

thanked Prometheus and then asked him to take it away. But he took part of a newly killed deer and roasted it over the fire. When the people smelled it, they flung themselves on the meat and ate it greedily.

"This is called 'fire,'" Prometheus said. "You must handle it carefully. It can change your whole life. You must feed it twigs, but don't let it get too big. If it escapes, use this magic called 'water.' Fire fears water. If you touch the fire with water, it will fly away until you need it again." **⊙**

Prometheus went from cave to cave teaching people about fire.

IN OTHER WORDS Prometheus takes a spark of fire from the sun and gives it to humans. At first, humans are afraid of fire, but Prometheus shows them how to cook meat. They decide that fire is good and they want to have it.

One day Zeus looked down from the mountain and was amazed. Everything had changed. Zeus saw huts, houses, villages, towns, and even a castle or two. He saw men cooking their food and carrying torches at night. He saw men using fire to make plows, swords, and spears. They were making ships and riding out to battle, like the gods themselves.

Zeus was full of rage. He seized his largest thunderbolt. "So they want fire," he said to himself. "I'll give them fire—more than they can use. I'll burn the earth up completely." But then another thought came to him, and he stopped. "No," he said to himself, "I shall have **vengeance**—and some fun, too. Let them destroy themselves with their new skills. This will be interesting to watch. But I'll take care of them later. First, I must deal with Prometheus."

He called his giant guards and had them capture Prometheus. They tied him to a mountain peak with large chains. Then, Zeus sent two large birds to fly 70 around him forever, ripping at his belly and eating his liver. **PAUSE & REFLECT**

Men knew a terrible thing was happening on the mountain, but they did not know what. The wind shrieked, screaming like a giant in torment and sometimes like fierce, angry birds.

For many hundreds of years Prometheus lay there. Finally, another brave hero was born. He climbed up the mountain and freed Prometheus. His name was Heracles (HAIR uh kleez).

IN OTHER WORDS Zeus notices that men have built houses, towns, ships, and weapons. They are also going to war against each other. Zeus decides to watch the humans destroy themselves.

► Circle the sentences that tell you how Zeus punishes Prometheus.

PAUSE & REFLECT

With a classmate, discuss the following question: Was Zeus right to punish Prometheus? Support your opinion with details from the myth.

SET A PURPOSE FOR READING
Read "Orpheus and Eurydice" to discover how Orpheus tries to use music to save his dear Eurydice.

Orpheus *and* Eurydice

Based on the Greek myth retold by

OLIVIA COOLIDGE

BACKGROUND In Greek mythology, Orpheus (AWR fee uhs) was the son of Calliope (kuh LY uh pee), goddess of epic poetry, and Apollo (uh POL oh), god of music and the sun. Apollo was said to have given the child Orpheus a harp that goddesses taught him to play. In the following story, Orpheus tries to use his musical power to help bring Eurydice (yu RID ih SEE), his wife, back from the dead.

VOCABULARY
The word **inconsolable** (in kuhn SOH luh buhl) is an adjective that means *unable to be comforted.*

VISUAL VOCABULARY

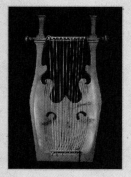

A **lyre** (lyr) is a small handheld harp.

The story of Orpheus shows the Greek love of music. In this story, Orpheus made beautiful songs. When he sang, the trees would crowd around to shade him. Wild beasts became gentle and sat harmless by him. Even gods of the woods listened to him as though under a magic spell.

Orpheus' music came from the love and longing in his heart. He loved a woman named Eurydice. All nature joyfully celebrated their wedding day. But that morning,
10 Eurydice was bitten by a snake and died.

Orpheus was **inconsolable**—he was so sad that he could not be comforted. Finally, that evening, Orpheus took his **lyre** and set out for the underworld. That was where the soul of dead Eurydice had gone.

On the path down to the underworld, Orpheus played his lyre and sang. Everyone stopped to listen. Ghosts followed him silently. Even monsters listened to his beautiful voice without moving. **D**

20 The hall of Hades,[1] ruler of the underworld, opened as Orpheus sang. Hades looked serious and unmoved. But tears shone on his cheeks. Even his hard heart was touched by the love in the music.

IN OTHER WORDS Orpheus plays and sings music so beautiful that even trees and animals listen. He loves a woman named Eurydice, but on their wedding day, Eurydice dies. Deeply saddened, Orpheus decides to rescue her from the world of the dead. He plays and sings his music as he travels the path to the underworld.

▶ What effect does Orpheus' music have on Hades? <u>Underline</u> the statement that tells you.

When the song ended, Hades spoke. "Go back to the light of day," he said. "Do not turn back. The spirit of Eurydice will follow you. But if you look at her, she will return to me." **E**

Orpheus walked away from the hall of Hades. He listened for a sound behind him, but he could not hear anything. He wondered if Hades was tricking him.
30 Suppose he came up to the light again and Eurydice was not there! The monsters had already heard his song. If he tried to enter the underworld a second time, his spell would be less powerful. He could never go back to the underworld. Perhaps he had lost Eurydice by believing Hades.

Worried that he was going farther from his bride, Orpheus **ascended** toward the light of day. But he could

---

1. **Hades** (HAY deez)

D LANGUAGE COACH
A **compound word** is a word made up of two or more other words, such as *steamboat*. If you don't know the meaning of a compound word, you can often figure it out from the words that form it. Circle the compound word in line 15. Then draw a line between the two words that make up the circled compound.

E GREEK MYTHS
What special powers does the god Hades seem to have?

_____

_____

_____

_____

_____

VOCABULARY
The word **ascend** (uh SEND) is a verb that means *to go up*.

● ASK QUESTIONS

Answer the question in the chart below. If you have any other questions about what happened in this myth, record them below as well. Then reread the myth carefully, looking for answers.

Questions
How are Orpheus and Eurydice brought back together?

↓

Answers

not go out without his love. Quickly he turned. He saw Eurydice's shadow behind him, and the sad look on her
40 face. He called, "Eurydice!" He tried to put his arms around her, but her shadow disappeared. A little whisper seemed to say "Goodbye." Then she was gone.

IN OTHER WORDS Hades tells Orpheus that Eurydice will follow him, as long as he does not not look back for her as he leaves the underworld. He begins walking but does not hear her behind him. Thinking that Hades has tricked him, Orpheus turns to see if Eurydice is really following him. He sees her shadow and hears her voice. Then she is gone.

Orpheus went quickly down the path to the underworld. But he could not get back in. When he came up to earth again, he sang of his lost Eurydice. His song was sad but beautiful. He could not stand to be around people, so he sent them away from him. Finally he was killed by women who were angry that he did not pay attention to them. At last he could go down to the underworld again.

IN OTHER WORDS Orpheus tries to follow Eurydice, but he cannot get back into the underworld. He continues to mourn Eurydice in his sad, beautiful songs. One day, some women become jealous of his love for Eurydice and kill him.

50, There he met the ghost of Eurydice. Now they walk together, and where the path is narrow, the ghost of Orpheus goes ahead and looks back at his love. ●

Literary Analysis: Characteristics of Greek Myths

The characteristics of Greek myths can be found in "Prometheus" and "Orpheus and Eurydice." Choose one of the myths. In the chart below, give examples of as many of each characteristic as you can.

READING 3 Analyze genre in different cultural and historical contexts. **3B** Describe conventions in myths. **6** Understand the structure and elements of fiction.

Myth:		
explains how something came to be	shows consequences of behavior	includes gods or other beings with special powers and certain flaws

Review your notes from "Prometheus" and "Orpheus and Eurydice" and the middle column of your completed chart. Think about the behaviors that are rewarded and those that are punished in each myth. What kind of behavior did the Greeks hope to encourage with these myths? Record your thoughts below.

_____

_____

_____

_____

_____

_____

RC-7(B) Ask literal and interpretive questions of text.
RC-7(C) Reflect on understanding to monitor comprehension.

Reading Strategy: Ask Questions

Think about the questions you asked as you read and the strategies you used to answer the questions. Use the chart below to analyze how you answered your questions. Did you reread? Read more slowly? Read ahead? Why did the strategy work?

Question/Answer	→	Strategy Used	Why It Worked
Q: A:	→		
Q: A:	→		
Q: A:	→		

Do you THINK before you act?

Imagine you could ask Prometheus or Orpheus this question. Choose one of these characters and, with a classmate, discuss how you think the character would answer. Base your opinion on what happens in the myth.

Vocabulary Practice

State whether the words in each pair are synonyms (words that mean the same) or antonyms (words that mean the opposite).

1. aptitude/talent _____

2. inconsolable/comforted _____

3. ascend/climb _____

4. infinitely/slightly _____

5. vengeance/mercy _____

Academic Vocabulary in Speaking

The word **attribute** (AT ruh byoot) is a noun that means *an element or characteristic that is a natural part of someone or something.*

A sense of humor is the main **attribute** Ivan looks for in a friend.

TURN AND TALK With a partner, talk about the differences between Zeus and Prometheus, focusing on their attributes or personality traits. Be sure to use the word **attribute** in your conversation.

READING 3 Analyze genre in different cultural and historical contexts. **3B** Describe conventions in myths. **6** Understand the structure and elements of fiction.

Texas Assessment Practice

DIRECTIONS Use "Prometheus" and "Orpheus and Eurydice" to answer questions 1–6.

1 Zeus' behavior is characteristic of a Greek myth when he —

- **A** discusses fire with Prometheus
- **B** vows to punish Prometheus
- **C** worries for the safety of humans
- **D** describes humans as innocent

2 Prometheus displays a special power when he —

- **F** screams in the wind in pain
- **G** defies Zeus' decisions
- **H** teaches humans to cook meat
- **J** uses the sunrise to start a fire

3 The myth "Prometheus" tries to explain —

- **A** how humans discovered fire
- **B** why vultures are disliked
- **C** why humans are different from animals
- **D** how light comes from the sun

4 The qualities that Orpheus represents in "Orpheus and Eurydice" are —

- **F** strength and bravery
- **G** simplicity and kindness
- **H** selfishness and pride
- **J** love and devotion

5 The myth "Orpheus and Eurydice" shows that the Greeks valued —

- **A** nature
- **B** music
- **C** honesty
- **D** family

6 Which behavior is most likely prized by the culture that gave us these two myths?

- **F** Generosity
- **G** Boldness
- **H** Obedience
- **J** Responsibility

READING 3 Analyze genre in different cultural and historical contexts. **3B** Describe convention in epic tales (e.g., the quest, the hero's tasks).

Beowulf

Epic poem translated by Burton Raffel

What are you willing to FIGHT for?

Sometimes, standing up for what you believe in takes courage. Courage often means conquering your own fears before taking a bold action. In the epic poem *Beowulf*, you'll read about Beowulf the warrior, who is very clear about what he's fighting for and why.

TURN AND TALK Have you ever had to overcome fear before taking action? Where do you find strength when you are afraid? Think of a strategy, or plan, that can help you deal with fear. List the steps of your strategy in the side column. Then, with a partner, imagine a situation in which courage might be needed, and discuss how your plan would help you.

Literary Analysis: Characteristics of the Epic

In literature, an **epic** is a long, narrative poem, or poem that tells a story. An epic poem usually tells about a series of **quests,** or journeys, undertaken by a great hero who is considered important in his or her culture. Epics are often written using very formal language instead of sounding like a story you might tell friends. As you read the excerpt from *Beowulf,* look for these characteristics of an epic:

- a hero with amazing strength, courage, and loyalty
- strange creatures and fantastic lands
- hero's tasks, or dangerous battles, in which the hero is tested

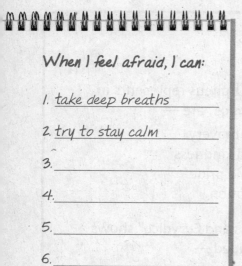

When I feel afraid, I can:

1. *take deep breaths*

2. *try to stay calm*

3. _____

4. _____

5. _____

6. _____

Reading Strategy: Paraphrase

Have you ever retold part of a favorite story or described for a friend a scene from a movie you've seen? When you restate ideas in your own words, you are **paraphrasing.** A good paraphrase has the following characteristics:

- It is made up of your own words instead of copying the author's original words.

- It captures the correct meaning of the original words.

- It contains all of the main ideas and supporting details from the original words.

- It is not just a short summary. Paraphrased text tends to be as long as the original text or longer.

Putting a story into your own words can help you understand the plot, or story events, and the characters. Paraphrasing is especially helpful when you read an epic poem such as *Beowulf*. This classic epic contains unfamiliar words, names, and speech patterns that may be difficult to understand at first. Putting lines or passages into your own words will help deepen your understanding of Beowulf and his quest.

As you read *Beowulf*, you will note lines or passages that are difficult to understand. Then, you will try to restate them in your own words. The chart below gives an example of how to paraphrase some challenging lines from *Beowulf*.

READING RC-7(E) Paraphrase texts in ways that maintain meaning and logical order within a text.

Passage from Poem	Paraphrase
I drove Five great giants into chains, chased All of that race from the earth.	Beowulf fought five giants and captured them all. Then he killed off their entire race.

SET A PURPOSE FOR READING
Read this excerpt to discover how a hero tries to convince a king that he is ready for battle.

BEOWULF

Epic poem translated by
BURTON RAFFEL

A PARAPHRASE

Reread the sentence that begins "Now Grendel's" (line 3) and ends "fleeing together" (line 8). In the box below, paraphrase these lines in your own words.

Paraphrase
Now the people are hearing about Grendel. Sailors have told them that . . .

BACKGROUND Beowulf (BAY uh wulf) is a great fighter. He crosses the sea to kill the monster Grendel, a creature that kills and eats human beings. In this excerpt, Beowulf has arrived at the court of Hrothgar (HROTH gahr), king of the Danes in Denmark. Beowulf tries to persuade the king to choose him to fight Grendel. In his speech, Beowulf describes his past victories and his strength as a warrior.

"Hail, Hrothgar!
Higlac is my cousin and my king; the days
Of my youth have been filled with glory. Now
    Grendel's
Name has echoed in our land: Sailors
5   Have brought us stories of Herot, the best
Of all mead halls,[1] deserted and useless when the
    moon
Hangs in skies the sun had lit,
Light and life fleeing together. **A**

---

1. **Herot, the best of all mead halls:** Herot is the great wooden building built by King Hrothgar for his men. Mead is a drink made from honey, water, yeast, and malt. A mead hall was a large room where warriors could gather to feast, listen to stories, and sleep in safety.

IN OTHER WORDS Beowulf greets Hrothgar. He points out that King Higlac is a "cousin," or relative. He also says that when he was young he did many great things. Beowulf knows that the monster Grendel is taking over the king's land. People can't go out at night because they are afraid of Grendel.

My people have said, the wisest, most knowing
10   And best of them, that my duty was to go to the
        Danes'
  Great King. They have seen my strength for
        themselves,
  Have watched me rise from the darkness of war,
  Dripping with my enemies' blood. I drove
  Five great giants into chains, chased
15   All of that race from the earth. I swam
  In the blackness of night, hunting monsters
  Out of the ocean, and killing them one
  By one; death was my errand and the fate
  They had earned. ❸

❸ PARAPHRASE
What does Beowulf mean when he says "death was my errand and the fate that they had earned"? Complete the sentence below in your own words.

Beowulf was sent . . .
_____
_____
_____

IN OTHER WORDS Beowulf says that many wise people told him to speak to Hrothgar. These people have seen Beowulf in action and know how strong he is. They have seen him fight in war and capture five giants.

► What has Beowulf hunted at night and what was the result? (Circle) the words that tell you this.

    Now Grendel and I are called
20   Together, and I've come. Grant me, then,
  Lord and protector of this noble place,
  A single request! I have come so far,
  Oh shelterer of warriors and your people's loved
        friend,

◯ EPIC

Epic poems usually include
(1) a hero with strength
and courage that are
superhuman, or well beyond
normal human abilities;
(2) strange creatures; and
(3) **hero's tasks,** in which
the hero is tested against
another warrior or a monster.
Find examples of these three
characteristics in lines 16–26
and <u>underline</u> them.

VISUAL VOCABULARY

A **linden** (LIN duhn) **shield**
was a shield made from the
strong, lightweight wood of
the linden tree.

That this one favor you should not refuse me—
25   That I, alone and with the help of my men,
   May purge all evil from this hall. **◯**

IN OTHER WORDS   Now Beowulf is ready to fight a new enemy,
Grendel. Beowulf compliments Hrothgar, saying that the king
takes care of his warriors and is loved by his people. Then Beowulf
asks Hrothgar for the chance to fight Grendel, to get rid of the evil
in the land.

   I have heard,
Too, that the monster's scorn of men
Is so great that he needs no weapons and fears none.
Nor will I. My lord Higlac
30   Might think less of me if I let my sword
Go where my feet were afraid to, if I hid
Behind some broad **linden shield**: My hands

Alone shall fight for me, struggle for life
Against the monster. God must decide
35 Who will be given to death's cold grip. **PAUSE & REFLECT**

IN OTHER WORDS Beowulf has heard that Grendel is so unafraid
of men that he doesn't bother to use weapons. Beowulf says he
won't use weapons either, because he wants his king, Higlac, to
be impressed by his bravery.

▶ How does Beowulf plan to kill Grendel? <u>Underline</u> the words
that tell you.

PAUSE & REFLECT
Are you convinced that
Beowulf is ready and able to
battle Grendel? Why or why
not? Share your opinion with
a partner, and bracket [ ]
phrases in the poem that
support your opinion.

READING 3 Analyze genre in different cultural and historical contexts. **3B** Describe conventions in epic tales (e.g., the quest, the hero's tasks). **RC-7(E)** Paraphrase texts in ways that maintain meaning and logical order within a text.

Literary Analysis: Characteristics of the Epic

Review the list of characteristics of the epic on page 246. In the chart below, list the traits that show that Beowulf is an epic hero. Give examples of each trait from the poem.

Beowulf's Traits	Examples from Poem
amazing courage	"Dripping with my enemies' blood"
amazing strength	

Reading Strategy: Paraphrase

Choose a short passage from *Beowulf*—a few lines or a complete sentence or two. Then paraphrase it below.

_____

_____

_____

To check your paraphrase, ask yourself these questions:

• Is it made up of my own words?

• Does it capture the meaning of the original passage?

• Does it contain all of the main ideas and supporting details from the original passage?

• Is it about the same length as or longer than the original passage?

TURN AND TALK Now, have a partner read your paraphrase and try to figure out which passage in the text it retells. Then switch roles.

What are you willing to FIGHT for?

Beowulf chose to sail to another land to battle a monster and help those in danger. Would you put yourself in danger to help people you do not know?

READING 3 Analyze genre in different cultural and historical contexts. 3B Describe conventions in epic tales (e.g., the quest, the hero's tasks).

TURN AND TALK Review the plan you came up with on page 246 for managing fear. Would it be enough to conquer fear in a truly dangerous situation? Discuss your thoughts with a partner.

Academic Vocabulary in Speaking

The word **physical** (FIZ ih kuhl) is an adjective that means *having to do with the body or material things*.

Physical exercise is important for a healthy life.

The word **task** (task) is a noun that means *a job or piece of work to be done*.

Rob found that organizing his coin collection was a big **task**.

TURN AND TALK With a partner, imagine how Beowulf's battle with Grendel might go, and why. Be sure to use the words **physical** and **task** in your conversation.

Texas Assessment Practice

DIRECTIONS Use *Beowulf* to answer questions 1–4.

1 An epic is —
- **A** a short poem about nature
- **B** a long, narrative poem
- **C** a short play about a monster
- **D** a long report about a real quest

2 A paraphrase of an epic is —
- **F** a line or passage from the epic
- **G** an oral reading of the epic
- **H** a movie made about the epic
- **J** a retelling of the epic in your own words

3 Which is not typical of an epic hero?
- **A** He has amazing strength.
- **B** He meets strange creatures.
- **C** He worries about his abilities.
- **D** He is tested in dangerous battles.

4 A good paraphrase of a passage —
- **F** should capture its correct meaning
- **G** should be brief
- **H** should include only main ideas
- **J** should copy the author's style

READING 3 Analyze genre in different cultural and historical contexts. **3B** Describe conventions in myths and epic tales (e.g., the hero's tasks).

Young Arthur

Based on the medieval legend retold by Robert D. San Souci

Is there a job you were BORN to do?

Some people believe that we all have a destiny, a future that we can't change even if we want to. Others think that life is what we make of it. In the legend you're about to read, a boy named Arthur discovers his destiny.

TURN AND TALK Make a list of people who have changed history through their dedication to a goal or job. Then jot down ideas about your own future goals or career. Afterward, with a small group of classmates, discuss whether people are born to do a particular job.

Literary Analysis: Characteristics of Legends

A **legend** is a story about a hero that is handed down from the past. Legends are often based on real people and events. As the stories pass through the generations, the characters, setting, objects, and events become less factual and more imaginary.

A legend has several important characteristics:

- It tells about a hero who may have unusual powers.
- It focuses on the hero's struggle to defeat a powerful force.
- It highlights a positive quality or way of behaving.

The King Arthur legends, for example, are probably based on a real-life king who lived in the year AD 500. The character of King Arthur showed heroic traits such as courage, honor, and fairness that made him a model for others to follow. He had special powers that helped him overcome enemies and difficult challenges.

As you read this excerpt from the medieval legend, identify the conflict young Arthur faces and how he proves his goodness.

People who have changed history:

1. Abraham Lincoln
2. _____
3. _____
4. _____
5. _____

What I might like to do in the future:

1. become a scientist
2. _____
3. _____
4. _____
5. _____

Reading Skill: Identify Chronological Order

In a legend, events are often presented in **chronological order,** or the order in which they take place. As you read, look for words and phrases that signal when events happen, such as *when, eventually, this time,* and *in the days that followed.* As you read, you will mark the sequence of events on a timeline like the one shown below.

RC-7(E) Summarize texts in ways that maintain meaning and logical order within a text.

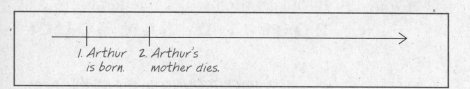

Vocabulary in Context

Note: Words are listed in the order in which they appear in the story.

Melancholy (MEL uhn kol ee) is a noun that means *sadness or depression.*
> *The jester tried to help the queen overcome her **melancholy.***

Reclaim (rih KLAYM) is a verb that means *to get back or recover.*
> *Merlin's plan allowed Arthur to **reclaim** his title of "King."*

Taskmaster (TASK mas tuhr) is a noun that means *a person who sets tasks for others to do.*
> *A shy child needs a gentle teacher, not a harsh **taskmaster.***

Flinching (FLINCH ing) is a noun that means *drawing back from difficulty or danger.*
> *The brave warrior will bear his punishment without **flinching.***

Vocabulary Practice

Review the words and sample sentences above. Then, with a partner, discuss what you think "Young Arthur" will be about. On the lines below, write down what you think will happen in the story.

_____

_____

_____

_____

Young *Arthur*

Based on the medieval legend retold by
ROBERT D. SAN SOUCI

BACKGROUND In the Middle Ages, a king's oldest son was next in line to become king. If the enemies of a king wanted to take over his kingdom, they might try to kill his son. This story is about the famous Arthur, a king's son, when he was a boy. Legends like this one often include magical people and tell about things that could never happen in real life. An important magician, Merlin, often appears in stories about Arthur.

VOCABULARY

The word **melancholy** (MEL uhn kol ee) is a noun that means *sadness or depression*.

Ⓐ CHRONOLOGICAL ORDER

Reread lines 1–13 and (circle) the words and phrases that signal the sequence of events. Begin a timeline on your own paper with the first two story events.

King Uther heard a loud knock at his door. A smiling servant entered. "You have a son," he told the king. Uther went into the queen's bedroom. "The boy's name shall be Arthur," he said, "and he will be a great king. For Merlin the magician has predicted that he will one day rule the land."

Sadly, Uther's queen died soon after Arthur's birth. Sadness wore out the king's spirit. He lost interest in ruling, and Merlin was unable to awaken him from his
10 **melancholy**. "There is fighting throughout the land," Merlin warned. "Your enemies are starting to rebel. Give me the baby for safekeeping since you have enemies even inside your own castle." Ⓐ

Uther agreed. Merlin took the baby to Sir Ector and his wife, who lived far from the castle. He told them nothing about the child, except that his name was Arthur. The couple's infant son had recently died, and they welcomed Arthur and treated him as their own.

Soon war divided the kingdom. King Uther, **reclaiming** 20 his old spirit and his desire to rule, rallied his knights and nobles to fight for him. With Merlin always beside him, he drove back his enemies.

Later, the king's enemies poisoned him. As he was dying he spoke, "Arthur shall be king after me."

Young Arthur, hidden from those enemies, was raised in Sir Ector's house. He learned to read and write along with his foster brother, Kay, who was older. By the time he was fifteen, Arthur was a tall, handsome, smart boy. **B**

IN OTHER WORDS King Uther (OO thur) has a son named Arthur. Troubles in the kingdom make the king afraid that someone might try to hurt the baby, so Merlin takes Arthur to live with Sir Ector. King Uther dies and Arthur grows up with Ector's son, Kay.

When Kay became a knight, he decided to train Arthur 30 in how to be a knight, too. But Sir Kay was jealous of the way their father treated Arthur, so he was a harsh **taskmaster**. Arthur came away from his lessons in sword fighting with many bruises and cuts. When he complained, Kay replied, "A knight must be thick-skinned and ready to put up with wounds without showing pain or **flinching**." Yet if Arthur so much as touched Kay, the knight would shout loudly for the doctor. When Arthur became Kay's apprentice—his student—Arthur felt in his heart that he was already a knight.

40 One Christmas Eve, Merlin the magician appeared again and called for everyone to come to London's central

C LEGENDS

Which of the characters you've met so far have positive qualities? Which characters have negative qualities? List their names under the headings below. Draw brackets [ ] around words on this page and the previous page that support your opinion.

Positive

↓

Negative

D LEGENDS

Why does Kay tell Arthur to get away from the sword?

_____

_____

_____

_____

_____

square. There, he pushed a large sword halfway into a huge stone. Written on the sword's blade in bright gold letters were the words: "Whoever pulls out the sword from this stone is the true King of England." **C**

In the days that followed, knights and nobles, farmers and bakers, and many other people pulled at the sword. But no one could even loosen it.

50 Later a great tournament[1] was held in London. Among those who came were Sir Ector, Sir Kay, and young Arthur, who served Kay. Arthur was so eager to see the games that he forgot to pack Kay's sword. Kay was quite upset when the mistake was discovered.

"You will be sorry if your error costs me a victory today," said Kay.

IN OTHER WORDS Merlin pushes a sword into a stone, saying that the real king will be able to pull the sword out of the stone. Sir Ector, Kay, and Arthur attend a tournament in the city, but Arthur forgets to bring Kay's sword.

Even Sir Ector was mad at Arthur. He told him to go back and get the missing sword.

Arthur left in a hurry. As he was riding away, he noticed the sword in the stone. "Surely that sword is as good as the 60 one left at home," he said. "I will borrow it."

He got off his horse, walked up to the sword, and pulled. The sword easily slid out of the stone. Arthur was in a hurry to get back to the tournament, so he did not notice the words on the blade. He ran back to the tournament where Sir Kay was waiting.

Kay shook with excitement when he saw the words on the sword. When Arthur asked what was wrong, Kay shouted, "Go! Get away! You have caused enough trouble." **D**

---

1. **tournament** (TOOR nuh muhnt): in medieval times, a sporting event in which knights wearing armor fought against each other.

70 But Arthur was curious. He followed as Kay ran to Sir Ector. "Look, Father!" cried Kay. "Here is the sword from the stone. That means I must be king of all the land!"

Sir Ector and the others saw the sword and read the words on the blade. They began to shout, "The sword from the stone! The king's sword!"

Hearing this, Arthur thought he had stolen a king's weapon. As people hurried toward Kay, Arthur got on his horse and rode away. He was sure he had committed
80 a crime.

As he rode, Arthur wondered whether Kay might be arrested for stealing the sword. "A true knight would not run away," he said to himself, "and I am a true knight in my heart." He was afraid, but he was also determined to do what was right. He turned his horse around. **PAUSE & REFLECT**

IN OTHER WORDS Arthur sees the sword in the stone and decides to borrow it. When he brings the sword to Kay, Kay acts as if he has pulled the sword out of the stone. The people around him act as if Kay is now the king. Arthur runs away, afraid he has done something wrong.

Back in the city Kay stood on the stone, holding the sword. Suddenly Merlin appeared at the edge of the crowd.
90 "Are you the one who pulled the sword from the stone?" Merlin asked.

"I am the one holding it," Kay replied.

"The real king could pull it free a hundred times," said Merlin. "Put the sword back into the stone and pull it out again."

PAUSE & REFLECT

Reread lines 70–86. Underline words that show Arthur's thoughts and feelings. Why does Arthur decide to turn around and go back to Sir Ector? What does this decision reveal about his personality?

_____

_____

_____

_____

_____

_____

_____

_____

VISUAL VOCABULARY

A **pommel** (POM uhl) is the knob on the end of a sword.

ⓔ CHRONOLOGICAL ORDER

Circle the time words and phrases on this page. After Sir Ector pays Arthur respect, who else does? List the final events on your timeline.

_____

_____

Kay put the sword back in the stone. But when he tried to pull it free, it would not move.

All of a sudden everyone looked at Arthur, who was pushing his way through the crowd. Arthur yelled, "It 100 wasn't Kay's fault! I brought him the sword!" Merlin smiled and said, "Climb up and draw the sword from the stone." Arthur grabbed the **pommel**, the knob on the end of the sword, and easily pulled the sword out.

Then Merlin called out, "This is Arthur, son of Uther, Britain's true king."

Sir Ector and Kay were amazed. They fell to their knees to show their respect. All around, there was growing confusion and disagreement. Some people cried, "It is the will of heaven! Long live the king!" Others cried, "It 110 is Merlin's plan to make a little boy king so that he can secretly rule us!"

The cries of "Long live King Arthur!" soon won out. ⓔ

IN OTHER WORDS All of the people realize that Arthur—not Kay—is the true king.

▶ Underline the sentence that tells you how Arthur shows that he is the king.

Literary Analysis: Characteristics of Legends

Most legends include a hero who faces a struggle or conflict. This character often has unusual powers and traits or qualities that others admire. Review Arthur's story. Pay attention to his conflict, his special powers, and his good traits. Then fill in the web below with these details about Arthur.

READING 3 Analyze genre in different cultural and historical contexts. **3B** Describe conventions in myths and epic tales (e.g., the hero's tasks). **RC-7(E)** Summarize texts in ways that maintain meaning and logical order within a text.

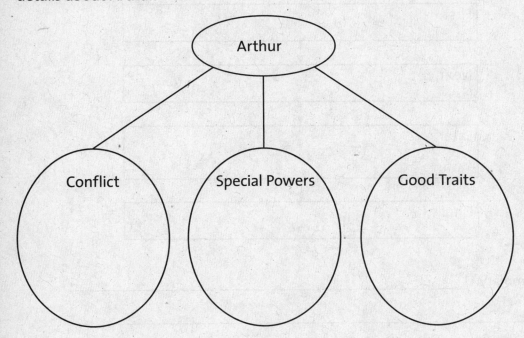

Arthur

Conflict

Special Powers

Good Traits

Is there a job you were BORN to do?

What ideas about destiny, or fate, are reflected in the legend of Arthur? Are they different from or similar to the ideas you discussed as part of the activity on page 254? Look over the ideas you listed. Explain whether you feel born to do a certain job or will choose it.

_____

_____

_____

_____

_____

_____

_____

READING 3 Analyze genre in different cultural and historical contexts.

Reading Skill: Identify Chronological Order

Review the events you listed on your timeline as you were reading. Decide which events are most important to the story, and write them in the sequence chart below. Then use your completed chart to write a summary of the story that shows the order of events.

First,

↓

Next,

↓

Later,

↓

Finally,

Summary: _____

_____

_____

Vocabulary Practice

Discuss each question with a partner, and use the vocabulary words to explain your answers.

1. If you were able to **reclaim** your lost dog from an animal shelter, would you be **melancholy**? Why or why not?

2. If your soccer coach were a **taskmaster**, do you think her instructions could cause **flinching** among the players? Why or why not?

Academic Vocabulary in Speaking

The word **conduct** (kuhn DUHKT) is a verb that means *to manage, direct, or control.*

> *The principal sat at the front of the room to **conduct** the meeting.*

The word **status** (STAT uhs) is a noun that means *the position or rank of someone or something compared with others.*

> *Her **status** as a student meant she couldn't eat lunch in the teacher's lounge.*

TURN AND TALK Discuss this legend with a partner. How did Arthur's **status** change in the story? How will he **conduct** the kingdom? Use **conduct** and **status** in your conversation.

Texas Assessment Practice

DIRECTIONS Use "Young Arthur" to answer questions 1–4.

1 Arthur is a good example of a hero in a legend because he —

- **A** believed he was a knight
- **B** has admirable traits
- **C** was the son of a king
- **D** does whatever he is told

2 Events presented in chronological order are told —

- **F** randomly
- **G** from least dramatic to most dramatic
- **H** from most important to least important
- **J** in the order in which they occur

3 A legend is —

- **A** a story passed down through many generations
- **B** a factual report of real events and people
- **C** a make-believe story
- **D** a story about magicians and magic objects

4 Why did people think Kay was the king?

- **F** Because he was Arthur's stepbrother
- **G** Because he was holding the sword from the stone
- **H** Because he had killed King Uther
- **J** Because Merlin had protected him

UNIT 7

Writing a Life
BIOGRAPHY AND AUTOBIOGRAPHY

Be sure to read the Reader's Workshop on pages 778–783 in *Holt McDougal Literature*.

Academic Vocabulary for Unit 7

You will see these Academic Vocabulary words as you work through this book. You will also be asked to use them as you write and talk about the selections in this unit.

Demonstrate (DEM uhn strayt) is a verb that means *to show clearly.*

Our computer teacher will **demonstrate** how the software works.

What skill could you **demonstrate** to friends or family? _____

_____

Goal (gohl) is a noun that means *something a person is trying to do or achieve.*

Kim's **goal** is to break the school record for the high jump.

Describe a **goal** you have set for yourself: _____

_____

Impact (IM pakt) is a noun that means *the effect of one thing on another.*

National elections have an **impact** on the country's politics.

What **impact** would enrolling in a new school have on you? _____

_____

Link (lingk) is a verb that means *to connect or join.*

Biographies often **link** a person's experiences with success.

Can you **link** a book you once read to a hobby you now have? _____

_____

Undertake (uhn duhr TAYK) is a verb that means *to begin or agree to do a task.*

In movies, spies often **undertake** difficult missions.

What type of volunteer project would you be willing to **undertake**?

_____

_____

READING 7 Make inferences and draw conclusions about the structural patterns and features of literary nonfiction. **9** Analyze author's purpose in cultural, historical, and contemporary contexts.

Eleanor Roosevelt
Based on the biography by William Jay Jacobs

What is your DUTY to others?

Everyone has things they have to do. Maybe it's homework or a job. But many of our duties, or responsibilities, are to others. We have to help our friends, family, and neighbors. In "Eleanor Roosevelt," you'll learn how a famous First Lady changed the world by helping others.

TURN AND TALK Make a list of the duties you have to people in your life. Then, with a partner, discuss the duties we have to people we *don't know*. What are our responsibilities to people in our community, our city, or even our country?

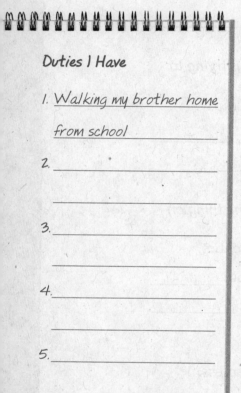

Duties I Have

1. *Walking my brother home from school*

2. _____

3. _____

4. _____

5. _____

Literary Analysis: Biography

A **biography** is the story of a person's life told by another person, called a biographer. Some biographers reveal their personal opinions of their subjects. However, they also balance these opinions with facts. Biographies are often entertaining and enjoyable to read. But entertainment is not the primary **purpose,** or goal, of a biography. Instead, a biographer wants to accomplish one or all of the following goals:

• provide information about the person's life

• reveal important aspects of his or her personality

• show us what others thought of the person

• explain the importance of his or her life and work

As you read, you will take notes about the art of writing a biography. Then, you will be asked to choose details that show how William Jay Jacobs accomplishes some of the goals above in his biography of Eleanor Roosevelt.

Reading Skill: Identify Chronological Order

A biography normally presents events in **chronological order,** or the order in which they happened. Phrases such as *the first few years* may show the order of events. As you read "Eleanor Roosevelt," you will create a timeline on a blank sheet of paper like the one shown to keep track of the order of events.

READING 7 Make inferences and draw conclusions about the structural patterns and features of literary nonfiction.

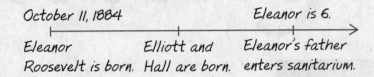

October 11, 1884   Eleanor is 6.

Eleanor Roosevelt is born.   Elliott and Hall are born.   Eleanor's father enters sanitarium.

Vocabulary in Context

Note: Words are listed in the order in which they appear in the selection.

Dominate (DOM uh nayt) **is a verb that means** *to have control over someone or something*.

> Eleanor's grandmother was always telling her what to do and tried to **dominate** and control her.

Brooding (BROO ding) **is an adjective that means** *full of worry*.

> Eleanor was sad, and her **brooding** silence showed it.

Prominent (PROM uh nuhnt) **is an adjective that means** *well-known or important*.

> Eleanor was one of the most **prominent** and beloved women of her time.

Migrant (MY gruhnt) **is an adjective that means** *moving from place to place*.

> Franklin and Eleanor tried to help **migrant** farm workers, who moved from one town to the next in search of work.

Vocabulary Practice

Discuss the following questions with a partner, using the boldface words in your answers.

1. When might it be okay for a **prominent** person to **dominate** a conversation?

2. Why might a **migrant** worker seem to be **brooding**?

Eleanor Roosevelt

Based on the biography by
WILLIAM JAY JACOBS

BACKGROUND Eleanor Roosevelt was First
Lady, or wife of the president, from 1933 to
1945. She was born into a wealthy family,
but she knew what it felt like to be an
outsider. In this biography, you will learn
how Eleanor helped people who suffered
because they had lost jobs, had no money,
or were treated unfairly.

Ⓐ BIOGRAPHY
Why do you think Jacobs,
the writer, chose to begin his
biography with a summary
of Eleanor Roosevelt's life?

_____

_____

_____

_____

_____

_____

Eleanor Roosevelt was the wife of President Franklin
Delano Roosevelt. But she was more than just a
president's wife.

She was a sad and lonely child. People teased her about
her looks and called her an ugly duckling.

But Eleanor Roosevelt refused to give up. Instead, she
devoted her life to helping others. Today she is remembered
as one of America's greatest women. Ⓐ

Eleanor was born in New York City, where her family
10 owned a house. They also owned a large house in the
country, on the Hudson River. A servant took care of
Eleanor when she was a child and taught her to speak
French. Eleanor's mother was Anna Hall Roosevelt, a

woman who wore expensive jewelry and fine clothing. Her father was Elliott Roosevelt. He had his own hunting lodge, and he liked to sail and to play tennis and polo. Elliott's older brother was Theodore Roosevelt. He became president of the United States in 1901. The Roosevelt family was one of America's oldest and wealthiest families.

20   Almost from the day of Eleanor's birth, October 11, 1884, people noticed that she was not a pretty child. Her mother and other relatives were beautiful, but Eleanor was plain looking. **ⓑ**

   When Eleanor was born, her parents had wanted a boy. She felt unwanted, and she became shy and withdrawn. She was a frightened, lonely little girl.

   The one joy in the early years of her life was her father. He used to dance with her, and he would throw her into the air while she laughed and laughed. He called her "little 30 golden hair" or "darling little Nell."

IN OTHER WORDS Eleanor Roosevelt was born into a wealthy and important family. But she was not like the rest of her family. The other members of her family did not think she was beautiful, and she felt unwanted.

   Then, when she was six, her father went to live at a medical center in Virginia. He had a drinking problem that he was trying to overcome. Eleanor missed him greatly.

   Next, her mother began to have painful headaches. Eleanor would sit for hours holding her mother's head in her lap and gently stroking her forehead. Nothing else seemed to take away the pain. Even at the age of seven Eleanor was glad to be helping someone.

   The next year, when Eleanor was eight, her mother died. 40 Soon after that, Eleanor's brother Elliott suddenly became ill, and he died, too. Eleanor and her baby brother, Hall, were taken to live with their grandmother. **ⓒ**

ⓑ IDENTIFY CHRONOLOGICAL ORDER

In lines 20–23, Jacobs begins his use of chronological order. Underline the date of Eleanor's birth. Begin your timeline with this date and event.

ⓒ IDENTIFY CHRONOLOGICAL ORDER

Reread lines 31–42. Circle the words and phrases that show the order of events and the passing of time. Continue your timeline with events from when Eleanor was six and when she was eight.

◐ BIOGRAPHY

What sentence in this paragraph tells you how important Eleanor's father's letters were to her? <u>Underline</u> that sentence. With a partner, discuss whether you think Eleanor lived up to her father's hopes for her.

_____

_____

_____

_____

_____

_____

VISUAL VOCABULARY

Field hockey (feeld HOK ee) is a game played between two teams of eleven players. The players use hooked sticks to hit a small hard ball into the opposing team's goal.

A few months later, tragedy struck again: Eleanor's father died. Eleanor had lost her mother, a brother, and her father all within eighteen months.

Eleanor carried her father's letters with her for the rest of her life. In them, he had told her to be brave and to become well educated. He wrote that he hoped she would grow up into a woman he could be proud of, a woman who helped 50 people who were suffering. ◐

The first few years after her father's death were very hard. For months, Eleanor pretended that he was still alive. She made him the hero of stories she wrote for school. Sometimes, alone and unhappy, she just cried.

Some of her few moments of happiness came from visiting her uncle, Theodore Roosevelt. A visit with Uncle Ted meant playing games and running around outdoors with the many Roosevelt children. He often read old stories and poetry to the children, and Eleanor learned how much 60 fun it was to read books aloud.

Still, Eleanor was unhappy most of the time. Her grandmother was old and often confused. She didn't show Eleanor and her brother much love.

IN OTHER WORDS Eleanor's childhood was filled with loss and sadness.

▶ Three events had an impact on Eleanor's young life. Reread lines 31–63, and bracket [ ] the sentence that best summarizes these events.

Just before Eleanor turned fifteen, Grandmother Hall decided to send her to Allenswood, a girls' school in England. At school, Eleanor worked to toughen herself physically. She did not like team sports, but she played **field hockey** to improve her self-control. She played hard and won the respect of her teammates.

70   Eleanor also learned to think for herself at Allenswood. She was growing up, and the joy of young womanhood was changing her personality.

Eleanor left Allenswood just before she turned eighteen. Grandmother Hall made her go to dances and parties. She wanted Eleanor to take her place in the social world with other wealthy young women.   **PAUSE & REFLECT**

Away from Allenswood, Eleanor began to worry about her looks again. The old teasing began again, especially from Uncle Ted's daughter, "Princess" Alice Roosevelt.

80   As always, Eleanor did as she was told. She went to all of the parties and dances. But she also began working with poor children in New York. She took children to museums and to musical concerts. She tried to get their parents interested in politics. She wanted them to work for better schools and cleaner, safer streets.   **E**

IN OTHER WORDS Eleanor went to a private school in England. There, she played sports and was liked by her teammates. Instead of finishing school in England, Eleanor returned home to take her place in the world of wealthy young women. She began to work with poor children in New York City.

Eleanor's life reached a turning point when she fell in love with her fifth cousin, Franklin Delano Roosevelt.

For a time they met secretly. Then they went to parties together. Franklin saw Eleanor as a person he could trust.
90   He knew that she would not try to **dominate** him.

On March 17, 1905, Eleanor and Franklin were married. Uncle Ted, who was now president of the United States, took the place of Eleanor's father in the wedding.

PAUSE & REFLECT
How do you think the position of women in our society has changed during the last one hundred years? Discuss this question with a partner or in a small group.

E BIOGRAPHY
Reread lines 70–85. In this section, Jacobs includes many details about Eleanor's personality. Underline the words and phrases that describe Eleanor. What are some of her strengths and weaknesses?

_____
_____
_____
_____
_____
_____
_____

VOCABULARY
The word **dominate** (DOM uh nayt) is a verb that means *to have control over someone or something.*

Circle a sentence in which the author tells about Grandmother Hall trying to **dominate** Eleanor.

VOCABULARY

The word **brooding** (BROO ding) is an adjective that means *full of worry*.

In May 1906, Eleanor gave birth to their first child. During the next nine years, Eleanor and Franklin had five more children, one of whom died as a baby. Eleanor was still shy and afraid of making mistakes, but she was so busy that she didn't spend time thinking about it.

Before long, Eleanor and Franklin began to have
100 problems with their marriage. She was serious and shy, and he enjoyed light talk and flirting with women. Instead of losing her temper, Eleanor hid her anger. She did not talk to Franklin at all. Faced with her **brooding** silence, he only grew angrier and more distant.

IN OTHER WORDS Eleanor fell in love with her fifth cousin, Franklin Roosevelt. They married and had six children, but one died as a baby. They had problems with their marriage, and Eleanor showed her unhappiness by not talking to Franklin.

VOCABULARY

The word **prominent** (PROM uh nuhnt) is an adjective that means *well-known or important*.

Meanwhile, Franklin's career in politics grew quickly. In 1910 he was elected to the New York State Senate. In 1913 President Wilson appointed him Assistant Secretary of the Navy, and the Roosevelt family moved to Washington, D.C.

In 1917 the United States entered World War I. Like
110 many socially **prominent** women, Eleanor helped with the war effort. Sometimes she worked fifteen or sixteen hours a day. She made sandwiches for soldiers who passed through the nation's capital, and she knitted sweaters.

In 1920 the Democratic Party chose Franklin as its candidate for vice-president of the United States. His party lost the election, but he became a well-known figure in national politics.

In the summer of 1921, disaster struck the Roosevelt family. Franklin fell ill with polio—a disease that used
120 to kill or cripple thousands of children and many adults each year. **F**

F IDENTIFY CHRONOLOGICAL ORDER

Reread lines 105–121. Circle each year listed. Add these years to your timeline. Then, put the events that occurred in each of these years into your own words on the timeline.

Franklin lived, but he lost feeling in his legs and could not use them. He had to be lifted and carried from place to place. He had to wear heavy steel braces from his waist to the heels of his shoes.

Many people told him to give up politics. But this time, Eleanor stood up for her ideas. She argued that he should not be treated like a sick person, that he should not be treated like someone waiting to die.

130　　Franklin agreed. He slowly recovered his health, and his energy returned. In 1928 he was elected governor of New York. Four years later, he was elected president of the United States. **G**

IN OTHER WORDS Franklin was elected a state senator. Later he was given a position in the national government. Then, he became ill and lost the use of his legs.

▶ How did Eleanor react to Franklin's illness? Put brackets around the sentence that tells you.

Eleanor changed during Franklin's illness. To keep him in the public eye, she became involved in politics herself. She made speeches to raise money for the Democratic Party. Then, after becoming interested in the problems of working women, she gave time to the Women's Trade Union League (WTUL).[1] **H**

140　　Through the WTUL, Eleanor met a group of remarkable women—women doing exciting work that made a difference in the world. They taught her about life in poor areas. She hoped that she could do something to help poor people. Instead of staying with her wealthy friends alone, she joined people working for social change.

When Franklin was sworn in as president, the nation was facing its deepest depression. The United States was in trouble. One out of every four Americans was out of work,

---

1. **Women's Trade Union League:** an organization that promoted laws to protect the rights of women who worked in factories.

G BIOGRAPHY

Reread lines 122–133. What do these events tell you about Eleanor and her relationship with Franklin?

_____

_____

_____

_____

H LANGUAGE COACH

An **idiom** is a phrase that has a meaning other than its individual words. The phrase *in the public eye* (line 135) means "often seen in public and in the media." With that meaning in mind, why do you think Eleanor's actions were so important?

_____

_____

_____

VOCABULARY

The word **migrant** (MY gruhnt) is an adjective that means *moving from place to place.*

PAUSE & REFLECT

How does Eleanor's role, or position, as First Lady compare to First Ladies today? With a partner, discuss what you know about modern First Ladies compared with what you have learned about Eleanor Roosevelt.

❶ **BIOGRAPHY**

Reread lines 159–172. Underline the words and phrases that tell you what Eleanor was like. Based on these words, how do you think the writer feels about Eleanor? Explain.

_____

_____

_____

_____

and people were losing hope. People stood in lines in front
150 of soup kitchens for something to eat. Mrs. Roosevelt knew
of once-wealthy families who were forced to eat stale bread
from thrift shops or to go from house to house begging for
money. Eleanor served soup in the kitchens. She traveled
across the country learning about the suffering of coal
miners, shipyard workers, <u>migrant</u> farm workers, students,
and housewives. Travel was hard for Franklin because of
his illness, so she became his eyes and ears. She told him
what the American people were really thinking and feeling.

Eleanor also urged Franklin to support laws that would
160 create social change. One such law was the National Youth
Administration (NYA). It provided money to help poor
young people stay in school.

Eleanor lectured widely, wrote a regular newspaper
column, and spoke often on the radio. She fought for equal
pay for women. Like no other First Lady before her, she
became a link between the president and the American
public. **PAUSE & REFLECT**

Eleanor fought for people who were treated unfairly. When
she entered a hall where black people and white people were
170 seated in separate sections, she made it a point to sit with the
black people. Her example was an important step in showing
the nation that all people should be treated the same. ❶

IN OTHER WORDS After Franklin's illness, Eleanor became more
active in politics. She worked to help poor people and people who
were treated unfairly.

On December 7, 1941, military planes from Japan
bombed the American naval base at Pearl Harbor, Hawaii.
This event led the United States to enter World War II.

Eleanor again joined the war effort. She helped the Red Cross raise money, and she gave blood. In addition, she visited American soldiers on islands throughout the South Pacific. When she visited a hospital, she stopped at every
180 bed. To each soldier she said something special, something that a mother might say. At first, the military leader Admiral Nimitz thought such visits would be a nuisance, an irritation, but he became one of her strongest admirers. Nobody else, he said, had done so much to help raise the spirits of the men.

By the spring of 1945, the war in Europe seemed near its end. Then, on April 12, a phone call brought Eleanor the news that Franklin had died. After Franklin's funeral, Eleanor placed flowers on his grave every day that she
190 was home.

With Franklin dead, Eleanor Roosevelt might have dropped out of the public eye. Instead, she found new ways to live a useful, interesting life—and to help others. Now, her successes were her own, not the result of being the president's wife.

In December 1945, President Harry S. Truman asked her to go to London to begin the work of the United Nations.[2] Truman said that the nation needed her; it was her duty. Eleanor agreed. Some people thought she wasn't
200 qualified for the job, but she proved them wrong. ❶

Eleanor pushed for a ruling that would help war refugees. Fighting had forced them to leave their home countries during World War II. Now, some refugees did not want to return home. Eleanor thought that people should have the right *not* to return to their native lands if they did not wish to. In an emotional speech she said, "We [must] consider first the rights of man and what makes men more free—not governments, but man!"

❶ **IDENTIFY CHRONOLOGICAL ORDER**
Reread lines 176–200. (Circle) each day, month, or year listed. Add the times and events to your timeline.

---

2. **United Nations:** Founded in 1945, the United Nations promotes peace and security between countries; in 2009, the UN included 192 member countries.

Eleanor thought the United Nations should stand for
210 personal freedom—the rights of people to free speech,
freedom of religion, and human needs such as health care
and education.

IN OTHER WORDS During World War II, Eleanor again helped with
the war effort. Then, just as the war was about to end, Franklin
died. Eleanor did not drop out of politics. Instead, she agreed to
help the United States in its work with the United Nations. At the
United Nations, Eleanor continued to fight for human rights.

Even after retiring from her work at the United Nations,
Eleanor continued to travel. She dined with presidents and
kings, but she also visited poor areas in India, factories in
Yugoslavia, and farms in Lebanon and Israel.

Everywhere she went, she met people who wanted to
greet her. They wanted to touch her, to hug her, to kiss her.

Eleanor's doctor told her to slow down, but that was hard
220 for her. She continued to write her newspaper column and to
appear on television. She still started work at seven-thirty in
the morning and often continued until well past midnight.

Eventually, she was forced to stop some of her activities
and spend more time at home.

On November 7, 1962, at the age of seventy-eight, Eleanor
died in her sleep. She was buried next to her husband. **Ⓚ**

Adlai Stevenson, who represented the United States at
the United Nations, remembered Eleanor as "the First Lady
of the World." As Stevenson said, "She would rather light a
230 candle than curse the darkness." **Ⓛ**

IN OTHER WORDS Eleanor stayed active in her later years. She
died in 1962 at age 78.

▶ Eleanor Roosevelt felt unwanted as a child. With a partner,
discuss how people felt about her later in her life.

**Ⓚ IDENTIFY
CHRONOLOGICAL
ORDER**

Circle the date of Eleanor's
death. Make this date the
last entry in your time line.

Ⓛ BIOGRAPHY

Jacobs ends his biography
with a quotation. Underline
the quotation, and circle
who said it. Why do you
think Jacobs chose to end
with a famous quotation?
Discuss your ideas with
a partner.

Literary Analysis: Biography

Think about the way William Jay Jacobs presented his subject in this biography. Complete the chart below to evaluate his purpose for writing and his opinion of Eleanor Roosevelt. Answer each question Yes or No. Include examples from the selection to support your answers.

READING 7 Make inferences and draw conclusions about the structural patterns and features of literary nonfiction. **9** Analyze author's purpose in cultural, historical, and contemporary contexts.

Did Jacobs give information about Eleanor's life? Yes	**Examples:** *Jacobs tells us when Eleanor was born (October, 11, 1884), who she married (Franklin Roosevelt), and how she worked at the United Nations.*
Did Jacobs reveal Eleanor's personality? _____	**Examples:**
Did Jacobs show what others thought about Eleanor? _____	**Examples:**
Did Jacobs explain the importance of Eleanor's life and work? _____	**Examples:**

What do you think is the writer's personal opinion of Eleanor Roosevelt? Support your idea with examples from the selection.

_____

_____

_____

_____

_____

_____

READING 7 Make inferences and draw conclusions about the structural patterns and features of literary nonfiction.

Reading Skill: Identify Chronological Order

Review the timeline you made as you read this selection. Then, write down the most important details about Eleanor Roosevelt's life in the chart. List at least three important events in each box.

Childhood

↓

Franklin's Presidency

↓

Later Life

What is your DUTY to others?

Review your notes about what our responsibilities are to other people. What duty to others do people of today's generation have? Discuss your answer with a partner.

Vocabulary Practice

Write the letter of the item you associate with each boldface word.

_____ **prominent**　　　**A.** a traveling worker

_____ **brooding**　　　**B.** an undefeated team

_____ **migrant**　　　**C.** an unhappy person

_____ **dominate**　　　**D.** a famous family

Academic Vocabulary in Speaking

The word **demonstrate** (DEM uhn strayt) is a verb that means *to show clearly*.

> In front of the whole class, Robert **demonstrated** how his science project worked, carefully describing each part.

You might also be familiar with another meaning of the word **demonstrate**: *to take part in a public protest*.

> The political group **demonstrated** out in front of the court, marching in a large and noisy circle.

TURN AND TALK With a partner, talk about how Eleanor chose to **demonstrate** her concern for her fellow Americans. Be sure to use the word **demonstrate** in your conversation.

READING 7 Make inferences and draw conclusions about the structural patterns and features of literary nonfiction. **9** Analyze author's purpose in cultural, historical, and contemporary contexts.

Texas Assessment Practice

DIRECTIONS: Use "Eleanor Roosevelt" to answer questions 1–4.

1 The main purpose of this biography is to —
- **A** give an account from Eleanor's point of view in her own words
- **B** entertain readers with interesting stories
- **C** explain the importance of Eleanor Roosevelt's life and work
- **D** show how much like other women of her time Eleanor Roosevelt was

2 Events in this selection are presented in —
- **F** the order of their importance to Eleanor Roosevelt
- **G** random order
- **H** chronological order
- **J** the order in which the author learned about them

3 Which words best describe Eleanor Roosevelt's personality when she was a young girl?
- **A** Angry and stubborn
- **B** Outgoing and considerate
- **C** Curious and creative
- **D** Shy and lonely

4 Which event was a major turning point in Eleanor's life?
- **F** When she spoke at the United Nations General Assembly
- **G** When her uncle, Theodore Roosevelt, gave her away at her wedding
- **H** When her husband fell ill with polio
- **J** When Japanese forces attacked Pearl Harbor

READING 10D Synthesize and make logical connections between ideas within a text and across two or three texts representing different genres. **RC-7(E)** Summarize and synthesize texts in ways that maintain meaning and logical order within a text and across texts.

A First Lady Speaks Out

- Letter, page 281
- Autobiography, page 282

Background

In "Eleanor Roosevelt," you read William Jay Jacobs's description of Eleanor Roosevelt's life. Now you will hear from Mrs. Roosevelt herself. Her letter reveals her response to an organization that refused to allow an African American singer to perform. Eleanor Roosevelt's autobiography reveals her thoughts about herself.

Skill Focus: Synthesize

Have you ever formed an idea about someone from what one person told you? Did your opinion change when you actually met the person or heard someone else's opinion? When you put together information from more than one source, you **synthesize.** As a result, you get a better understanding of a subject. Think about the picture or idea you got of Eleanor Roosevelt from Jacobs's biography. As you learn more from the following selections, notice whether your ideas change. You will use these steps to synthesize:

- Sum up what you learned about Mrs. Roosevelt from reading the biography of her.

- Make notes of additional information you learn as you read her letter and autobiography. Include your own ideas or opinions of her as well.

You will record your notes in a chart like the one below.

Source	Important Ideas
"Eleanor Roosevelt"	*She was a sad and lonely child.* *She spent her life helping others.*
Letter to the Daughters of the American Revolution	
Autobiography	

Letter to the President General of the Daughters of the American Revolution

Based on the letter by **Eleanor Roosevelt**

THE WHITE HOUSE WASHINGTON

February 28, 1939

My dear Mrs. Henry M. Robert Jr.:

I have never been a very useful member of the Daughters of the American Revolution.[1] Therefore, it will make very little difference to you whether I quit.

5   However, I strongly disagree with your decision to prevent a great performer from singing in Constitution Hall. You have set a very poor example for other people. You had a chance to lead in a reasonable way. It seems to me that your organization has failed.

10   I know that many people will not agree with me. Still, leaving your group seems to be the right thing to do.

Very sincerely yours,
Eleanor Roosevelt

IN OTHER WORDS Mrs. Roosevelt says she is quitting an organization because it will not allow a great African American singer to perform in its concert hall.

▶ Mrs. Roosevelt says that the group has "failed." With a partner, discuss how it has failed.

---

1. **Daughters of the American Revolution:** an organization of women whose families once fought against the British in the Revolutionary War.

SET A PURPOSE FOR READING

Read Eleanor Roosevelt's letter and an excerpt from her autobiography to learn more about her values and her life experience.

Ⓕ OCUS ON FORM

A letter is a handwritten or printed text usually sent by mail. Letters by famous people help you better understand their private thoughts, feelings, and concerns.

Ⓐ SYNTHESIZE

Reread lines 5–11. What event prompted Mrs. Roosevelt to write this letter? In your chart, note what you learn about her from her response to this event.

Source
Letter to the D.A.R.

↓

Important Ideas

ⓕOCUS ON FORM

An autobiography is the story of a person's life, as told by that person. It is written in the first-person point of view. In the first-person point of view the author uses the words *I*, *me*, and *my* to describe himself or herself.

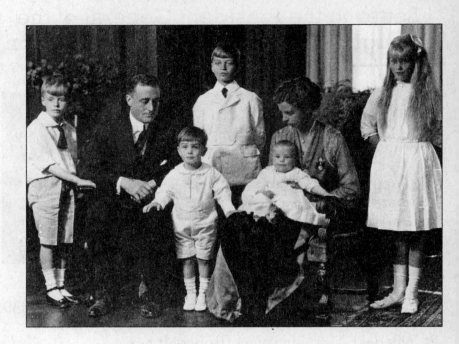

~ F R O M ~

THE AUTOBIOGRAPHY OF ELEANOR ROOSEVELT

Based on an excerpt from the autobiography by ELEANOR ROOSEVELT

When I was a young girl, I felt the pain of being an ugly duckling as only a young girl can feel it. This pain led me to be shy and afraid. I was afraid of almost everything, I think. I was afraid of mice, of the dark, of dangers that I would make up, and of my own failings. My main goal, as a girl, was to do my duty. This had been drilled into me as far back as I could remember. But it wasn't about my duty as I saw it, but my duty as set down for me by other people. I never
10 even thought about fighting against this. Anyhow, my one very strong need in those days was to be accepted, to be loved. So I did whatever was asked of me, and

I hoped that my actions would bring me closer to the love I so much wanted. **B**

IN OTHER WORDS Eleanor Roosevelt explains that she was once afraid of almost everything. She was especially afraid of her own failings, so she took her responsibilities very seriously. She tried to please everyone. She hoped that pleasing other people would lead them to love her.

As a young woman, my sense of duty was still as strong as it had been when I was a girl. However, it had changed its focus. My husband and my children became the center of my life, and their needs were my new duty. I am afraid now that I thought of these new
20 duties in much the same way as I had my childhood duties. I was still shy and still afraid of doing something wrong. I was afraid of making mistakes, of not living up to the standards set by my husband's mother, of failing to do what was expected of me.

As a result, I was so focused on duty that I became too critical, too hard on other people. I was so focused on raising my children properly that I was not wise enough just to love them. Now, looking back, I think I would rather spoil a child a little and have more fun
30 out of it. **PAUSE & REFLECT**

IN OTHER WORDS Eleanor continued to have a strong sense of duty as an adult. She focused on the needs of her family.

► Reread lines 15–30. Then, with a partner, discuss how Eleanor's sense of duty affected her as a mother.

B SYNTHESIZE

In "Eleanor Roosevelt," the biography by William Jay Jacobs, you learned about Eleanor's childhood. Reread lines 1–14 and underline words and phrases that provide additional information about her childhood. Add the information to your chart.

Source
Autobiography of Eleanor Roosevelt

↓

Important Ideas

PAUSE & REFLECT

Reread lines 15–30. Circle three examples of new information and insights that Mrs. Roosevelt shares about her adulthood. Discuss what you learn about Eleanor Roosevelt with a partner.

READING 10D Synthesize and make logical connections between ideas within a text and across two or three texts representing different genres. RC-7(E) Summarize and synthesize texts in ways that maintain meaning and logical order within a text and across texts.

Practicing Your Skills: Synthesize

Review your notes about Eleanor Roosevelt. Then **synthesize** the information you've learned by making a statement about the kind of person Eleanor Roosevelt was. Include information from all three selections to support your judgment.

What Eleanor Roosevelt Was Like

_____

_____

_____

_____

_____

↑   ↑   ↑

Biography	Letter to Daughters of the American Revolution	Autobiography
_____	_____	_____
_____	_____	_____
_____	_____	_____
_____	_____	_____
_____	_____	_____

Academic Vocabulary in Speaking

The word **impact** (IM pakt) is a noun that means *the effect of one thing on another.*

   The **impact** of the heavy branch dented the car's roof.

TURN AND TALK With a partner, talk about the **impact,** or effect, that Eleanor Roosevelt had as First Lady and afterward. Be sure to use the word **impact** in your conversation.

READING 10D Synthesize and make logical connections between ideas within a text and across two or three texts representing different genres. **RC-7(E)** Summarize and synthesize texts in ways that maintain meaning and logical order within a text and across texts.

Texas Assessment Practice

DIRECTIONS Use the texts from "A First Lady Speaks Out" to answer questions 1–4.

1 Eleanor Roosevelt's main reason for writing to Mrs. Henry M. Robert Jr. was to —

- **A** ask how she could be more helpful to her organization
- **B** quit the organization and explain her reasons for doing so
- **C** convince the organization to let an African American singer perform at Constitution Hall
- **D** express her agreement with fellow members of the organization

2 The letter shows that Eleanor Roosevelt —

- **F** stood up for what she believed in
- **G** didn't want to upset anyone
- **H** was very involved in the D.A.R.
- **J** was a big fan of the singer

3 How do Roosevelt's descriptions of herself as a child fit with the descriptions in Jacobs's biography of her?

- **A** The descriptions provide opposite ideas about Mrs. Roosevelt.
- **B** The descriptions are from exactly the same viewpoint.
- **C** The descriptions focus on different events.
- **D** The descriptions are very similar.

4 One of the main points in Roosevelt's autobiography is —

- **F** how much she enjoyed raising her children
- **G** the importance of duty in her life
- **H** her pride in her accomplishments
- **J** regret for her past mistakes

READING 9 Explain the difference between the theme of a literary work and the author's purpose in an expository text. **10D** Make logical connections between ideas within a text and across two or three texts representing similar or different genres.

from **It's Not About the Bike**

Autobiography by Lance Armstrong with Sally Jenkins

from **23 Days in July**

Based on the nonfiction account by John Wilcockson

What is a WINNER?

Can you be a winner if you're not competing against other people? In the following selections, you will find out how Lance Armstrong faced two very different challenges and came out a winner in both.

TURN AND TALK Which is more difficult? Winning a game or sports event or winning in some kind of personal challenge, such as overcoming a fear? Discuss these ideas with a partner and write your ideas on the lines at left.

Which is more difficult?

Winning a game or sports event is difficult because ___

___

___

Winning a personal challenge is difficult because ___

___

___

Which is more difficult? ___

___

___

Elements of Nonfiction: Author's Purpose and Theme

An **author's purpose,** or reason for writing, may be to share thoughts or feelings, to give information, to persuade, or to entertain. The writer may also want to communicate a **theme,** or a message about life or people in general. To learn how to identify the author's purpose and the theme in a piece of writing, see the chart below.

Author's Purpose	Theme
Think about • the subject the writing is about • the kinds of details the author chooses • the effect the writing has on you	Think about • what the title means • the challenges characters face • the lessons characters learn

Reading Skill: Make Inferences

To understand what you read, it helps to **make inferences**, or logical guesses. You base these guesses on clues in the writing and on what you already know. As you read the two selections, you will add clues a writer gives you to your own knowledge to make an inference like the one below.

RC-7(D) Make complex inferences about texts.

Clue		What I Know		Inference
Lance Armstrong talks to the nurse many times about cycling.	+	People like to talk about the things that are important to them.	=	Cycling is very important to Lance Armstrong.

Vocabulary in Context

Note: Words are listed in the order in which they appear in the selections.

Terse (turs) is an adjective that means *speaking little* or *communicating with only a few words*.

> The shy baseball player was **terse,** giving one-word answers to the reporter's questions.

Stance (stans) is a noun that means *position*.

> A rider's **stance** on the bicycle is important, because a low position helps the bicycle move faster.

Prestigious (pres TIJ uhs) is an adjective that means *having the reputation of being greatly valued or important*.

> The winner of the **prestigious** race was cheered as a hero.

Vocabulary Practice

Review the words and sample sentences above. Then use the words to make a prediction about what kinds of information you might read in these selections.

_____

_____

_____

_____

SET A PURPOSE FOR READING
Read "It's Not About the Bike" to discover how a nurse helped Lance Armstrong during his struggle with cancer.

A AUTHOR'S PURPOSE AND THEME

The **theme** of a work is the message the author wants to communicate. Reread the title and lines 1–12. What do you think Armstrong's theme might be?

_____

_____

_____

_____

_____

VOCABULARY

The word **terse** (turs) is an adjective that means *speaking little* or *communicating with only a few words.*

It's *NOT* About the Bike

Autobiography by
LANCE ARMSTRONG

BACKGROUND In 1996 professional cyclist Lance Armstrong learned that he had cancer. This selection describes his relationship with a nurse who helped him during his treatment. After recovering from cancer, Armstrong returned to cycling. In 1999 he won his first Tour de France, the world's most famous bicycle race.

There are angels on this earth and they come in subtle forms, and I decided LaTrice Haney was one of them. Outwardly, she looked like just another efficient, clipboard-and-syringe-wielding[1] nurse in a starched outfit. She worked extremely long days and nights, and on her off hours she went home to her husband, Randy, a truck driver, and their two children, Taylor, aged seven, and Morgan, four. But if she was tired, she never seemed it. She struck me as a woman utterly lacking in ordinary resentments, 10 sure of her responsibilities and blessings and unwavering in her administering of care, and if that wasn't angelic behavior, I didn't know what was. **A**

Often I'd be alone in the late afternoons and evenings except for LaTrice, and if I had the strength, we'd talk seriously. With most people I was shy and **terse**, but

---

1. **syringe-wielding** (suh RINJ WEELDing): carrying a device used for giving shots.

I found myself talking to LaTrice, maybe because she
was so gentle-spoken and expressive herself. LaTrice
was only in her late 20s, a pretty young woman with a
coffee-and-cream complexion, but she had self-possession
20 and perception[2] beyond her years. While other people our
age were out nightclubbing, she was already the head nurse
for the oncology research unit.[3] I wondered why she did
it. "My satisfaction is to make it a little easier for people,"
she said.

IN OTHER WORDS Lance Armstrong tells about LaTrice Haney,
a nurse who helped him while he was being treated for cancer.
Lance was able to talk freely with the gentle LaTrice.

► Which sentence gives one reason LaTrice is a successful nurse?

She asked me about cycling, and I found myself telling
her about the bike with a sense of pleasure I hadn't realized
I possessed. "How did you start riding?" she asked me.
I told her about my first bikes, and the early sense of
liberation,[4] and that cycling was all I had done since
30 I was 16. I talked about my various teammates over the
years, about their humor and selflessness, and I talked
about my mother, and what she had meant to me.
I told her what cycling had given me, the tours of
Europe and the extraordinary education, and the wealth.
I showed her a picture of my house, with pride, and invited
her to come visit, and I showed her snapshots of my cycling
career. She leafed through images of me racing across the
backdrops of France, Italy, and Spain, and she'd point to a
picture and ask, "Where are you here?" **B**

B MAKE INFERENCES
Reread lines 25–39. <u>Underline</u>
the questions that LaTrice
asks Lance. Then fill out the
inference chart below to
make an inference about
how LaTrice's questions
might help Lance.

Clues

↓

What I Know

↓

Inference

---

2. **perception** (puhr SEP shuhn): the ability to understand people and situations.
3. **oncology** (on KOL uh jee) **research unit:** the part of a hospital that focuses on
   the study of cancer.
4. **liberation** (lib uh RAY shuhn): being set free.

40   I confided that I was worried about my sponsor, Cofidis,[5] and explained the difficulty I was having with them. I told her I felt pressured. "I need to stay in shape, I need to stay in shape," I said over and over again.

"Lance, listen to your body," she said gently. "I know your mind wants to run away. I know it's saying to you, 'Hey, let's go ride.' But listen to your body. Let it rest."

IN OTHER WORDS LaTrice asks Lance how he started cycling, and he tells her all about his beginnings in the sport, his early career, his travels, and his success. When he says that he worries about not staying in shape, she tells him that he must let his body rest.

ⓒ AUTHOR'S PURPOSE AND THEME
Reread lines 47–64. An author may have more than one purpose for writing. Think about why Armstrong gives this information about the bicycle. Place a checkmark ✔ next to two purposes he might have had for writing these lines.

_____ to inform the reader about bicycles and cycling
_____ to entertain the reader with stories about cycling
_____ to persuade the reader to begin cycling
_____ to express some of his thoughts and feelings about cycling

    I described my bike, the elegant high performance of the ultralight tubing and aerodynamic[6] wheels. I told her how much each piece cost, and weighed, and what
50 its purpose was. I explained how a bike could be broken down so I could practically carry it in my pocket, and that I knew every part and bit of it so intimately that I could adjust it in a matter of moments.

    I explained that a bike has to fit your body, and that at times I felt melded to it. The lighter the frame, the more responsive it is, and my racing bike weighed just 18 pounds. Wheels exert centrifugal force[7] on the bike itself, I told her. The more centrifugal force, the more momentum.[8] It was the essential building block of speed.
60 "There are 32 spokes in a wheel," I said. Quick-release levers allow you to pop the wheel out and change it quickly, and my crew could fix a flat tire in less than 10 seconds.

    "Don't you get tired of leaning over like that?" she asked. ⓒ

---

5. **Cofidis** (KOH fih dis): the sponsor of the French cycling team that Armstrong then rode for.
6. **aerodynamic** (air oh dy NAM ik): able to move through the air easily.
7. **centrifugal** (sen TRIF yoo guhl) **force**: the force that seems to cause a revolving object to move away from the object it is revolving around.
8. **momentum** (moh MEN tuhm): forward motion resulting from movement.

Yes, I said, until my back ached like it was broken, but that was the price of speed. The **handlebars** are only as wide as the rider's shoulders, I explained, and they curve downward in half-moons so you can assume an aerodynamic <u>stance</u> on the bike.

IN OTHER WORDS Lance talks in great detail about how a racing cycle is designed and the reasons for the parts to be designed as they are.

▶ <u>Underline</u> three details in lines 47–69 that show the importance of speed to the design of a racing cycle.

---

70   "Why do you ride on those little seats?" she asked.

The seat is narrow, contoured to the anatomy, and the reason is that when you are on it for six hours at a time, you don't want anything to chafe your legs. Better a hard seat than the torture of saddle sores. Even the clothes have a purpose. They are flimsy for a reason: to mold to the body because you have to wear them in weather that ranges from hot to hail. Basically, they're a second skin. The shorts have a chamois padded[9] seat, and the stitches are recessed[10] to avoid rash.

80   When I had nothing left to tell LaTrice about the bike, I told her about the wind. I described how it felt in my face and in my hair. I told her about being in the open air, with the views of soaring Alps, and the glimmer of valley lakes in the distance. Sometimes the wind blew as if it were my personal friend, sometimes as if it were my bitter enemy, sometimes as if it were the hand of God pushing me along. I described the full sail of a mountain descent,[11] gliding on two wheels only an inch wide. ⓓ

---

9. **chamois** (SHAM ee) **padded:** padded with soft leather made from the skin of goats, sheep, or deer.
10. **recessed** (ree SESSD): set lower than or back from the rest.
11. **descent** (dih SENT): a passing down from a higher place to a lower place.

VISUAL VOCABULARY
Handlebars (HAN dl bahrz) are curved metal bars with handles on the ends, used for steering a bicycle.

VOCABULARY
The word **stance** (stans) is a noun that means *position*.

ⓓ **MAKE INFERENCES**
Reread lines 70–88. What can you infer about why Lance rides his bike? Write the inference below, and <u>underline</u> clues in the selection that support this inference.

_____

_____

_____

_____

"You're just out there, free," I said.

90 "You love it," she said.

"Yeah?" I said.

"Oh, I see it in your eyes," she said.

IN OTHER WORDS Lance goes on to describe the purpose for the design of the bicycle's seat and the clothes bicyclists wear. He then tells LaTrice how he feels as he rides, and she says that she can tell that he loves it.

I understood that LaTrice was an angel one evening late in my last cycle of chemo.[12] I lay on my side, dozing on and off, watching the steady, clear drip-drip of the chemo as it slid into my veins. LaTrice sat with me, keeping me company, even though I was barely able to talk.

"What do you think, LaTrice?" I asked, whispering. "Am I going to pull through this?"

100 "Yeah," she said. "Yeah, you are."

"I hope you're right," I said, and closed my eyes again. LaTrice leaned over to me.

"Lance," she said softly, "I hope someday to be just a figment of your imagination.[13] I'm not here to be in your life for the rest of your life. After you leave here, I hope I never see you ever again. When you're cured, hey, let me see you in the papers, on TV, but not back here. I hope to help you at the time you need me, and then I hope I'll be gone. You'll say, 'Who was that nurse back in Indiana? Did
110 I dream her?'"

---

12. **chemo** (KEEM oh): short for *chemotherapy,* a form of treatment for people with cancer.

13. **figment** (FIG muhnt) **of your imagination:** something not real; a made-up image.

It is one of the single loveliest things anyone has ever said to me. And I will always remember every blessed word. (PAUSE & REFLECT)

IN OTHER WORDS LaTrice tells Lance that she believes he will get well. She hopes that one day he will be able to look back on her only as part of his past.

PAUSE & REFLECT
Reread the last two paragraphs. Then, with a partner, discuss why Lance decides the nurse is an "angel."

23

DAYS IN JULY

Based on the nonfiction account by
JOHN WILCOCKSON

BACKGROUND Lance Armstrong won his
seventh Tour de France in 2005, but the
2004 race was special because no cyclist
had ever won six Tours. This selection was
written by a reporter who covered the
2004 race.

The city of Paris looks beautiful. Her golden domes are
glowing in the late-afternoon sunshine. Rainbows shimmer
in the spray of fountains. A short distance away, the
thousand-foot-high Eiffel Tower stands out against a solid
blue sky.

Another Tour de France has just ended, this one
culminating in a historical sixth straight victory for a
young man from Texas. He stands now on the top step
of the winner's stand at the finish line. Lance Armstrong
10 holds a yellow cap over his heart as the "Star Spangled

Banner" rings out proudly over the brown cobblestone streets.

At the foot of the covered, most **prestigious** viewing stand, Armstrong's coach Chris Carmichael reminds me of how hard Armstrong works: "I told you back in March, it wasn't even going to be close. You gotta know the intensity of this guy. Nobody has got his intensity. Nobody."

Armstrong had said the night before, "Winning in '99
20 was a complete shock and surprise for me. Not that I've gotten used to winning the Tour de France, but I do know what it means and I know what it feels like. . . . This one is very, very special for me. They're all special, but this one is something that in '99 I never believed possible. I never thought I'd win a second one, or a third, or however many. This one is incredibly special. I'm humbled by it. A lot of people just one month ago thought it wouldn't be possible for me to do it. We tried to stay calm, the team tried to stay calm . . . and we were confident that we had a good
30 chance." **E**

IN OTHER WORDS The writer describes the scene after Lance Armstrong wins his sixth Tour de France bicycle race in a row. Armstrong—the first cyclist ever to win six Tour de France races—says this win is special.

I think back to December, and remember something Armstrong told me in Austin, Texas: "I'm doing three or four hours of exercise every day right now. Yesterday I was in [Washington] DC, so I got up early—I'd just come back from Europe—and I went down to the gym for an hour and a half . . . yes, lifting weights. It was pouring with freezing rain outside, so I went back to the room, and

VOCABULARY
The word **prestigious** (pres TIJ uhs) is an adjective that means *having the reputation of being greatly valued or important.*

E AUTHOR'S PURPOSE AND THEME
Reread lines 13–30. What might be the author's purpose for including each of these quotations by Carmichael and by Armstrong?

Carmichael:

_____

_____

_____

Armstrong:

_____

_____

_____

Ⓕ MAKE INFERENCES
Reread lines 31–39. (Circle) three details about Armstrong's training. What inference can you make about Armstrong based on these clues and on what you know?

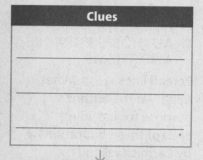

Clues
_____
_____
_____

↓

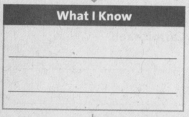

What I Know
_____
_____

↓

Inference
_____
_____

PAUSE & REFLECT

In 1996, Armstrong beat cancer. In 2004, he became a six-time winner of the Tour de France. Think about what you learned about Armstrong from both selections. With a partner, discuss the personal qualities that you think helped Armstrong win such big victories.

rode my bike for an hour on the rollers. It's not easy to ride rollers. I hate that." Ⓕ

40   But he doesn't hate this: a half-million people lining the most glorious street in the world. When he and his team are introduced to start their lap of honor, the modern "anthem" of the British rock group Queen thumps into the warm Paris air:

"*We are the champions, my friend. . . . We are the champions. We are the champions. We are the champions . . . of the world.*"

Girlfriends perch on boyfriends' shoulders to get a better view. Banners unfold, one saying, "The eyes of Texas are
50 upon you." Thousands of fans from all over the United States line the barriers. Most of them are dressed in yellow, the color Armstrong wears as the overall leader of the Tour. Two guys from Texas in the crowd say, "We did it. And next year we'll come again!" . . .

Lance is having fun. The celebrations will continue all night, maybe for the rest of his life. A life that almost ended in 1996. Six Tour de France wins have come along since his recovery from cancer.

"I really love this event," Armstrong says. "I think it's
60 an epic sport. It's something I will sit around the TV and watch in ten years, and in twenty years." He will always be a fan of the Tour, but right now he's the champion.

It's after 7 P.M. and the crowds are starting to leave. One of the last to go is a friendly, middle-aged American. He rolls up his Texas flag, grabs his wife's hand, and says to the world, "He's the man!"   **PAUSE & REFLECT**

IN OTHER WORDS The writer describes the celebration as Armstrong and his team take their lap of honor. Cycling fans line the streets, and music plays from loudspeakers.

▶ Reread the lines 55–66. (Circle) the sentence that tells what makes Armstrong's record-breaking victory even more amazing.

Elements of Nonfiction: Author's Purpose and Theme

Use details from *It's Not About the Bike* and *23 Days in July* to fill in the chart below.

READING 9 Explain the difference between the theme of a literary work and the author's purpose in an expository text. **10D** Make logical connections between ideas within a text and across two or three texts representing similar or different genres.

It's Not About the Bike	23 Days in July
Meaning of Title:	Subject:
Challenges Characters Face:	Author's Choice of Details:
Lessons Characters Learn:	Selection's Effect on Reader:
↓	↓

Theme	Author's Purpose

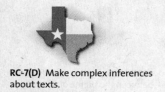

RC-7(D) Make complex inferences about texts.

Reading Skill: Make Inferences

Make an inference based on the quotation from each selection and on your own knowledge.

1. "I talked about my mother, and what she had meant to me." ("It's Not About the Bike," line 32)
My Inference about Lance Armstrong:
2. "Most of them are dressed in yellow, the color Armstrong wears as the overall leader of the Tour." ("23 Days in July," lines 51–52)
My Inference about the fans:

What is a WINNER?

Review your notes on page 286 about the difficulty of winning a sports event compared to winning a personal challenge. Now that you have read the selections about Lance Armstrong, have you changed your mind about this question? Explain which you think is more difficult now, and why.

_____

_____

_____

_____

Vocabulary Practice

Fill in each blank with the correct word: **terse, stance,** or **prestigious.**

1. In baseball, having a proper _____ is important for a batter to hit the ball well.

2. The Pulitzer Prize is one of America's most _____ awards for writing.

3. A person whose answers to questions are _____ may be hard to interview.

Academic Vocabulary in Speaking

The word **goal** (gohl) is a noun that means *something a person is trying to do or achieve.*

> My sister is working hard so she can reach her **goal** of saving enough money to buy a new guitar.

TURN AND TALK Lance Armstrong works toward different **goals** in each selection. With a partner, identify these **goals**, and discuss how they are alike and different. Use the word **goal** in your discussion.

READING 10D Make logical connections between ideas within a text and across two or three texts representing similar or different genres.

Texas Assessment Practice

DIRECTIONS: Use "It's Not About the Bike" and "23 Days in July" to answer questions 1–6.

1 In "It's Not About the Bike," why is Lance Armstrong in the hospital?

- (A) To recover from a racing accident
- (B) To find out whether he has cancer
- (C) To visit cancer patients
- (D) To get treatments for cancer

2 Lance calls LaTrice an angel because —

- (F) she helps him talk more easily
- (G) he thinks she is not human
- (H) she gives him great care and support
- (J) he knows he will never see her again

3 Which of the following states a theme from "It's Not About the Bike"?

- (A) Remarkable support may come during the most difficult times.
- (B) A friend will always be there for you.
- (C) Serious goals call for serious training.
- (D) You should never lose hope for achieving your dreams.

4 Why does LaTrice tell Lance, "I hope I never see you ever again"?

- (F) She wants him to win a big race.
- (G) She hopes he won't need more cancer treatments.
- (H) She does not like him as a person.
- (J) She wants to leave her job as a nurse.

5 Which word best describes the feelings of the crowd in "23 Days in July"?

- (A) Resentful
- (B) Thrilled
- (C) Jealous
- (D) Brave

6 You can guess that the author's purpose for writing "23 Days in July" is to —

- (F) express his own excitement
- (G) persuade readers that Armstrong is the best
- (H) give facts and descriptions of an event
- (J) entertain readers with a fun story

READING 5 Understand and draw conclusions about the structure and elements of drama. Explain a playwright's use of dialogue and stage directions. **7** Describe the structural and substantive differences between a diary and a fictional adaptation of it.

Clara Barton: Battlefield Nurse
Drama by Jeannette Covert Nolan

from The War Diary of Clara Barton
Based on the diary entry by Clara Barton

How can we CHANGE what's wrong?

People who fight for change are sometimes thought to be troublemakers. In the play and diary entry you're about to read, you'll learn about one such person, Clara Barton.

TURN AND TALK On the lines at left, list people who worked to bring about change. Then, with a partner, talk about the people on each of your lists. Discuss what you know about the difficulties each person faced and what he or she did to overcome those difficulties.

People Who Fought for Change

Nelson Mandela _____

_____

_____

_____

_____

_____

_____

Literary Analysis: History-Related Writings

History-related writings focus on people or events from history. The play you're about to read, *Clara Barton: Battlefield Nurse*, is a type of history-related writing, a **historical drama.** Historical dramas

• are fictional texts, written in the form of plays

• are *based* on real people and events from the past

• include action and dialogue—conversations between characters—to create interesting stories and increase dramatic effect

The second selection you will read, *The War Diary of Clara Barton*, is another type of history-related writing, a **diary.** A diary

• records a writer's thoughts, feelings, and experiences

• provides details about life during the writer's time

• does not necessarily use facts; instead, a diary presents the writer's viewpoint, opinions, and interpretations

Reading Strategy: Compare and Contrast

When you **compare and contrast** texts on the same topic, you think about similarities and differences among the texts. When you compare, you ask, "How are these similar to each other?" When you contrast, you ask, "How are these different from each other?"

After you read the following play and diary, you will be asked to **compare and contrast** how the two texts present similar characters, actions, settings, and events. Comparing and contrasting the two texts will help you understand how fiction writers, such as playwrights, create dramatic effects by mixing factual details with imagined ones.

To compare the two texts, you will consider details such as those in the chart below.

READING 5 Understand and draw conclusions about the structure and elements of drama. Explain a playwright's use of dialogue and stage directions. **7** Describe the structural and substantive differences between a diary and a fictional adaptation of it.

Details About Key Elements		
	Clara Barton: Battlefield Nurse	*War Diary of Clara Barton*
Characters	Captain Neal	Officer who lived with rich owners of a big mansion
Characters' Actions	Captain Neal blocks Clara's attempts to help soldiers.	
Setting		
Events		

CLARA BARTON
Battlefield Nurse

Drama by

JEANNETTE COVERT NOLAN

BACKGROUND Clara Barton was a nurse who cared for the sick and injured during the American Civil War. Although women serve in the military today, they were not welcomed on the battlefield at the start of the Civil War. Barton worked hard to persuade the US Army to allow nurses to care for soldiers injured in battle. Her efforts earned her the title "Angel of the Battlefield." Clara Barton later became famous for starting the American Red Cross, an organization that provides aid to people during wars and natural disasters.

CHARACTERS

Captain Neal, of the U.S. Army Medical Corps

Sergeant Fisk
Pvt. Joe Brown ⎱ orderlies

Pvt. Carl Jenkins

Mrs. Almira Fales

Clara Barton

George, Clara's handyman

Courier[1]

Messenger

Offstage Voice

Ⓐ

---

1. **courier** (KOOR ee uhr): a special messenger.

Time: *The evening of December 13, 1862.*[2]

Setting: *A room in a small building on the grounds of Lacy House, a plantation mansion in Falmouth, Virginia.*[3] **Ⓑ**

At rise:[4] *Captain Neal sits at table, going through stacks of paper. Sergeant Fisk looks out window. Bursts of gunfire can be heard intermittently.*

Captain Neal (*suddenly*). What's this?

Fisk (*turning*). Sir?

Captain Neal. This packet of letters.

10 **Fisk.** Letters the men in Lacy House want sent to their families, sir. They're for the return mail tonight. A courier is coming from Washington, as you know.

Captain Neal (*irritably, breaking in*). How should I know? I arrived here only yesterday, and I don't have the hang of things yet. I begin to wonder if I ever will! (*leafs through letters*) They're all in the same handwriting.

Fisk. Clara Barton's handwriting, sir. Those men are among the worst wounded; they can't write, can't hold a pen. They tell Miss Barton what to say, and she writes it down 20 for them. **Ⓒ**

Captain Neal (*with exasperation*). Miss Barton? I might have guessed! That woman is a nuisance!

Fisk (*surprised*). Clara Barton, a nuisance, sir?

Captain Neal. An infernal nuisance! She has no respect for rank or discipline, no official capacity—no right to be here. Yet she behaves as though she had invented the place!

---

2. **December 13, 1862:** the Battle of Fredericksburg, one of the early battles of the American Civil War. The battle was fought in and near Fredericksburg, Virginia, on December 13–15, 1862. Confederate (Southern) troops defeated Union (Northern) troops during this battle.

3. **Lacy House . . . Virginia:** During the Battle of Fredericksburg, a Union Army hospital was set up at Lacy House, a large, elegant house not far from the fighting.

4. **At rise:** as the curtain rises.

Ⓑ HISTORY-RELATED WRITINGS

How can you tell that the selection you are about to read is history-related writing?

_____

_____

_____

_____

Ⓒ COMPARE AND CONTRAST

Who are the main characters identified in the opening of the play? Where and when does the action take place?

Characters: _____

_____

_____

_____

Setting: _____

_____

_____

_____

D HISTORY-RELATED WRITINGS
Reread lines 27–42 On the lines below, write what you know about Clara Barton so far.

What these lines tell me about Clara Barton: _____

_____

_____

_____

_____

PAUSE & REFLECT
Reread lines 21–42. Compare Fisk's view of Clara Barton with Captain Neal's. Do they see her actions in the same way? Explain.

_____

_____

_____

_____

_____

_____

_____

_____

Fisk. Well, sir, in a way she did. She's been in Falmouth more than a week, working round the clock, organizing the hospital, ever since our troops started assembling.

30 **Captain Neal.** That's her usual procedure. If a battle is anticipated, Miss Barton moves in with the vanguard regiments.[5] Or if the skirmish occurs without forewarning, she moves in as soon as the news reaches Washington. In either circumstance she rushes into the field, establishes herself and assumes control of the situation.

Fisk. She brought five wagonloads of supplies with her, sir. Food, blankets, bandages, medicines—

Captain Neal (*in scoffing tone*). She always brings supplies.

Fisk. They say she buys them with her own money. **D**

40 **Captain Neal.** Yes, and with donations solicited from her friends all over the country. She's not timid. She'll stop at nothing. (*abruptly*) Sergeant, are you married?

PAUSE & REFLECT

IN OTHER WORDS Captain Neal, an Army medical officer, looks over a bundle of letters. Wounded soldiers have been telling Clara Barton what to write, and she's been writing the letters for them. The captain says that Clara causes trouble. Fisk says that Clara is just helping the soldiers.

▶ Reread lines 21–42. <u>Underline</u> the words that show the captain's attitude toward Clara Barton.

Fisk (*taken aback*). Married? (*proudly*) Why, yes, sir.

Captain Neal. And how does your wife spend her time?

Fisk. Why, minding the house and the kids, sir.

Captain Neal. As well she should! I'm sure your wife wouldn't dream of neglecting her home and family to make a spectacle of herself on a battlefield, picking up the dead, nursing the injured. Nor should mine!

5. **vanguard regiments** (VAN gahrd REJ uh muhnts): the troops moving at the head of the army.

50 **Fisk.** But Miss Barton isn't married, sir.

Captain Neal (*sharply*). What has that to do with it? I know plenty of unmarried ladies who are content to stay in their homes, where they belong, and leave the rough tasks to men.

Fisk (*slightly puzzled*). They say Miss Barton never was much of a homebody, sir. She had a job in Washington before the war; she was a clerk in the government Patent Office.[6]

Captain Neal (*interrupting*). And she ought to be there now.
60 Instead, she traipses down to Falmouth, takes over the Lacy Plantation House, (*pointing to door, left*) turns it into a hospital—and proposes to manage it! **E**

Fisk. Without any permission at all?

Captain Neal. Oh, she probably obtained some sort of permission, but with or without permission, it wouldn't matter to Clara Barton. She never stands on ceremony. She just rushes in with her wagonloads of supplies, her handful of volunteer assistants—

IN OTHER WORDS Captain Neal says that Clara should behave like other women. Fisk defends Clara. They talk about whether Clara has permission, or official approval, to work with the Army hospital. Captain Neal complains that she doesn't always bother to get permission.

► With a partner, discuss clues in the text that tell you why the captain might feel that Clara does not belong near the Army. What does Captain Neal think Clara should do instead?

Fisk (*more puzzled*). She accomplished a lot of good, sir.

70 **Captain Neal.** What's good about a woman on the field? It's against nature, against Army rules! (*impatiently*) She seems

---

6. **Patent Office:** a government office that grants patents, documents giving inventors exclusive rights to make, use, or sell an invention.

E HISTORY-RELATED WRITINGS

In lines 50–62, Captain Neal explains how he thinks women should act during a war. On the lines below, explain Captain Neal's view.

What Captain Neal's words tell me: _____

_____

_____

_____

_____

_____

to bewitch people to do her bidding. They seem to be in awe of her. But I am not! I officially represent the Medical Corps at this post now, and I will not be bluffed by a fussy little woman like—(*Pvt. Joe Brown enters up right, carrying huge covered basket. As he opens door, explosion of cannon is heard off.*)

Brown. Whew! That was a whopper! Those Confederate gunners[7]—

80 **Captain Neal.** Shut the door, soldier!

Brown. Yes, sir. (*shuts door and sets basket on floor*)

Captain Neal. Where have you been, Brown?

Brown. Out trading with neighborhood farmers for fresh milk and eggs. Fared right well, too.

Captain Neal. Did I say anything to you about fresh milk and eggs?

Brown. No, sir. Miss Barton did. She said I was to take some of that canned stuff from her stores and trade it for—

Captain Neal (*coldly*). Let me remind you, Brown, that

90 you're a Medical Corps orderly, not Miss Barton's errand boy. **F**

Brown (*in confusion*). Yes, sir—no sir—(*pauses as another explosion is heard off*)

IN OTHER WORDS Private Brown enters the room. Clara Barton had asked Brown to trade some of her canned food for fresh milk and eggs. Captain Neal is angry that a soldier is taking orders from Clara. Brown begins to speak when a cannon is heard firing.

Captain Neal (*rising; anxiously*). Fisk, go see what's happening in Fredericksburg! Get me a report! (*as Fisk nods*) No, nevermind, I'll go myself! I have to know what's going on—(*exits quickly right*)

---

7. **Confederate** (kuhn FED uhr it) **gunners:** soldiers from the South in charge of artillery and cannons.

F COMPARE AND CONTRAST

In lines 80–91, a low-ranking soldier, Private Brown, reveals that he has been following Clara Barton's orders. This upsets Captain Neal, who is an officer. Underline the sentences that tell you what Clara ordered Brown to do.

Brown. Air's pretty thick in here, eh, Sergeant?

Fisk (*nodding*). Pretty thick, Joe

100 **Brown.** The old man's sure got his dander up.

Fisk. I think he's worried.

Brown. Everybody's worried. The Johnny Rebs are giving us Yanks[8] the very devil.

Fisk. Captain Neal's brother is in the midst of it. His artillery battery[9] is in an exposed position that the Confederates have been shelling for hours.

Brown. Lieutenant Ralph Neal? I know him. He's just a boy.

Fisk (*sighing*). A boy of nineteen. (*pause*) How old are 110 you, Joe?

Brown. Twenty—but a veteran. (*steps to window, looks out*) Every man out there is somebody's brother or son or sweetheart. **G**

Fisk. And another thing—the Captain is at odds with Miss Barton.

Brown. What about?

Fisk. I think he resents the fact that she was here before he was, and he doesn't like playing second fiddle.

IN OTHER WORDS The captain leaves. Fisk tells Brown that the captain is just nervous about his nineteen-year-old brother's safety. Fisk also tells Brown that the captain doesn't like Clara Barton. The captain doesn't like "playing second fiddle," or being less important than Clara.

G HISTORY-RELATED WRITINGS

The dialogue in lines 102–113 contains information about the war's events and people. On the lines below, explain what the dialogue reveals about soldiers and the war.

What these lines tell me about soldiers and the war: _____

_____

_____

_____

_____

_____

_____

---

8. **Johnny Rebs . . . Yanks:** slang for Confederate soldiers (Rebels) and Union soldiers (Yankees).

9. **artillery** (ahr TIL uh ree) **battery:** an army unit that uses cannons and other big guns.

○ COMPARE AND CONTRAST
Reread lines 119–130. In lines 121–122, Brown shows that he disagrees with Captain Neal's opinion of Clara Barton. Brown says that Clara is "an angel." Draw brackets [ ] around the sentences that explain why Brown feels as he does.

VISUAL VOCABULARY

A **valise** (vuh LEES) is a traveling bag or suitcase that holds clothes or other personal items.

Brown. Jealous, eh?

120 **Fisk.** Maybe. He's certainly critical of everything.

Brown. But why? Miss Barton—why, Sergeant, she's an angel!

Fisk. Captain Neal isn't a bad fellow.

Brown. I'll take Miss Barton!

Fisk *(grinning).* You're one of those people she's bewitched, Joe.

Brown. I'm one she nursed back to health last year. There are hundreds of us; we owe our lives to her. (*Knock is heard at right door. Fisk opens it to Mrs. Almira Fales, dressed in*
130 *traveling costume and carrying a small valise.*) ○

Mrs. Fales. I'm looking for Miss Barton. Do you know where she is?

Fisk. In the hospital, ma'am. Will you have a seat? I'll call her for you. (*exits left*)

Mrs. Fales (*sitting on bench, puts valise on floor*). What's the news, young man?

Brown. Not very cheerful, ma'am. The day seems to be going badly for us.

Mrs. Fales. I feared so. Well, I suppose we can't win every
140 engagement.

Brown. No, ma'am. Though that would be nice, wouldn't it? (*glancing appraisingly at her*) Traveling's kind of inconvenient in these times for a lady.

Mrs. Fales. Oh, I travel whenever and wherever I please.

IN OTHER WORDS Brown tells Fisk that he likes Clara Barton because she nursed him (Brown) back to health. Mrs. Fales enters the room, looking for Clara Barton.

Brown. Are you some kin[10] to Miss Barton?

Mrs. Fales. No. But I know Miss Barton—and admire her. (*smiling reminiscently*) Miss Barton and I met on the way to a battlefield. It was in August, at Bull Run.[11] You see, Mr.—

150 **Brown.** Brown—the name is Joe Brown, ma'am.

Mrs. Fales. You see, Mr. Brown, my sons are soldiers. I knew they were at Bull Run. Somehow I had the notion they'd been hurt, perhaps killed. There was no reliable information about the battle, no list of casualties. My husband and I were frantic. Finally I decided I would just go down there and find out about our boys. It was on the road I met Miss Barton. I had heard of her and the magnificent service she's performing. I asked if I could work with her at Bull Run. She had a few men working 160 with her, but we were the only women in the outfit. (*shaking her head*) And how we worked! The battle was over, the ground literally strewn with human wreckage— and not enough doctors from the Medical Corps. ❶

Brown (*shaking head*). There never are enough, ma'am.

Mrs. Fales. We had several days and nights of it, working at top speed in the most adverse conditions. At last we got the field cleared, the dead buried, and the wounded shipped by train to hospitals in the surrounding cities. I learned most about nursing from Miss Barton. She is an expert.

IN OTHER WORDS Mrs. Fales tells Brown that she met Clara Barton on the way to a battlefield called Bull Run. She and Clara worked as nurses after the battle.

▶ With a partner, retell Mrs. Fales's story about her actions at Bull Run.

---

10. **kin:** relative, family.
11. **Bull Run:** the site of a famous Civil War battle in which Confederate forces defeated Union forces; nearly 5,000 men were killed, wounded, captured, or determined to be missing in action.

❶ **HISTORY-RELATED WRITINGS**

Reread lines 151–163. What does Mrs. Fales's dialogue tell you about Civil War battles? What does it tell you about events after a battle has ended?

What Mrs. Fales's dialogue tells me about Civil War battles: ____

_____

_____

_____

_____

_____

What Mrs. Fales's dialogue tells me about events after a battle has ended: _____

_____

_____

_____

_____

_____

170 Brown (*fervently*). An angel!

Mrs. Fales. Yes, she seemed just that. Then, a week ago, when I heard she was in Falmouth, I made up my mind to come and help—if she'll have me.

Brown (*enthusiastically*). Oh, I reckon she will, ma'am, and gladly. (*tentatively*) But—your sons?

Mrs. Fales. They survived Bull Run. So far they've been spared, thank goodness! (*Captain Neal enters right. Brown salutes.*)

Brown. Mrs. Fales is here to see Miss Barton, sir.

180 Captain Neal (*nodding gruffly*). Madam.

Mrs. Fales. How do you do, sir?

Captain Neal. Well, Brown, is this your rest period? Be off!

Brown (*clicking his heels*). Yes, sir. (*moves toward door*)

Captain Neal. What about your milk and eggs?

Brown. Oh, yes, sir! I almost forgot. (*Exits with basket. Captain Neal eyes Mrs. Fales curiously, then sits at table and busies himself with pen and paper. Clara Barton enters left.*)

Mrs. Fales (*rising*). Clara!

Clara. Almira Fales!

190 Mrs. Fales (*pleased*). So you remember me?

Clara (*warmly*). As if I ever could forget! (*clasping Mrs. Fales' hands*) Is it possible you've come to volunteer?

Mrs. Fales. Yes, I have.

Clara (*happily*). Oh, I'm so grateful! Do sit down. I'm so happy you're here.

IN OTHER WORDS Mrs. Fales says she is there to help Clara. Captain Neal returns and tells Brown to get back to work. Clara Barton enters the room and greets Mrs. Fales.

► Reread lines 185–195. (Circle) the words that tell you how Clara Barton feels about Mrs. Fales.

Mrs. Fales (*sitting with Clara on the bench*). You're looking well, Clara.

Clara. I am well. Always tired, but well. (*smiles*) My health seems to thrive on abuse.

200 **Mrs. Fales.** And still wearing that red bow in honor of your father.

Clara. In memory of him, now. My father died recently.

Mrs. Fales (*sadly*). Oh, I'm so sorry to hear that.

Clara. Thank you, Almira. (*sighing*) Red was his favorite color; it's mine, too.

Mrs. Fales. The badge of bravery. (*leans forward, intently*) You are so often in danger, Clara! Are you never afraid?

Clara. Afraid? Constantly! I just try to hide my fear—with a bright red ribbon. ❶

210 **George** (*entering left, carrying wooden tool kit; gruffly*). Miss Barton, I've built those extra bunks you were talking about.

Clara. Thank you, George. I'd like you to meet Mrs. Fales, a good friend of mine, and a good nurse. (*to Mrs. Fales*) George is my right-hand man.

IN OTHER WORDS Clara Barton tells Mrs. Fales that she wears a red bow in honor of her dead father. Clara admits that she is always afraid. A worker named George enters. Clara introduces him as her "right-hand man," or assistant. He has built bunks, or beds, for wounded soldiers.

❶ **COMPARE AND CONTRAST**
Reread lines 198–209 Underline details that describe what Clara Barton is like.

George (*grinning cordially at Mrs. Fales*). You'll be welcome, ma'am. (*to Clara*) I made space for the poor chaps. Reckon we'll get 'em, too. The stretcher-bearers are out now.

Clara. I'll inspect the bunks. Will you come with me, Almira? (*They rise and exit left. George starts to follow, but* 220 *Captain Neal stops him with a gesture.*)

Captain Neal. Are you a carpenter?

George (*with a laugh*). Carpenter, porter, chief cook, and bottle washer, jack-of-all-trades.

Captain Neal. I have some carpenter's chores for you to do, at your leisure.

George. Well, sir, I don't have much leisure—and I'd be obliged to ask Miss Barton.

Captain Neal (*sharply*). No, you would not! I am in charge here. Miss Barton has no connection with the Army—

230 **George.** She's tried to connect herself with the Army, sir, but those people in Washington won't let her do what she wants to do.

Captain Neal. Nor will I, here at Lacy House. **Ⓚ**

George. So you're one of 'em? Well, sir, you'll just have to get your own carpenter. I'm working for Miss Barton! (*exits quickly through door right*)

Clara (*reopening door left*). The bunks are fine, George. . . . Oh, George is gone?

Captain Neal (*dryly*). Yes, he's gone—quite suddenly,

240 **Clara.** Well, I must get Mrs. Fales settled.

Ⓚ COMPARE AND CONTRAST

In lines 219–233, George reveals one reason Clara has trouble getting things done. Draw brackets [ ] around that reason.

IN OTHER WORDS Captain Neal asks George to do some work for him. George tells the captain that he works only for Clara Barton. The captain is angered by George's loyalty to Clara Barton.

Captain Neal. Just a moment, Miss Barton! Why is that lady in Falmouth?

Clara (*smiling*). I think you know why. Weren't you eavesdropping?

Captain Neal (*incensed*). Miss Barton, I do not intend to have Lacy House turned into an institution for interfering females!

Clara. Oh, Captain, how I wish there were more interfering females. They make such splendid nurses.

250 **Captain Neal.** Then they should enlist as nurses in the Army.

Clara. I thought of doing that, but those women are sent to work in city hospitals; they can never go into the field. I would like the Army to sponsor me as a field nurse, where I know I'm most effective.

Captain Neal (*sternly*). Where you have no authority to be. The Army does not approve of women in military encampments. The battlefield is not a place for women.

Clara. How silly! So many lives are sacrificed because of the
260 Army's rigidity. **PAUSE & REFLECT**

IN OTHER WORDS Captain Neal tells Clara that Mrs. Fales is not welcome. He believes that women who want to help soldiers should join the Army.

▶Clara Barton refused to join the Army. <u>Underline</u> the lines that tell you why she did not enlist in the Army.

Voice (*offstage*). Miss Barton! Miss Barton is needed!

Clara. Excuse me, please, Captain. (*exits*)

PAUSE & REFLECT

Men such as George, Private Brown, and Sergeant Fisk all seem to value Clara Barton's work. Captain Neal, on the other hand, considers her a source of trouble. Why might the men have such differing opinions?

_____

_____

_____

_____

_____

_____

_____

_____

_____

_____

Captain Neal. Miss Barton is needed! All day, by everyone! But if I have my way, Miss Barton may soon find there are such things as rules and regulations.

Fisk. (*entering*). Excuse me, Captain, but there's heavy firing on our artillery positions.

Captain Neal (*anxiously*). How bad is it?

Fisk. A great many casualties, it would seem. (*goes to window and looks out*) The stretcher-bearers are busy with the wounded. (*Guns boom in distance.*)

Jenkins (*entering right*). Sergeant, where do we take these Graycoats?

Captain Neal. Graycoats?

Jenkins (*noticing Captain Neal, salutes him*). Yes, sir. The Confederate Johnnies. Are they to be put in the hospital with our boys? ●

Captain Neal. Who said they were to be brought to Lacy House?

280 **Jenkins.** Miss Barton, sir.

Captain Neal. The hospital is crowded!

Jenkins. Not too crowded, Miss Barton said.

Captain Neal. Go outside and wait there! (*Jenkins salutes and exits.*) Fisk, call Miss Barton.

Fisk. Yes, sir. (*exits*)

● HISTORY-RELATED WRITINGS

Reread lines 272–277. Underline the words the characters use to describe Confederate soldiers. How might the author have made sure to use historically accurate terms?

_____

_____

_____

_____

_____

_____

_____

_____

_____

_____

_____

_____

_____

_____

IN OTHER WORDS Clara Barton leaves the room. Fisk and the captain watch as wounded soldiers are brought in from battle. Jenkins enters and asks where to put the wounded "Graycoats"— enemy soldiers. He tells them that Clara Barton said to bring the soldiers to their hospital.

Captain Neal (*to himself*). Now she has gone too far. Much too far. (*After a moment, Fisk reenters, escorting Clara.*) I'll talk privately with Miss Barton, Sergeant. (*Fisk exits right.*) Miss Barton, since when have we adopted a policy of
290 rescuing our sworn enemies?

Clara (*calmly*). I have always done it, Captain.

Captain Neal. You have done it?

Clara. I have never withheld aid to any man lying on any battlefield, merely because his uniform was gray rather than blue. I never stop to ask him his race, politics, or religion, either. If he is a human being—suffering, I give him all the help I can.

Captain Neal (*angrily*). This is ridiculous. Do you for an instant suppose that our men who fall on a Southern
300 battlefield are shown such mercy?

Clara. Of course, I suppose that! I know it is true! And you must surely know it, too. I think the Confederates' ideas and convictions are wrong. But I am not so deluded as to think they aren't human!

Jenkins (*opening door; thrusting in his head*). Miss Barton, the Sergeant said you were in here. Shall we take the Rebs into Lacy House? It's getting dark and raining a little.

Clara. Yes, Jenkins.

Captain Neal. Just a minute, orderly. We cannot
310 accommodate those men.

Clara. We can accommodate them, Captain. And we must!

Captain Neal. Our facilities are limited.

Clara. George built more bunks—and he can build more, many more.

Ⓜ COMPARE AND CONTRAST

In lines 286–304, Captain Neal and Clara argue about how to treat enemy soldiers. What does the argument show about how Captain Neal feels about the enemy? What does the argument show about how Clara feels about the enemy?

How Captain Neal feels about the enemy: _____

_____

_____

_____

_____

_____

How Clara feels about the enemy: _____

_____

_____

_____

_____

_____

_____

Captain Neal. By taking in these Confederates, we may be depriving men who fell inside our lines.

Jenkins. These men fell inside our lines, sir.

Clara. Indeed, Captain, should we have allowed them to lie there and die? How could we turn them away? (*to Jenkins*) 320 Take them into Lacy House! (*Jenkins has been looking bewilderedly from Clara to Captain Neal, he exits.*)

IN OTHER WORDS Captain Neal asks Clara why they should help their enemies. Clara says she does not ask whether a man is an enemy or not; she just helps him. The Captain says there is no room at the hospital. Clara tells him that George has built more bunks.

▶ Reread lines 293–304. Underline the words or phrases that tell you why Clara Barton thinks it is best to help enemy soldiers.

Captain Neal (*furiously*). Miss Barton, this situation is intolerable! (*Fisk enters.*) Sergeant, didn't I tell you—

Fisk (*apologetically*). The mail, sir. The courier from Washington. (*stands aside*)

Courier (*entering, placing mail pouch on table*). Anything to go back, Captain?

Captain Neal. Yes. (*He picks up packet of letters that Clara has written for the soldiers, tosses it to Courier, who salutes and* 330 *exits, followed by Fisk. Glancing briefly through contents of the mail pouch, he pounces upon one letter, opens and scans it hurriedly. Holding the letter, Captain Neal turns to Clara.*) Miss Barton, I am not a cruel man—

Clara. Oh, I'm sure of that. Merely short-sighted and old-fashioned in your prejudices. And obstinate. But I am obstinate,[12] myself.

---

12. **obstinate** (OB stuh nit): stubborn.

Voice (*offstage*). Miss Barton! Miss Barton is needed!

Clara. Excuse me, Captain. (*starts toward door left*)

Captain Neal. Since the moment of my arrival in Falmouth,
340 I have known there would be this crisis.

Clara (*turning back*). Crisis?

IN OTHER WORDS Captain Neal is interrupted by a mail carrier, or
courier. The mail carrier delivers mail from Washington, D.C., and
picks up the letters that Clara Barton helped the soldiers write.

►With a partner, summarize the stage directions
in lines 326–332.

Captain Neal. Between us. I have seen it as inevitable that
while you were here, some members of the small staff in
Lacy House, perhaps most of them, would ignore me and
look to you for direction—

Clara (*quietly*). Only because I was here first.

Captain Neal (*raising his voice*). You are everywhere first,
Miss Barton! It is uncanny. (*more calmly, with an effort at
controlling his temper*) Therefore, I have known that one of
350 us must go. And I have not doubted which one it would be.

Clara (*matter-of-factly*). Is that your opinion? Mine is
just the contrary, Captain. I don't see why we both can't
remain, and on good terms, too. If there is a crisis between
us, it is not of my making.

Captain Neal (*with sarcasm*). Oh, no? PAUSE & REFLECT

Clara. I wish only to work with you—with anyone who
serves the end of justice and mercy. Very often I've been
thrown into contact with a man like you—prejudiced,
suspicious of me and my methods, even my motives; but

PAUSE & REFLECT

Stage directions often
provide hints about what
a character is like. Reread
the stage directions in
lines 346–355. With a
partner, discuss what the
stage directions reveal about
Clara and Captain Neal.
Then, write your answers
below.

What the stage directions show
about Clara: _____

_____

_____

_____

_____

What the stage directions show
about Captain Neal: _____

_____

_____

_____

_____

Ⓝ HISTORY-RELATED WRITINGS

How might the dialogue between Clara and Captain Neal represent her real-life struggles to gain acceptance by the military?

_____

_____

_____

_____

_____

Ⓞ HISTORY-RELATED WRITINGS

Reread lines 374–382. What do these lines tell you about the way people communicated with each other at the time of the Civil War?

_____

_____

_____

_____

_____

_____

_____

_____

_____

_____

360 still we have worked together well enough. And sometimes we have become fast friends. I have many friends among the Medical Corps doctors. I don't see why you and I can't arrange some sort of compromise—

Captain Neal (*harshly*). It is too late for compromise.

Voice (*offstage*). Miss Barton!

Clara. Too late, Captain?

Captain Neal. This letter—

Brown (*opening door at left*). Miss Barton, that fellow with the malaria[13] has got a chill, a violent chill—

370 **Captain Neal** (*shouting*). Get out! Get out! Ⓝ

Clara (*above Captain Neal's shouting*). Give him a dose of quinine,[14] Brown. See that he swallows it. I'll come presently.

Brown. Yes, ma'am. (*closes door*)

Captain Neal. Miss Barton, I've received a letter from Washington. (*holding up letter*) From my superior officers. It is the reply to a telegram I dispatched last night—just twelve hours after my arrival. I am lucky to have a reply so promptly.

Clara (*uneasily*). And what does it say?

Captain Neal. The tone of this letter is unequivocal.[15] It 380 states very definitely that you are to be relieved of all duty in the Falmouth area. At once. In plain words, Miss Barton, you are dismissed. Ⓞ

___

IN OTHER WORDS Captain Neal tells Clara that they cannot work together. Clara says that she works well with other Army officers. The captain then explains that he has a letter ordering Clara to leave.

► Reread lines 374–382. Underline the words that show that the captain already knows what is in the letter.

___

13. **malaria** (muh LAIR ee uh): a disease carried by mosquitoes.
14. **quinine** (KWY nyn): a type of medicine; used to treat malaria.
15. **unequivocal** (uhn ih KWIV uh kuhl): clear; without question.

Clara (*incredulously*). You wired to the War Department, complaining of me?

Captain Neal. I did.

Clara. You complained of my skill at nursing?

Captain Neal. Not that. You may be a very good nurse.

Clara (*vehemently*). I am a good nurse!

Captain Neal. I complained of you as a meddler.

390 **Clara** (*angrily*). In plain words, Captain, you let your dislike of me override your judgment regarding the welfare of this hospital.

Captain Neal (*emphatically*). There is nothing more to be said on the subject. You are relieved of all duty. I'll have a wagon made ready to convey you safely to the railroad station. Of course, the other lady, Mrs. Fales, will accompany you. **℗**

Clara (*angrily*). But I won't go! I can't desert the men, the wounded men in Lacy House. I know them—know them 400 all by name!

Captain Neal (*firmly*). You will go, Miss Barton. Under the circumstances it would be most awkward for you to remain. Your dismissal is from Washington, and it is specific and urgent.

Clara. Who will do the work in my place? I've snatched back from death's door many patients whom your doctors and nurses had given up as lost.

Captain Neal (*sneeringly*). I'm not interested in a recital of your triumphs.

410 **Clara** (*angrily*). How absurdly, blindly biased you are, Captain!

Captain Neal (*with controlled anger*). Sergeant Fisk will fetch a wagon. You must have a bag, or something to pack?

℗ HISTORY-RELATED WRITINGS
Reread lines 393–397. What do these lines tell you about the kinds of transportation that were available at the time of the Civil War?

_____

_____

_____

_____

_____

_____

Q COMPARE AND CONTRAST

Reread lines 412–424. In this passage, what does Captain Neal realize about Clara Barton?

_____

_____

_____

_____

_____

What has changed about his opinion of her?

_____

_____

_____

_____

_____

Clara (*sadly, realizing her defeat*). Yes, I have a bag. (*starts toward left door, speaks over her shoulder*) I came with five wagon-loads of supplies. For days they were the only supplies available, and they're not yet exhausted. I hope you will accept what's left—for the sake of the hospital. Lint, medicines, muslin sheets—such articles have value, even if 420 I have none.

Captain Neal (*stiffly*). I will accept them, Miss Barton. (*As she exits, he paces up and down, muttering.*) A strange woman. Most women would have cried. She didn't. No tears. She has courage—the courage of a man! **Q**

IN OTHER WORDS Captain Neal tells Clara that she must leave immediately. Clara questions his reasons. She asks who will be the nurse if she leaves. She tells the captain that she will go but also says that she will leave the rest of her supplies for the wounded soldiers. The captain is impressed by Clara Barton's courage since she doesn't back down from him.

Fisk (*entering from door right*). May I come in, sir?

Captain Neal (*barking*). Why not? (*a slight pause, as sound of cannon is heard off*) You're to fetch a wagon and drive Miss Barton and the other lady to the railroad station. They're catching the night train.

430 **Fisk** (*regretfully*). I'm sorry, sir. Miss Barton was so set on staying.

Captain Neal (*wryly*). More eavesdropping!

Fisk (*meekly*). Well, I was just at the door, sir, I couldn't have avoided—

Captain Neal. No matter. Go fetch a wagon.

Fisk (*lingering*). It does seem too bad, when Miss Barton's so popular with everybody—

Captain Neal (*roaring*). Fetch a wagon!

Fisk. Yes, sir. (*turns toward door right and collides with*
440 *Messenger, who rushes in, breathless*)

Messenger. Captain Neal? I'm from General Burnside's
headquarters. We are in full retreat across the bridge,
sir, falling back on all fronts. The Rebels have swept
everything before them. (*pausing, panting*) And your
brother, sir— PAUSE & REFLECT

Captain Neal. My brother!

Messenger. Lieutenant Neal—

Captain Neal. What about him? (*seizing Messenger by the
sleeve*) What about Lieutenant Neal?

450 **Messenger.** Shot, sir.

Captain Neal. Killed?

Messenger. Wounded, sir.

Captain Neal (*tugging roughly at Messenger's sleeve*). Is
it—serious?

Messenger. Yes, sir. Serious. But the doctor in
Fredericksburg did an emergency operation. They're
bringing him to Lacy House, sir.

Captain Neal (*releasing Messenger's sleeve*). Fisk! Fisk!

Fisk (*at door*). Yes, sir. Just off to fetch the wagon, sir.

460 **Captain Neal.** Wagon! (*wildly*) Blast the wagon! Fetch Miss
Barton! Get her in here! (*shouts*) Miss Barton! (*Clara,
wearing her traveling cloak and bonnet, enters.*)

Clara. Did you call me?

Captain Neal (*rushing to her*). I did call you, Miss Barton.
My brother—(*He buries his face in his hands.*)

PAUSE & REFLECT

In lines 441–445, a
messenger arrives with news
about the battle. What has
happened? _____

_____

_____

_____

_____

_____

_____

_____

_____

_____

Messenger. It's Lieutenant Neal, ma'am. Seriously wounded.

IN OTHER WORDS Captain Neal tells Fisk to take Clara to the train station. A messenger arrives and announces that the captain's brother has been shot and wounded in battle. The captain orders Clara Barton to come back to Lacy House where his wounded brother is being brought.

► Reread lines 441–463. Underline the sentence that tells you the captain has changed his mind about Clara.

Clara. The Captain's brother? Oh, dreadful! But— not dead?

470 **Messenger.** No, ma'am. Not yet.

Clara. Well, with proper nursing I'm sure—

Messenger. That's what the doctor said. With you here, the doctor said—

Captain Neal (*looking up; emotionally*). Miss Barton, my brother is so young!

Clara (*quietly*). Most of them are, aren't they? (*They exchange looks, then slowly, she takes off her bonnet and throws it on to bench.*) The doctor seems to think that something can be done.

480 **Captain Neal.** Miss Barton, if you will do your best for my brother—

Clara. I'll give him the same care I give all the men neither more nor less. **Ⓡ**

Captain Neal. I understand, Miss Barton. I understand— and I could ask for nothing better.

Mrs. Fales (*entering left, in traveling costume, carrying her valise*). Well, Clara, I'm ready, if we must go.

Ⓡ COMPARE AND CONTRAST

In lines 468–483, Captain Neal asks Clara Barton to help his brother. She agrees to help. What does Captain Neal's action tell you about him? What does Clara Barton's action tell you about her?

What Captain Neal's action tells me: _____

_____

_____

_____

_____

What Clara Barton's action tells me: _____

_____

_____

_____

_____

_____

Clara. We're not going.

Mrs. Fales (*puzzled*). Not going?

490 **Clara.** We're staying—at Captain Neal's request.

Mrs. Fales. But I thought he—

Clara. The Captain wants us to work with him—and he's in command, isn't he?

Mrs. Fales (*perplexed*). I don't know. And I don't believe he knows either! (*to herself*) A very snappish man!

Clara (*smiling*). Sh-h! We must get into our work uniforms. (*They exit.*)

Captain Neal (*to Fisk and Messenger*). Why are you standing there gaping? I have a letter to write. A letter which must 500 be sent tonight. To Washington. (*hesitantly, as if with effort*) A letter acknowledging that I've been in error, and recommending that Miss Clara Barton be permanently attached to the United States Army, as an Army nurse—in the field, or wherever she chooses to be. (*Fisk and Messenger exit right. Captain Neal sits at table and writes rapidly. Lights dim slightly; shot is heard off.*) **S**

Clara (*entering at left*). Captain, your brother is in the hospital, and conscious. Would you like to speak to him?

Captain Neal (*springing up*). Will he pull through? Do you 510 think there's a chance?

Clara. I think there's a chance.

IN OTHER WORDS Captain Neal asks Clara to do her best for his brother. Clara tells him that she treats all the soldiers the same. The captain writes a letter. Clara Barton tells him that his brother is likely to survive.

► Reread lines 498–506. With a partner, discuss what the captain's letter is likely to say.

S COMPARE AND CONTRAST

Reread lines 498–506. What does this event tell you about Captain Neal?

What this event tells me about Captain Neal: _____

_____

_____

_____

_____

_____

⊤ HISTORY-RELATED WRITINGS

Reread lines 519–530. In these lines, what do you learn about the goals of the American Red Cross?

_____
_____
_____
_____
_____
_____
_____
_____
_____
_____
_____
_____
_____
_____
_____
_____
_____

Captain Neal. And you'll help him? (*Clara nods.*) I do want to speak to him! (*pauses*) I'd like you to read this letter.

Clara (*dismayed*). The letter from Washington?

Captain Neal (*quickly*). No, no, it's not the one I received! It's a letter I'm just in process of writing and haven't quite finished. But since it concerns you—(*hands letter to her, then crosses to door left and exits*)

Clara. I do think the Captain's heart is in the right place.
520 (*Sits on bench and reads letter silently. She smiles, still holding letter.*) Sometimes I have a vision, or what seems a vision. I see my country whole and healed once more, North and South reunited, one people, never again to be divided by war and hatred. (*pauses*) I see beyond the present, far, far into a future when this humble work of mine has found boundless, universal support. I see the work growing, embracing all the civilized nations of the world through both war and peace. (*During her speech, room has gradually darkened. On rear wall, spotlight shines
530 on emblem of Red Cross.*) ⊤

Voice (*offstage*). Miss Barton!

Clara (*rousing, turning her head*). Yes?

Voice. Miss Barton is needed!

Clara (*rising, standing a moment under Red Cross emblem, then hurrying to exit*). Coming!

IN OTHER WORDS Captain Neal asks Clara to read the letter he wrote. He leaves Clara alone. Clara thinks out loud and imagines the country united after the war. The play ends with someone calling for Clara's help again.

▶ Underline the stage directions that help show that Clara's thoughts are linked to the organization she started.

---

from The War Diary of **Clara Barton**

Based on the diary entry by CLARA BARTON

**SET A PURPOSE
FOR READING**
Read "*from* The War
Diary of Clara Barton" to
learn about events during
the Civil War as seen
through Barton's own
eyes.

BACKGROUND During the Civil War, Clara Barton kept a diary of her thoughts, feelings, and experiences. In one part of her diary, Barton describes the Battle of the Wilderness. Fought near Fredericksburg, Virginia, the battle involved more than 100,000 Union troops and about 60,000 Confederate troops. Neither side won a clear victory, but the number of casualties—wounded and dead soldiers—was very high. Many soldiers burned to death when the forest caught fire.

○ **COMPARE AND CONTRAST**

Reread lines 1–12. What does Clara Barton think about the officers in charge of the city?

Barton's opinion of the officers:

_____

_____

_____

_____

No one has forgotten the sadness of the Battle of the Wilderness. But you may never have heard about how much worse the officers in charge of the city made things. These officers were in charge of the care, food, shelter, comfort, and lives of wounded men.

Since then, one of the highest officers there has been convicted as a traitor. Another officer there lived with the rich owners of a big mansion. Yet he bragged that it was too hard for the rich people of Fredericksburg
10 to open up their homes to "dirty, lousy, common soldiers," and he said that he was not going to make them do it. ○

I heard him say this. Then, in one old hotel, I saw five hundred men dying and starving, begging for a cracker to keep them alive. I saw them beg for a drink of water. I saw two hundred army wagons lined up in the rain for hours. Each one was filled with wounded men. The dark spot in the mud under many a wagon showed where some poor fellow's life had dripped out
20 in those dreadful hours.

IN OTHER WORDS Clara Barton explains that after the battle, officers made things worse for wounded men. Instead of wounded soldiers being sent to people's homes to recover, the soldiers were forced to crowd together in a hotel. They did not even have anything to eat or drink.

▶ With a partner, discuss the meaning of "The dark spot in the mud under many a wagon showed where some poor fellow's life had dripped out in those dreadful hours."

I remembered one man who might be able to help, if I could get back to Belle Plain to tell him. An army wagon took me ten miles through the fields and swamp to Belle Plain. A steamboat took me from there to Washington. Landing at sunset, I sent for Henry Wilson, chairman of the Military Committee of the Senate. A messenger brought him to me at eight o'clock. He was sad and horrified, as was every other patriot at that time. **Ⓥ**

30   He listened to the story of suffering and betrayal. He left me quickly, looking shocked. At ten o'clock he stood in the War Department.[1] The people in charge there did not believe his report. Some frightened person must have lied to him. Military authorities had not reported such suffering to them.

Mr. Wilson insisted that the officers in charge of the battle were not to be trusted. Still the Department officials doubted him.

Finally he told them: Either you will send someone
40   tonight to investigate the cruelty against our wounded men at Fredericksburg, or the Senate will send someone tomorrow. **Ⓦ**

This threat got them into action.

That night the Quartermaster-General[2] and staff rode to Fredericksburg. By noon the wounded men were being fed from the food of the city and the houses were opened to the "*dirty, lousy* soldiers." In three days I returned with carloads of supplies.

---

1. **War Department:** a department of the U.S. government; now called the Department of Defense.
2. **Quartermaster-General:** the officer in charge of supplies for the entire army.

Ⓥ COMPARE AND CONTRAST

In the play you learned about an officer, Captain Neal. In Barton's diary, you learn about a politician, Senator Wilson. Reread lines 21–29. What is Senator Wilson like? Is he similar to or different from Captain Neal?

What Barton's diary tells me about Wilson: _____

_____

_____

_____

Ⓦ HISTORY-RELATED WRITINGS

Clara Barton describes what happened when Senator Wilson made his report to the War Department. Why, according to Clara Barton, did officers in charge of the battle lie about how bad conditions were?

Why officers lied about conditions: _____

_____

_____

_____

_____

The private thoughts of a diary entry can provide insights into a real-life figure's personality. Based on Clara Barton's diary entry, what was Clara Barton like?

What Clara Barton was like: _____

_____

_____

_____

_____

_____

Every man who left Fredericksburg by boat or by
50 car owes it to the firm decision of one man: Mr. Henry Wilson! ⊗

IN OTHER WORDS Clara takes a wagon and a boat to Washington to meet with Mr. Wilson. Wilson demands that the War Department help the soldiers. Officials there don't believe him at first, but they finally agree to look into the problem.

► With a partner, discuss how the wounded soldiers were helped. Underline the sentences that show the kind of help the soldiers finally received.

Literary Analysis: History-Related Writings

Clara Barton: Battlefield Nurse and *The War Diary of Clara Barton* are different types of history-related writing. To examine how the historical drama and the diary give readers a view of both the place and time of the Civil War and of Clara's character, complete the following charts.

READING 5 Understand and draw conclusions about the structure and elements of drama. Explain a playwright's use of dialogue and stage directions. **7** Describe the structural and substantive differences between a diary and a fictional adaptation of it.

Clara Barton: Battlefield Nurse

What the stage directions tell me about place and time:

_____

_____

_____

What the dialogue tells me about Clara Barton:

_____

_____

_____

The War Diary of Clara Barton

What Clara's descriptions tell me about the place and time:

_____

_____

_____

What Clara's words tell me about her:

_____

_____

_____

READING 5 Understand and draw conclusions about the structure and elements of drama. Explain a playwright's use of dialogue and stage directions. **7** Describe the structural and substantive differences between a diary and a fictional adaptation of it.

Reading Strategy: Compare and Contrast

These two selections present two pictures of historical events and people. Think about the people, settings, and events described in both selections. Then, list similarities and differences in the chart below.

	Similarities	Differences
Characters/Real-life People	Captain Neal and the selfish officer	
Characters' Actions	Captain Neal tries to stop Clara from helping soldiers; the selfish officer refuses to improve conditions for soldiers.	
Setting		
Events		

How can we CHANGE what's wrong?

Think about your list of people who fought for change. Who on that list is similar to Clara Barton? Write that person's name and explain how that person is similar to Clara Barton.

_____

_____

_____

Academic Vocabulary in Speaking

The word **undertake** (uhn duhr TAYK) is a verb that means *to begin* or *to agree to do a task*.

> It was time to begin helping soldiers, so she decided to **undertake** the task of gathering supplies.

The word **link** (link) is a verb that means *to connect or join*.

> A teacher used connecting cables to **link** the computers in the lab to each other.

TURN AND TALK With a partner, talk about a national or world problem that Barton might work to change today. Use the words **undertake** and **link** in your conversation.

READING 5 Understand and draw conclusions about the structure and elements of drama. Explain a playwright's use of dialogue and stage directions. **7** Describe the structural and substantive differences between a diary and a fictional adaptation of it.

Texas Assessment Practice

DIRECTIONS: Use *Clara Barton: Battlefield Nurse* and *The War Diary of Clara Barton* to answer questions 1–4.

1 Why does Captain Neal change his mind about Clara?

- (A) Clara describes her work to him, and he is convinced that she wants to help.
- (B) The War Department tells him to let Clara stay.
- (C) His brother may die, and he realizes that soldiers need Clara's help.
- (D) A servant finishes building bunks, and he learns how much Clara has done.

2 Based on Captain Neal's statements in lines 46–54, you can tell that women who lived during Clara Barton's time were —

- (F) expected to stay home and care for their families
- (G) unable to do difficult physical tasks
- (H) not allowed to travel during wartime
- (J) not interested in knowing about the war

3 In Clara's diary, why is she mad at the officers?

- (A) They have not gotten supplies to take care of hundreds of injured soldiers.
- (B) They have been working for the enemy and are traitors.
- (C) They will not allow the city to open its homes to soldiers.
- (D) They will not let her travel to Washington, D.C.

4 Based on both the play and the diary excerpt, what is one conclusion you can draw about Clara Barton?

- (F) Most military and political leaders considered her to be a troublemaker.
- (G) She personally saved hundreds of lives.
- (H) She worked tirelessly to better the conditions and lives of injured soldiers.
- (J) She felt that most officers disrespected their troops and treated them badly.

Included in this unit: TEKS 10, 10B, 10C, 11, 11A, 11B, 12, 12A, 12B, RC-7(A, E)

UNIT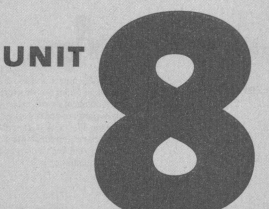

Face the Facts

INFORMATION, ARGUMENT, AND PERSUASION

Be sure to read the Reader's Workshops on pages 902–905 and 952–957 in *Holt McDougal Literature.*

Academic Vocabulary for Unit 8

You will see these Academic Vocabulary words as you work through this book. You will also be asked to use them as you write and talk about the selections in this unit.

Area (AIR ee uh) is a noun that means *a field of experience, activity, or knowledge.*
In what **area** is the author an expert?

What academic **area** interests you the most? Why? _____

_____

Domain (doh MAYN) is a noun that means *a place or field of activity over which someone or something has control.*
The new teacher's **domain** is math.

Who is the leader in the **domain** of your favorite sport? _____

_____

Hypothesis (hy POTH uh sis) is a noun that means *a reasonable guess that still needs to be proved true or false.*
How can you tell if a statement is a fact or a **hypothesis**?

What **hypothesis** would you make about the future of books? _____

_____

Objective (uhb JEK tiv) is a noun that means *a goal or something that is aimed for or worked toward.*
What is the **objective** of a persuasive essay?

What is your **objective** for a class you are taking this year? _____

_____

Resolve (rih ZOLV) is a verb that means *to figure out, solve, or make clear.*
How do the characters **resolve** their conflict?

Describe how you **resolve** a problem between friends: _____

_____

READING 10 Draw conclusions about expository text.
10B Distinguish factual claims from commonplace assertions and opinions.

Great White Sharks
Based on the magazine article by Peter Benchley

Can you tell FACT from fiction?

Writers sometimes create imaginary stories that can seem more real than life itself. But how do you know when a work of fiction is based on accurate information and when it's not? Peter Benchley was famous for writing both facts and fiction about great white sharks.

LIST IT Choose a movie or a book you have enjoyed that features nature or animals. List some of its key events or actions on the lines at the left. Then decide whether each detail could happen in real life.

Elements of Nonfiction: Evidence in Informational Text

The ideas in informational texts are usually supported by evidence like **facts.** Facts are statements that can be proved. Be sure you can tell the difference between facts and other types of evidence.

Evidence in Informational Text		
Fact	a statement that can be proved by a reliable source	*Sharks are known to eat a wide variety of foods.*
Opinion	a statement of personal belief that does not require proof or evidence	*I think sharks are vicious predators.*
Commonplace Assertion	a statement that many people think is true, but which may not be	*Everyone knows that sharks like to eat people.*

As you read, look for clues that will help you identify which types of evidence the author uses. Which type is the strongest?

Title:

Detail 1.

Could it happen?

Detail 2.

Could it happen?

Detail 3.

Could it happen?

Reading Skill: Recognize Author's Bias

Bias is the side of an issue that a writer favors. Writers reveal their bias through **loaded language**, words that are either strongly positive or strongly negative. As you read, watch for loaded language the author uses to stay aware of his possible bias.

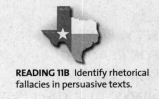

READING 11B Identify rhetorical fallacies in persuasive texts.

Loaded Language	Possible Author's Bias
"most wonderful of natural-born killers"	Benchley has a positive opinion of sharks even though they are killers.

Vocabulary in Context

Note: Words are listed in the order in which they appear in the article.

The word **demonize** (DEE muh nyz) is a verb that means *to unfairly treat something as evil.*

> Humans often **demonize** an innocent creature out of fear.

The word **anecdotal** (an ik DOH tuhl) is an adjective that means *based on observations rather than on scientific analysis.*

> The tourist gave **anecdotal** evidence instead of hard facts.

The word **travesty** (TRAV ih stee) is a noun that means *any treatment that makes a serious thing seem ridiculous.*

> The trial was a **travesty** because the jury was biased in favor of the defendant.

Vocabulary Practice

Review the vocabulary words and think about their meanings. Then discuss with a partner what you think Peter Benchley's view of great white sharks will be, based on these words. Share your predictions with a classmate.

SET A PURPOSE FOR READING

Read "Great White Sharks" to discover Peter Benchley's opinion of sharks.

GREAT WHITE SHARKS

Based on the magazine article by PETER BENCHLEY

BACKGROUND Peter Benchley wrote *Jaws*, a novel about a great white shark that attacks swimmers at a beach. *Jaws* became a hit movie of the same name. *Jaws* convinced many people that sharks are bloodthirsty animals that eat people. Over time, Benchley changed his mind about sharks. In this article, he admits that sharks are not the evil killers he once imagined.

Considering what we have found out about great white sharks in the past 25 years, I couldn't write *Jaws* today. Back then, most people thought that great white sharks ate people by choice. Now we know that almost every attack on a human is an accident. The shark mistakes a human for its prey.[1] Ⓐ

Ⓐ EVIDENCE

Reread lines 1–6. A **commonplace assertion** is a statement that many people assume is true but may not be. Underline the commonplace assertion that Benchley mentions. Draw brackets [ ] around the factual claim he makes to challenge that assertion.

---

1. **prey:** an animal that is hunted, usually as food.

Back then, we thought that a great white would always kill and eat its victim. Now we know that nearly three-quarters of all bite victims survive. Perhaps
10 that's because the shark knows that it has made a mistake and doesn't return for a second bite.

Back then, we believed that great whites attacked boats. Now we know that they sense movement, sound in the water, and electrical fields like those caused by running motors. When they approach a boat, they're just coming to investigate, to find out something about it.

Back then, it was OK to <u>demonize</u> an animal, or identify it as evil, especially a shark. People had done so since the beginning of time.

IN OTHER WORDS Many people once thought that great white sharks were dangerous killers that attacked humans on purpose, but this is incorrect. Most shark attacks on humans are accidents, and most victims survive them.

---

20 Today we know that these most wonderful of natural-born killers are *not* evil. They are victims in danger of serious decline. Much of the evidence is <u>anecdotal</u>, or based on personal experience rather than official studies. Fishermen and scientists who study nature are seeing fewer great whites. **B**

Scientists estimate that the numbers of some types of sharks have dropped 80 percent. White sharks are probably not reproducing fast enough to maintain their population. Despite their grace and power, great white
30 sharks are surprisingly fragile. . . .

VOCABULARY
The word **demonize** (DEE muh nyz) is a verb that means *to unfairly treat something as evil.*

VOCABULARY
The word **anecdotal** (an ik DOH tuhl) is an adjective that means *based on observations rather than on scientific analysis.*

B RECOGNIZE AUTHOR'S BIAS
Reread lines 12–25. Circle the examples of **loaded language** that you find here—words that sound either very good or very bad.

ⓒ RECOGNIZE AUTHOR'S BIAS

Reread lines 31–33. What words here reveal how Benchley feels about sharks? Fill in the chart below with the words and what you think they show about Benchley's bias, or attitude toward his subject.

Loaded Language
_____
_____
_____

↓

Possible Bias
_____
_____
_____
_____

VISUAL VOCABULARY

A **diver** (DY vuhr) is a person who uses special equipment to breathe and swim underwater.

PAUSE & REFLECT

Based on the article so far, how has Benchley's attitude toward great white sharks changed since he wrote *Jaws*? How has his attitude remained the same?

Today more people appreciate and value sharks for what they are: beautiful, graceful, efficient, and important to sea life and humans. ⓒ The change is largely due to television shows and films about sharks. They show the positive side of sharks, as well as the dangers sharks face from the way humans fish. Governments are learning that a dead shark may bring as much as fifty dollars to one fisherman, but a live shark can bring in thousands of dollars from tourists. **Divers** will fly halfway around
40 the world to see white sharks.

I can claim some credit for the change in attitude. *Jaws* was blamed for distorting, or giving the public an incorrect view of sharks—and for causing some people to hunt and kill them. But it also created a new interest in sharks. I receive more than a thousand letters a year from children who want to know more about them.

PAUSE & REFLECT

IN OTHER WORDS Sharks are not as dangerous as people once thought. Sharks themselves are in danger. Adult sharks don't produce young fast enough to replace sharks that die, and fishing kills many more. People today have more positive opinions about sharks than in the past.

► According to Benchley, what changed people's minds about sharks? Underline the statements that tell you.

The number of sharks changes depending on how much food there is. Also, sharks breed late in life, and a

female gives birth to only a few baby sharks. Scientists
50 aren't sure about the number, but seven or eight seems
to be a safe guess. At birth, baby sharks are already
four or five feet long and weigh 50–60 pounds. Still,
many don't survive the first year because other sharks,
including great whites, eat them. **PAUSE & REFLECT**

How big can sharks get? Fishermen around the
world say that they have seen 25-footers, 30-footers,
even 36-footers. None of these claims has been shown
to be true. The largest proven catch was a shark 19.5
feet long.
60   According to British biologist Ian Fergusson, no one
has ever proved that there is a great white shark longer
than 19.5 feet. He is irritated by the media's attempts
to excite audiences by claiming that sharks are bigger
than they really are. **D**

IN OTHER WORDS The number of sharks rises or falls
according to how much food there is, and sharks have few
babies. No one really knows how large sharks can become.
Some people often make unproven claims of seeing very
large sharks.

Scientists today have identified about 400 living
species of sharks. Of all known species, only four,
including great whites, attack human beings.

PAUSE & REFLECT
Why does Benchley include
these facts about baby
sharks? What point is he
trying to make?

_____

_____

_____

D EVIDENCE
Reread lines 60–64. An
opinion is a statement of
personal belief, feeling,
or thought that does not
require proof or evidence.
Underline the opinion in this
paragraph.

E RECOGNIZE AUTHOR'S BIAS

Reread lines 73–85. What words here show Benchley's bias about whether sharks are dangerous to people? Use those words to fill out the chart below.

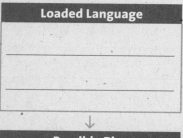

Loaded Language

↓

Possible Bias

VOCABULARY

The word **travesty** (TRAV ih stee) is a noun that means *any treatment that makes a serious thing seem ridiculous.*

In Australia, between 1876 and 1999, a total of 52 attacks by great whites were recorded. Of those 70 attacks, 27 were fatal. In the Mediterranean Sea since 1900 there have been 23 reliable reports of encounters with great whites.

A swimmer has a greater chance of being struck by lightning than of being killed by a shark. Around the world many, many more people die every year from bee stings, snakebites, falling off ladders, or drowning in bathtubs than from shark attacks.

People have actually seen sharks behave violently toward each other. But rather than actually hurting or 80 killing each other, sharks seem to threaten other sharks just to show their power. They don't act on those threats.

We must hope that we're learning enough about sharks to save them before we destroy them through ignorance and carelessness. **E**

Great white sharks have survived, almost unchanged, for millions of years. For human beings to drive them to extinction would be more than an ecological tragedy. It would be a moral <u>travesty</u>.

IN OTHER WORDS People have a greater chance of being injured or killed in many other ways than by a shark attack. As we learn more about sharks, Benchley hopes we will save them instead of causing them to disappear.

▶ Discuss with a partner why people are unlikely to die from shark attacks. Then (circle) three things Benchley lists as more likely to kill a human being than a shark.

Elements of Nonfiction: Evidence in Informational Text

In "Great White Sharks" Peter Benchley says that many people have the wrong idea about sharks. In the chart below, list the factual claims, opinions, and commonplace assertions that Benchley uses to support his point.

READING 10 Draw conclusions about expository text. **10B** Distinguish factual claims from commonplace assertions and opinions.

Types of Evidence	Examples
Factual Claims	
Opinions	
Commonplace Assertions	

Using this chart and your notes from "Great White Sharks," decide which type of evidence Benchley uses most. Then explain whether you found that evidence convincing. Use examples from the article to support your answer.

_____

_____

_____

_____

_____

_____

_____

READING 11B Identify rhetorical fallacies in persuasive texts.

Reading Skill: Recognize Author's Bias

Loaded language is usually very positive (good) or very negative (bad). Look back at your notes from the selections, and fill out the chart below. Use a + to indicate that an example of loaded language is positive and a – to show that it is negative. Then complete the sentence starter by circling the word that describes Benchley's bias and explaining how his use of loaded language shows that bias.

Examples of Loaded Language	+ or –	Author's Bias

In this article, Peter Benchley shows a positive/negative bias toward sharks by using loaded language in this way:

_____

_____

_____

Can you tell FACT from fiction?

If you were going to write a story about sharks, which facts from the article would you include? What would you make up? Why?

_____

_____

_____

Vocabulary Practice

Match the vocabulary word with the best example of its meaning.

1. **demonize**   **A.** pretending to reward a child but then taking the reward away

2. **anecdotal**   **B.** saying the opposing team are all cheaters

3. **travesty**   **C.** seeing a cyclist with no helmet and deciding that cyclists don't ride safely

Academic Vocabulary in Writing

The word **domain** (doh MAYN) is a noun that means *a place or field of activity over which a person has control.*

He was so good at basketball that the court was his **domain.**

WRITE IT Shark attacks occur because humans enter the **domain** in which a shark lives. Think about rules that would keep both people and sharks safe. Then write down your rules below. Be sure to use the word **domain** in your answer.

READING 10 Draw conclusions about expository text. **10B** Distinguish factual claims from commonplace assertions and opinions. **11B** Identify rhetorical fallacies in persuasive texts.

_____

_____

_____

Texas Assessment Practice

DIRECTIONS. Use "Great White Sharks" to answer questions 1–4.

1 Which statement is the best example of a fact?

- **A** Fishermen say that there are sharks as large as 36 feet long.
- **B** Great white sharks target and attack humans whenever possible.
- **C** Scientists estimate that populations of some species of sharks have dropped by 80 percent.
- **D** It is wrong that so many sharks do not survive their first year due to a lack of food.

2 Which statement is an opinion?

- **F** Only four species of sharks are known to attack humans with any frequency.
- **G** It would be an ecological tragedy if great white sharks became extinct.
- **H** There are about 400 known species of sharks in the world today.
- **J** Peter Benchley wrote the book *Jaws.*

3 Which statement includes loaded language?

- **A** Great whites are amazing creatures that are in danger of being lost to the world.
- **B** Fisherman and naturalists are seeing fewer great white sharks than in the past.
- **C** Great white sharks have few natural enemies.
- **D** Many ideas about great white sharks have changed in the last 25 years.

4 Which statement is a commonplace assertion?

- **F** Sharks have at times attacked swimmers.
- **G** Sharks seek out swimmers to eat them.
- **H** Great white sharks have been known to eat baby sharks.
- **J** Great white sharks are the most ancient and powerful animals in the sea.

READING 10C Use different organizational patterns as guides for forming an overview of different kinds of expository text.

Like Black Smoke: The Black Death's Journey
Based on the magazine article by Diana Childress

A World Turned Upside Down: How the Black Death Affected Europe
Based on the magazine article by Mary Morton Cowan

How do we fight DISEASE?

People didn't always know what we know today about preventing illness. The articles you are about to read tell about the bubonic plague, a disease that affected so many people during the Middle Ages that it changed a society.

LIST IT What can we do to encourage good health for ourselves and others? List five guidelines that people can follow to prevent diseases from spreading. Be ready to explain why you included each guideline.

Elements of Nonfiction: Cause-and-Effect Pattern of Organization

Nonfiction writers often use patterns of organization (awr guh nih ZAY shuhn), or arrangement, to help explain ideas. One commonly used pattern is **cause-and-effect organization,** which shows connections between events. This pattern

• uses words and phrases such as *caused, because, led to, for this reason, may be due to,* and *as a result* to signal the connection between causes and their effects

• can answer the questions "What happened?" (effect) and "Why did it happen?" (cause), as in the example below

Cause: Why Did It Happen?		Effect: What Happened?
Angel overslept.	→	Angel missed the bus.

As you read these two articles, notice how the writers use cause-and-effect patterns to explain key points.

Guidelines for Health

1. Wash hands often with

   soap and water.

2. _____

   _____

3. _____

   _____

4. _____

   _____

5. _____

   _____

Reading Strategy: Set a Purpose for Reading

Your **purpose for reading** is why you read something. Your main purpose in this lesson is to compare the information in two articles on the same subject. As you read, you will note which of the topics below are covered by each article.

READING 10 Analyze expository text. **RC-7(A)** Establish purposes for reading.

Topics Covered	"Like Black Smoke"	"A World Turned Upside Down"
Agricultural changes		
How disease spread		
Loss of life		
Trade routes		
Worker shortages		

Also make note of other purposes you discover as you read. These additional purposes will help you get the most from your reading.

Vocabulary in Context

Note: Words are listed in the order in which they appear in the articles.

Chronicle (KRON ih kuhl) is a noun that means *a record of events in the order in which they took place*.

  The **chronicle** explains the history of the plague.

Rampage (RAM payj) is a noun that means *a course of wild or dangerous action*.

  The plague's **rampage** across Europe caused many deaths.

Cope (kohp) is a verb that means *to struggle but manage with some success*.

  Villages could not **cope** with losses from the plague.

Recurrence (rih KUR uhns) is a noun that means *the act of happening again*.

  People lived in fear of a **recurrence** of the plague.

Vocabulary Practice

Review the words and sample sentences above. Then use the boldface words to discuss these questions with a partner.

1. How could you **cope** with a **recurrence** of an illness?

2. What kinds of details would you include if you were writing the **chronicle** of a **rampage**?

**Ⓐ SET A PURPOSE FOR
READING**
Read the article's title and
then (circle) its boldfaced
headings. What do you
expect to learn from this
article?

_____

_____

_____

_____

_____

_____

_____

_____

_____

_____

_____

_____

_____

_____

_____

_____

_____

_____

_____

Like Black Smoke
The Black Death's Journey Ⓐ
Diana Childress

BACKGROUND One of the most
important events of the Middle
Ages (A.D. 500 to A.D. 1500) was the
spread of the bubonic plague (boo
BON ik playg), or the Black Death.
People who caught the disease
suffered from fever and painful
swellings. The swellings were
followed by black spots on the skin.
Next came a severe, bloody cough,
and after that—death. At the time,
no one knew what caused the
disease.

"We see death coming into our midst like black
smoke," wrote a Welsh poet in the year 1349.
The plague terrified those who witnessed it. They
knew it was contagious, that people could "catch" it,
but no one could stop it.

Eastern Beginnings

The first sign of the Black Death is in the cemetery
of a town near Lake Issyk-Kul (is ik KUL) in Central
Asia. Many graves there are from the years 1338 and
1339. Three grave markers there provide a clue about
10 why so many people died. The headstones mention
the plague.

Did the Black Death start near this lake? No one knows for sure. Most medieval writers say that the plague began in the East. Historians today agree that the epidemic started in Asia—probably in the area near the border of India and China. In both areas, the plague has existed for a long time in small animals like squirrels and gerbils. **B**

IN OTHER WORDS The Black Death, or the plague, was one of the worst diseases to spread across the world. No one is sure where it started, but some believe it started near a large lake in Asia.

On the Move

How did the disease move from animals to humans?
20 Before the plague happened, earthquakes, floods, and famines destroyed parts of Asia. These disasters may have driven wild animals into villages and towns in search of food. **Fleas** then spread plague germs to rats. When rats died of the plague, their fleas jumped to humans.

The disease could spread more easily if a person's lungs started filling up with plague bacteria. Then, every cough and sneeze spewed germs into the air,
30 spreading the plague directly to others. **C**

If they are not among the lucky few who recover, people and rats soon die of

B LANGUAGE COACH
The word *epidemic* (ep ih DEM ik) in line 15 means "a sudden outbreak of a rapidly spreading disease." The word comes from two Greek **roots:** *epi-*, meaning "upon," and *demos*, meaning "people."

VISUAL VOCABULARY

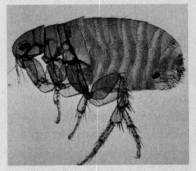

The **flea** (flee) is a small bloodsucking insect with powerful legs that allow it to jump great distances.

C CAUSE AND EFFECT
Use this illustration to help you understand how the plague spread. Place brackets [ ] around the text explanation in lines 19–31 that the illustration pictures.

the plague. However, infected fleas can wait in a rat's nest, barnyard manure, or bedding and clothing for many months without eating. One story of the time tells how four soldiers learned a hard lesson about where fleas could hide. They stole a blanket from an empty
40 house and slept under it. They were dead by morning.

Travelers and ships carried the Black Death in their baggage as they moved across Asia. By the year 1345, the plague had traveled from that Asian lake to cities like Sarai (suh RY) and Astrakhan (AS truh kan) in what is now southwestern Russia. **D**

IN OTHER WORDS Fleas from rats jumped on people and spread the plague. When some people who had the plague coughed or sneezed, they spread the disease.

▶ How did people traveling across Asia spread the disease? Underline the sentence that shows how they helped spread the plague.

From Asia to the Mediterranean

At the time, Italian traders from Genoa and Venice used the port at Kaffa, a city on the Black Sea. Since the mid-1200s, their ships had carried horses, furs, and slaves to Syria and Egypt and silks and spices
50 to Italy.

When the plague began to spread to the area, many of the Europeans tried to escape by sea, but the Black Death sailed with them.

D SET A PURPOSE FOR READING
What topics have been covered so far? In the chart below, place a checkmark ✔ next to any topic covered.

Topics Covered	
Agricultural changes	
How disease spread	
Loss of life	
Trade routes	
Worker shortages	

The next summer, plague broke out in the key port city of Constantinople (kon stan tuh NOH puhl). From there, it spread across the Mediterranean (med ih tuh RAY nee uhn) region. That fall, ships brought the plague to Alexandria, Egypt. Some boats came to Messina, Sicily, with sailors so ill that one <u>chronicle</u>
60 reports that the men had "sickness clinging to their very bones."

The epidemic reached Genoa, Italy, on New Year's Eve 1347 when three ships carrying spices from the East arrived. When the people of Genoa discovered that many of the sailors were sick, they chased the ships from the port. They even fired burning arrows at the ships. However, rats carrying the plague had already jumped off the ships onto the land. PAUSE & REFLECT

IN OTHER WORDS Ships carried fleas and rats infected with the plague from the Black Sea to Italy. Italian ships also sailed to Egypt and Turkey (Constantinople), taking the plague to those places. Townspeople tried to keep the sick sailors out of their towns. They did not know that rats that had jumped from the ship were also sick with the plague.

Following the Trade Routes

Next, the Black Death swept across Europe, North
70 Africa, and the Middle East. After it attacked the seaports, smaller boats carried it up rivers to towns and cities farther from the sea. It could not be stopped.

VOCABULARY
The word **chronicle** (KRON ih kuhl) is a noun that means *a record of events in the order in which they took place.*

PAUSE & REFLECT
<u>Underline</u> the sentences that tell how the people of Genoa reacted to the sick sailors. What does this tell you about Europeans' state of mind as the plague spread?

_____

_____

_____

_____

_____

E CAUSE AND EFFECT

Reread lines 69–77. <u>Underline</u> the sentence that explains how the plague spread inland—to towns not on a seacoast.

Some towns would not let in travelers from infected areas. People learned not to trust "plague goods," items that had come from areas where people were sick, but few noticed the dead rats—and no one thought of the fleas. **E**

Reports of plague in 1348 show how the disease spread. In the east, it hit Jerusalem and nearby cities, and even pilgrims visiting Mecca in Arabia. From Genoa and Venice it moved down the Italian boot toward Florence and Rome. Going west, it struck Marseilles (mahr SAY) in France, Tunis in North Africa, and Barcelona in Spain. By June, the disease hit Paris, causing the French royal family to flee. That summer, it overran Germany, Poland, and Hungary and crossed the sea to southern England.

The Black Death landed in Scandinavia on a ship carrying wool from London to Norway. The ship had

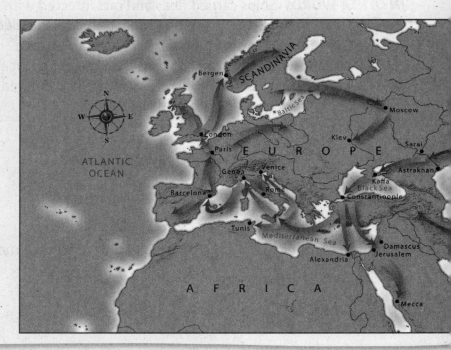

90 run aground near Bergen because all the crew had died. From there, plague spread across Norway, into Sweden, and across the Baltic Sea to Russia.

IN OTHER WORDS From the area around Italy, the Black Death moved across Europe and the Middle East. The plague hit cities in all directions. After starting out near a lake in Asia, it turned back toward Russia.

The Journey Ends

In the year 1350, the plague peaked in Scotland and Scandinavia. The following year, it stretched from Greenland to Yemen, at the tip of the Arabian peninsula. In 1353, it closed in on Moscow, killing both the head of the Russian church and other important Russians.

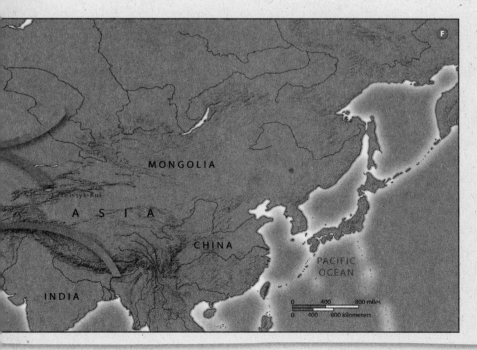

ⓕ CAUSE AND EFFECT
The seven continents are North America, South America, Europe, Asia, Africa, Australia, and Antarctica. On the map, ⟨circle⟩ the names of the continents that were affected by the Black Death. In what direction did the Black Death first travel?

_____

_____

_____

VOCABULARY

The word **rampage** (RAM payj) is a noun that means *a course of wild or dangerous action*.

Ⓖ SET A PURPOSE FOR READING

Reread lines 99–107. Place brackets [ ] around the statistic, or number fact, that shows the extent of the loss of life during the Black Death's spread. Then, look back at the chart you began filling out on page 348. Place checkmarks ✔ for any additional topics covered in this article.

Finally, the Black Death slowed down somewhere 100 in Kiev (KEE ef), having come back almost full circle—near its beginning in Kaffa. During its long, wild **rampage**, between one-third and one-half of the population of Europe, North Africa, and the Middle East died. No natural disaster before or since has caused such a terrible loss of human life over such a large area. It was one of the worst catastrophes in human history. Ⓖ

IN OTHER WORDS The Black Death continued to spread, traveling across Europe and Asia. It killed people in the far north (Scandinavia), on snowy islands (Greenland), and in hot deserts (Yemen). The Black Death finally stopped spreading in Russia. The plague was one of the worst disasters ever.

A WORLD TURNED UPSIDE DOWN: HOW THE BLACK DEATH AFFECTED EUROPE

Based on the magazine article by Mary Morton Cowan

BACKGROUND The spread of the bubonic plague, or the Black Death, not only frightened people, but it also changed the social conditions of the world in which they lived. The following article discusses changes caused by the plague's spread, including its effects on farming, cities, and technology.

Huge changes in population change the way society works. The bubonic plague killed up to one-third of the people in Europe in just four years. It changed Europe's social structure forever. 🄷

People in the Middle Ages lived under the feudal system, which was based on the ownership of land. The rich and powerful nobles lived in castles that had many acres of land around them. The nobles depended on peasants to farm their land. In turn, peasants

10 received protection, shelter, and a small area of land on which to grow their own food. Under this system,

🄷 **SET A PURPOSE FOR READING**

Reread lines 1–4. Paraphrase, or restate in your own words, the main idea that this article will explore.

_____

_____

_____

peasants would be peasants forever and could never become rich.

In the 300 years before the Black Death, the number of people in Europe tripled. More land was farmed, but food was still scarce. Some peasants left the farms, hoping for a better life in the city. The crowded cities, however, could not support so many peasants who had no skills of use in the city.

20 After gunpowder was invented, the lords had found it harder to defend their castles. In some years they had trouble growing food. Many had to <u>cope</u> with the result of a war between France and England. Yet, they remained in control.

Then, without warning, the Black Death swept through western Europe, killing 25 million people. People who survived the plague soon moved in and took over any property they could find. Cities and towns lost people by the thousands. In all, thousands 30 of villages were abandoned, left entirely without people. ❶

VOCABULARY

The word **cope** (kohp) is a verb that means *to struggle but manage with some success.*

<u>Underline</u> the sentence that tells you that the lords' efforts to *cope* with the war were successful.

❶ **CAUSE AND EFFECT**

Reread lines 25–31. <u>Underline</u> the effects of the Black Death that the author describes.

IN OTHER WORDS Before so many people got sick and died from the plague, the people on the bottom of society had no way of getting to the top. The Black Death killed so many people that the poorest people were able to take over rich people's homes, and many villages were left with no one living in them.

Agriculture also faced challenges. The tools and land were there, but now the workers were missing.

Food prices dropped. There was even extra food instead of shortages.

Because workers were scarce, peasants who did not die of the plague now had some control for the first time. Anger among the workers led to violence and revolt in the centuries that followed. The old feudal
40 system began to change.

The lack of skilled workers led to major problems in the economy. Unlike farmers, skilled workers must train for many years to learn their jobs. Now there were not enough people to take the place of skilled workers who died. Because fewer new things were being made, the prices of saddles, farm tools, and other goods increased. **J**

The smaller population did help in some ways. For example, it encouraged new inventions. One of those
50 was the printing press, developed around 1450. Just one printing press replaced hand-copying by hundreds of scribes—people whose job was to copy documents and books. **PAUSE & REFLECT**

The Black Death affected all of medieval society. When the disease returned a few years later, people were even more terrified. Its <u>recurrence</u> in the following decades was enough to keep Europeans in constant fear. A dark mood swept across Europe. Many people began to question the authority and teachings
60 of the church. In fact, they began to have doubts about everything they had believed up until then.

J CAUSE AND EFFECT
Reread lines 36–47. (Circle) the clue words that help you recognize the cause-and-effect pattern of organization.

PAUSE & REFLECT
According to this article, there were some benefits to having a smaller population. What other bad situations, personally or historically, can you think of that led to some good results?

_____

_____

_____

VOCABULARY
The word **recurrence** (rih KUR uhns) is a noun that means *the act of happening again.*

Ⓚ SET A PURPOSE FOR READING

What topics were covered in this article? In the chart below, place a checkmark ✔ next to the topics covered.

Topics Covered	
Agricultural changes	
How disease spread	
Loss of life	
Trade routes	
Worker shortages	

Yet, it was this questioning that led to major changes in religion, art, and science. Without a doubt, the Black Death forever changed Europe's economic and social structure. Ⓚ

IN OTHER WORDS The Black Death allowed some peasants to gain power. However, the peasants were not able to do all the jobs skilled workers had done before.

► Discuss with a partner the changes that happened when the plague came back in the years following its first outbreak.

Elements of Nonfiction: Cause-and-Effect Pattern of Organization

The writers of both articles use cause-and-effect organization to explain key points. To explore the relationship between causes and effects in the articles, complete the chart below.

READING 10C Use different organizational patterns as guides for forming an overview of different kinds of expository text.

"Like Black Smoke: The Black Death's Journey"

Cause: An infected person coughs.	→	Effect:
Cause:	→	Effect: Four soldiers were dead by morning.
Cause: Trade ships with sick sailors visited many ports.	→	Effect:

"A World Turned Upside Down: How the Black Death Affected Europe"

Cause: The Black Death swept through western Europe.	→	Effect:
Cause:	→	Effect: The prices of goods such as farm tools increased.
Cause: People began to question things they used to believe.	→	Effect:

READING 10 Analyze expository text. **RC-7(A)** Establish purposes for reading.

Reading Strategy: Set a Purpose for Reading

Your main purpose for reading was to compare information presented in the two articles. Review your notes about the topics covered in each selection. Then use the Venn diagram below to compare the articles. Place each topic from the charts on pages 348 and 356 where it belongs in the diagram.

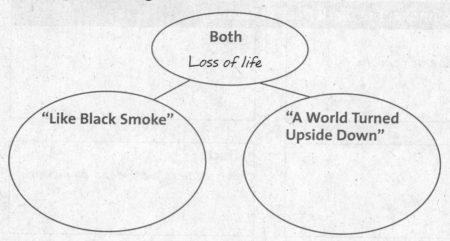

Both

Loss of life

"Like Black Smoke"

"A World Turned Upside Down"

How do we fight DISEASE?

If people in the Middle Ages had known what caused the Black Death, what steps could they have taken to slow its spread? You may find it helpful to look back at the Guidelines for Health that you listed on page 344.

_____

_____

_____

Vocabulary Practice

In each item, circle the letter of the word or phrase that is most similar in meaning to the given vocabulary word. Use a dictionary if you need help.

1. **chronicle: (a)** written history **(b)** clock **(c)** magnifying glass **(d)** photograph

2. **rampage: (a)** bull **(b)** reading lamp **(c)** violence **(d)** peace

3. **cope: (a)** teach **(b)** cry **(c)** move away **(d)** deal with

4. **recurrence: (a)** return **(b)** replacement **(c)** reflection **(d)** regret

Academic Vocabulary in Speaking

The word **hypothesis** (hy POTH uh sis) is a noun that means *a reasonable guess that still needs to be proved true or false.*

> I think I would enjoy studying more if I played music in the background, but I need to test my **hypothesis.**

TURN AND TALK The first article explains how the plague likely moved from humans to animals. With a partner, discuss whether this idea can be proved true or false. Be sure to use the word **hypothesis** in your conversation.

READING 10 Analyze expository text. **10C** Use different organizational patterns as guides for forming an overview of different kinds of expository text.

Texas Assessment Practice

DIRECTIONS Use "Like Black Smoke" and "A World Turned Upside Down" to answer questions 1–6.

1 Where do most historians think the Black Death started?
- **A** Asia
- **B** Africa
- **C** Europe
- **D** South America

2 How did boats spread the disease?
- **F** Those who had died were sent off on boats.
- **G** Boats took the plague from city to city.
- **H** Sailors did not wash their hands often enough.
- **J** Doctors traveled by boats to visit the sick in many countries.

3 Which of the following is not a cause-and-effect signal word or phrase?
- **A** Instead
- **B** Because
- **C** As a result
- **D** For this reason

4 How did the plague reach Scandinavia?
- **F** Wild animals in search of food brought it into villages.
- **G** A Sicilian ship carried it to Genoa.
- **H** Pilgrims carried it with them to Mecca.
- **J** A ship from London brought it to Norway.

5 What happened to food as a result of the plague?
- **A** There wasn't enough farmland left, so there were food shortages.
- **B** Food was of a lower quality, so survivors were unable to eat it.
- **C** There was extra food, and food prices dropped.
- **D** Landowners kept the food to themselves as peasants starved.

6 What was one positive effect of the plague?
- **F** People became more committed to their faith.
- **G** Villages were abandoned.
- **H** The feudal system was strengthened.
- **J** New technologies were developed.

READING 10D Synthesize and make logical connections between ideas within a text and across two or three texts representing similar or different genres. **12** Understand how to glean and use information in procedural texts and documents. **12A** Follow multi-dimensional instructions from text to complete a task, solve a problem, or perform procedures. **12B** Explain the function of the graphical components of a text.

Preparing for Emergencies

- Informational Brochure, page 361
- Poster, page 364
- Supply List, page 366

Background

Every year, millions of people are affected by natural disasters. Would you know what to do if a hurricane or other natural disaster threatened your town? Being able to follow the directions in procedural documents, such as those in this section, will help you stay safe.

Skill Focus: Follow Directions

When you **follow directions** you follow steps in a particular order and pay attention to the details in each step so you can complete a task. Directions may include written text, as well as images such as pictures, diagrams, or maps. A key or legend may be included to explain the meanings of words or symbols used in these images. As you read, you will need to **synthesize,** or put together, these different types of information so you can follow the directions correctly.

As you read directions, following the steps below can help you avoid mistakes or misunderstandings.

Action	Questions	Answers
Scan the title and headings.	What do they tell you the document is about?	*What to do during an emergency*
Read the directions through once.	What is my main task?	
Reread the instructions.	Are there numbered or bulleted lists of steps? What do they tell me about how to do this task?	
Examine any diagrams or other images.	What extra information do they provide?	
Check the key or legend, if there is one.	What does it explain?	

Disaster Strikes
Are You Ready?

Based on the informational brochure

Wherever you live, severe weather conditions may affect you. The following information will help you prepare for the threat of storms, including one of the most powerful, the hurricane. **Ⓐ**

Hurricanes are among the most dangerous of all storms. They bring high winds and waters to many areas along the sea. Their destructive paths can take them far inland, too, where they produce tornadoes and floods and do great damage. Five categories, or
10 levels, tell how dangerous each hurricane is. A storm's category is measured by its wind speed in miles per hour and its storm surge. A storm surge is a rise in

B FOLLOW DIRECTIONS
Reread lines 15–18. With a partner, discuss what you should do to find out what steps to take if a storm is coming.

coastal water, topped by waves. A storm surge can range from 4 feet to more than 20 feet.

To help people decide what they should do and where they should go, weather stations and government agencies use television, radio, and the Internet to broadcast information about how strong a storm is. A hurricane is an intense storm that looks like a spinning 20 cone and has a wind speed of 74 miles per hour or greater. Some hurricanes can have winds as high as 300 miles per hour. **B**

Depending on the path of a storm, its strength, and your location, you might have to seek shelter immediately right where you are. You may have to evacuate, or leave the area, right away and get to a safe place. These public warning terms will help you decide if you are in a situation that calls for quick action.

- **Hurricane Watch** Get prepared. Hurricane conditions may threaten a coastal area within 24–36 hours.

- **Hurricane Warning** Put your action plans in place now to protect people and property. A hurricane is expected near you in 24 hours or less. **C**

Before any weather emergency threatens your community, you should create a family emergency and evacuation plan and prepare an emergency supply kit. Also find out where your school or community shelters are and become familiar with the community evacuation plan.

C **FOLLOW DIRECTIONS**
Reread the bulleted items in lines 29–35. If a hurricane is coming near you in less than 24 hours, what should you do? Bracket [ ] the lines that tell you.

Emergency Procedures

Based on the poster

In some weather-related emergencies, students will be told to go outside and then will be sent home. In other cases, the school will provide shelter for students, staff, and community members.

A shelter can be a school's assembly area, gym, or hallways, or a special tornado shelter. The choice depends on the type of emergency.

D FOLLOW DIRECTIONS
Students in room 105 may take two different routes to leave the main building and gather in the assembly area. Draw a line on the map showing each route to the assembly area.

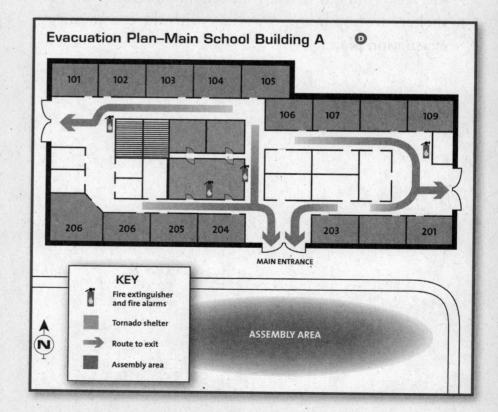

Evacuation Plan–Main School Building A D

| 101 | 102 | 103 | 104 | 105 |

| 106 | 107 | 109 |

| 206 | 206 | 205 | 204 | 203 | 201 |

MAIN ENTRANCE

KEY
- Fire extinguisher and fire alarms
- Tornado shelter
- Route to exit
- Assembly area

N

ASSEMBLY AREA

Evacuation Plan—Main School Building

What to Do in an Emergency

1. Identify all EXIT locations. **E**

10 2. Know the classroom evacuation route and any other routes to get out.

3. Know the locations of fire alarms and fire extinguishers. **F**

4. Know the evacuation routes for students with special needs.

5. Listen for warning sirens and/or announcements.

6. Close classroom windows, blinds, and doors that lead outside.

7. Turn off classroom lights, other electrical
20 equipment, and water faucets.

8. Put on or take along coats as directed.

9. Go to the nearest exit or to the chosen assembly area by following the route marked for your classroom.

PAUSE & REFLECT

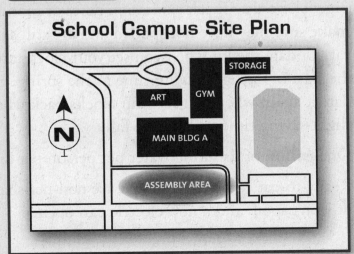

School Campus Site Plan

STORAGE

ART   GYM

N

MAIN BLDG A

ASSEMBLY AREA

E FOLLOW DIRECTIONS

Read step 1 and look at the school map. If you are in room 201, circle the nearest exit to you.

F FOLLOW DIRECTIONS

Remember that you must **synthesize** information by putting together different types of information. Look at the key for the map of the main school building. Find the symbol for the fire extinguisher. On the map, circle the fire extinguisher closest to room 107.

PAUSE & REFLECT

With a partner, discuss how having a map, in addition to written directions, helps you prepare for emergency evacuations at school.

Emergency Supply Kit G
Based on the supply list

Keep enough supplies in your home to survive on your own in a sheltered place for at least three days. If possible, keep these materials in a separate container or special closet you can get to easily. You should tell everyone in your home that these supplies are for emergencies only. Check expiration dates of food items to make sure they have not spoiled and are still safe to eat. Update the kit when you set your clocks ahead at the start of daylight-saving time in the spring, and 10 update it again when you set your clocks back when daylight-saving time ends in the fall.

- One **gallon** of drinking water per person per day

- Ready-to-eat canned foods that are non-perishable, or won't spoil, and a non-electric can opener

G FOLLOW DIRECTIONS
Sometimes you must **synthesize** the information in images and text. Look at the photograph and the title of this selection. With a partner, discuss how these two pieces of information fit together.

VISUAL VOCABULARY

A **gallon** (GAL uhn) is an amount equal to four quarts of liquid.

- First-aid kit

- Flashlight

- Battery-operated AM/FM radio, NOAA[1] all-hazards radio receiver, and extra batteries (You can also buy wind-up radios that do not need batteries.)

20 - Whistle

- Personal hygiene items such as soap, toothbrush and toothpaste

- Phone that does not rely on electricity

- Child-care supplies or other special care items

---

1. **NOAA:** the National Oceanic and Atmospheric Administration, a federal agency that provides updates on severe weather conditions.

READING 10D Synthesize and make logical connections between ideas within a text and across two or three texts representing similar or different genres. **12** Understand how to glean and use information in procedural texts and documents. **12A** Follow multi-dimensional instructions from text to complete a task, solve a problem, or perform procedures. **12B** Explain the function of the graphical components of a text.

Practicing Your Skills: Follow Directions

Now that you have read the selections, complete the chart.

Action	Questions	Answers
"Disaster Strikes: Are You Ready?"		
Scan the title and headings.	What do they tell you the document is about?	*What to do during an emergency*
Read the directions through once.	What is my main task?	
"Emergency Procedures" and "Emergency Supply Kit"		
Reread the instructions.	Are there numbered or bulleted lists of steps? What do they tell me about how to do this task?	
Examine any diagrams or other images.	What extra information do they provide?	
Check the key or legend, if there is one.	What does it explain?	

You have **synthesized** information from three procedural documents to help you know what to do in emergency weather conditions. What if you have to evacuate your home? Using information from the documents, put the steps below in the correct order. On each line, write the number of the step.

_____ Leave your house to go to the shelter.

_____ Close windows, blinds, and exterior doors of your house.

_____ Find at least two exits from your house and the shortest route to the local shelter. Mark them on your maps.

_____ Prepare an emergency supply kit. Find the address of your local community shelter.

_____ Listen to the radio to find out how close the storm is to you and when you need to leave for the shelter.

Academic Vocabulary in Speaking

The word **area** (AIR ee uh) is a noun that means *a field of experience, activity, or knowledge.*

When I found out that I enjoyed drawing, I realized that art is the **area** I most want to study.

TURN AND TALK Suppose a hurricane is threatening your town and your goal is to escape to safety. In addition to an emergency kit and your own clothing, you can take just one other item with you. With a partner, discuss what the item would be and why you would choose it. Be sure to use the word **area** in your conversation.

READING 12 Understand how to glean and use information in procedural texts and documents. **12A** Follow multi-dimensional instructions from text to complete a task, solve a problem, or perform procedures. **12B** Explain the function of the graphical components of a text.

Texas Assessment Practice

DIRECTIONS Use the three selections to answer questions 1–4.

1 How do diagrams or graphics help make directions easier to follow?

- **A** They tell you what needs to be accomplished.
- **B** They show the order of steps.
- **C** They provide a visual guide.
- **D** They explain the dangers of a hurricane.

2 What conditions cause a hurricane watch?

- **F** The intensity of a storm has increased.
- **G** A hurricane may hit within 24–36 hours.
- **H** The path of a hurricane may shift suddenly.
- **J** A hurricane has hit several nearby communities.

3 It is important to reread directions carefully because —

- **A** the directions may include illustrations
- **B** the directions may be complex and have several steps
- **C** the directions may not be detailed
- **D** you will probably have to explain the directions to someone else

4 When you synthesize, you —

- **F** identify headings and graphics
- **G** apply the writer's ideas to your own experiences
- **H** restate main ideas
- **J** put together information from several sources

READING 11 Analyze persuasive text.

Pro Athletes' Salaries Aren't Overly Exorbitant
Based on the editorial by Mark Singletary

Do Professional Athletes Get Paid Too Much?
Based on the article by Justin Hjelm

Are people paid FAIRLY?

A first-year New York City police officer earns about $45,000 a year. The president of the United States earns $400,000 a year. Many professional athletes receive more than $2 million a year—sometimes much more. Is this fair? In these newspaper articles, two writers give different opinions about the huge salaries that many professional athletes make.

TURN AND TALK With a group of classmates, discuss the salaries listed above. Then, on the lines at left, write down how important you consider the work done by police officers, the president, and athletes. Who *should* earn the most money?

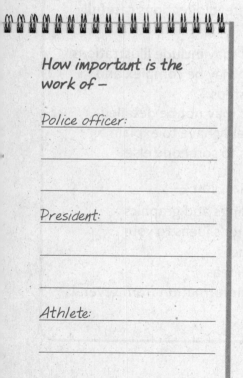

How important is the work of –

Police officer:

President:

Athlete:

Elements of Nonfiction: Argument

An **argument** takes a position on an issue or problem and supports that position with reasons and evidence. Strong arguments have the following elements:

- **Claim:** a clear statement of the writer's main idea or position

- **Support:** the reasons and evidence that back up the claim

- **Counterarguments:** arguments that answer the possible disagreements of someone with an opposing or different view

As you read, identify these elements in each argument.

Reading Skill: Evaluate Reasoning

A **rhetorical fallacy** (rih TOR ih kuhl FAL uh see) is a false or misleading statement that can weaken an argument. One rhetorical fallacy is **stereotyping**—thinking about a group of people as if they were all alike. Stereotyping can create false judgments based on where people are from, what they believe, or how they look. You can use a chart like the one below to keep track of stereotypes you notice as you read.

READING 11B Identify such rhetorical fallacies as stereotyping in persuasive texts.

Example of Stereotyping	Explanation
"I think pro athletes are selfish."	A false judgment based on the actions of a few athletes

Vocabulary in Context

Note: Words are listed in the order in which they appear in the selections.

Brevity (BREV uh tee) is a noun that means *shortness*.
Athletes need to make a lot of money in a short time because of the **brevity** of their careers.

Compensation (kahm pen SAY shuhn) is a noun that means *payment*.
Compensation should be higher for the very best athletes.

Appalling (uh PAWL ing) is an adjective that means *outrageous* or *terrible*.
The outrageously high salaries of some athletes are **appalling**.

Vocabulary Practice

Review the words and sample sentences above. Then, with a partner, discuss how you could complete each of the following sentences.

The **brevity** of the movie was disappointing because . . .

My **compensation** for babysitting was too low because . . .

That meal was **appalling** because . . .

SET A PURPOSE FOR READING
Read "Pro Athletes' Salaries Aren't Overly Exorbitant" to learn how the author supports his opinion.

Ⓐ ARGUMENT
The writer's claim is stated in the title. Restate the claim in your own words.

_____

_____

_____

_____

_____

Ⓑ EVALUATE REASONING
Reread lines 1–4. Then, underline the stereotype the writer uses. With a partner, discuss whether you think this use of a stereotype weakens the writer's argument.

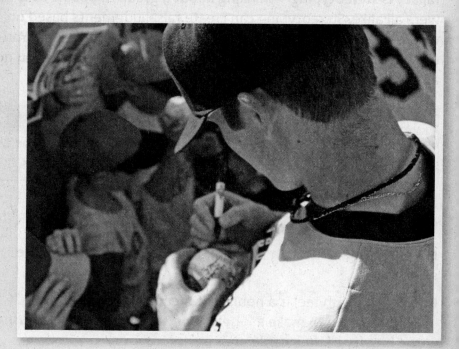

Pro Athletes' Salaries Aren't Overly Exorbitant[1] Ⓐ

Based on the editorial by MARK SINGLETARY

BACKGROUND Professional athletes in the U.S. are often paid much more than other professionals, including doctors and lawyers. The writer of this article supports the large salaries of pro athletes. He thinks that their high salaries are not such a bad thing.

These days, I'm seeing the salaries of professional athletes in a more positive light. I think pro athletes are selfish. And because of their huge salaries, in time professional sports will have to be reorganized. Ⓑ

---

1. **exorbitant** (ig ZOR bih tuhnt): much greater than is usual.

But the players are no more selfish than the owners who pay the salaries. And the owners are no more selfish than the television and radio stations that pay so much for the rights to broadcast games. Still, pro sports work best when what people will pay to view 10 or hear games matches the value of what athletes and owners have to sell. **C**

_____

IN OTHER WORDS The writer says that pro athletes, team owners, and those who broadcast professional sports all want the money that fans are willing to spend.

_____

It would be awesome to train and play on a major league team. But at some point the fun might turn into work. **D**

I'd probably think that I deserved the same pay as my teammates. And if I was a star player, I might end up asking for a little more than the average player. After all, I might think that fans were coming mainly to see me play.

20 Also, I would notice that television stations pay huge amounts to show my games. And I would see that companies want to spend money advertising where my team plays.

One argument for paying huge salaries to athletes is the <u>brevity</u>, or shortness, of their careers. One injury could end an athlete's career.

C ARGUMENT

Reread lines 5–11. What counterargument does the writer make about the players' selfishness?

_____

_____

_____

_____

_____

D LANGUAGE COACH

The use of *awesome* in line 12 is a **colloquialism** (kuh LOH kwee uhl izm). A colloquialism is a word or phrase that is conversational in tone, something you would use when talking with a friend. Colloquialisms are common in informal speech and writing.

VOCABULARY

The word **brevity** (BREV uh tee) is a noun that means *shortness*. Circle the word in line 26 that relates directly to the word *brevity*.

VOCABULARY
The word **compensation**
(kahm pen SAY shuhn) is a
noun that means *payment*.

**E EVALUATE
   REASONING**
Reread lines 37–41. Do you
see a possible stereotype? Fill
in the chart below to record
this example.

Example of Stereotyping

Explanation

Fans are important to the success of the ball club.
My teammates and I are responsible for winning
fans. If I am a star, I can assume the fans come to see
30 me play.

When the fans come to see the stars perform, the
team's value increases. I also know how much I make
and how that relates to others that play my game.

So, even though I may love the game, and playing
the game is huge **compensation**, I want things to be
fair.

IN OTHER WORDS The writer understands why an athlete
would want at least the same salary as other team members.
He also understands why star players would want more
money.

► Discuss with a partner why star athletes might feel that
they deserve more money than their teammates.

Being fair means that the athletes deserve what
the fans are willing to pay. The owners probably
don't care what the athletes make. They usually
40 pass the cost on to ticket buyers and businesses
that sponsor teams. **E**

It seems fair to pass along as much money
as possible to the players who make the games

entertaining. The smartest people in pro sports are those earning as much and passing along as much money as possible. They also are looking toward the future.

So, everyone benefits.

IN OTHER WORDS The writer says that athletes should be paid as much as fans are willing to pay them. Because pro sports is a business, people should take in as much money as they can. But they should pass along as much as they can, too.

Ⓕ ARGUMENT
The title of this article asks a question. Circle the writer's one-word answer in line 1. Then, restate the writer's claim in your own words below.

_____
_____
_____
_____
_____
_____
_____

DO PROFESSIONAL ATHLETES GET PAID TOO MUCH?

Based on the article by JUSTIN HJELM

BACKGROUND In this article, Justin Hjelm argues that professional athletes are paid too much for what they do. He suggests that it's society's fault.

YES. For nearly a hundred years, pro athletes have Ⓕ demanded and received larger salaries than most other people of their time. What's disturbing and wrong today is that even average players make huge amounts of money.

In 1979, baseball pitcher Nolan Ryan was the first athlete to get a $1-million-a-year contract. And now, just 25 years later, a $1-million contract offer is an insult.

10 Professional athletes have made too much money for too long now. Today, pro athletes are among the wealthiest people in America.

Sports are entertainment. It's sad that pro athletes can make over a million dollars a year while teachers, police officers, and fire fighters make much, much less.

Entertainment is a necessary thing, but it is not as important as many other jobs. What kind of message are we sending our children with these backward
20 values? **PAUSE & REFLECT**

PAUSE & REFLECT
Reread lines 13–20. Then, with a partner, discuss what the writer means by the phrase "backward values."

IN OTHER WORDS The writer argues that pro athletes make too much money for what they do. He says this is especially true when we compare their jobs to more important jobs.

For young people, sports seem like the better and easier career path. Would a child rather play basketball and make millions or go to school for years and end up making $50,000 a year?

Those who disagree say that it is not that simple. Becoming a pro athlete is very difficult. But fewer and fewer kids realize this.

The NBA draft[1] is proof of this. Ten years ago, a high school player rarely skipped college. Now, lots of
30 high schoolers try to be drafted. These players lose the chance to go to college. They struggle for years to get on a professional team. After that, without a college education, they struggle to find decent jobs. **G**

G ARGUMENT
In line 26, the writer claims that it is "very difficult" to become a pro athlete. Reread lines 28–33. Then underline the sentences that support that claim.

---

1. **NBA draft:** the process by which teams in the National Basketball Association select, or draft, players.

VOCABULARY

The word **appalling** (uh PAWL ing) is an adjective that means *outrageous* or *terrible*.

⊕ EVALUATE REASONING

What stereotype does the example of Kenny Anderson support? Do you think all athletes have this attitude?

_____

_____

_____

_____

_____

_____

Also troubling are the egos[2] of the athletes who get these giant paychecks. Kenny Anderson, who once played for the Boston Celtics, complained that he could not afford the insurance on his eight cars. This attitude is <u>appalling</u>. ⊕

Athletes are paid far too much, but I believe
40 it's our fault. We put too much importance on entertainment. Salaries in the sporting world were once carefully controlled. Today, greed and our thirst for entertainment are the main reasons pro athletes are paid too much.

IN OTHER WORDS We are sending the wrong message to young people. They want the huge salaries of pro athletes, but playing professional sports is not a realistic career for most people.

▶ With a partner, discuss how we may be at fault for the large salaries of professional athletes.

---

2. **egos** (EE gohz): here, inflated sense of self-importance.

Elements of Nonfiction: Argument

Singletary and Hjelm make very different arguments about how much professional athletes should be paid. In the chart below, list two more examples each writer uses to support his claim. Then, write a sentence or two explaining which writer you think makes a better argument.

READING 11 Analyze persuasive text.

ELEMENTS OF AN ARGUMENT	
Singletary	**Hjelm**
Claim: *Athletes deserve as much as fans are willing to pay.*	**Claim:** *Athletes are paid far too much.*
Support: *Television stations pay huge amounts to show games with certain players.* _____ _____ _____ _____	**Support:** *Entertainment is not as important as many other jobs.* _____ _____ _____ _____
Counterarguments: *Pro athletes are selfish, but they're no more selfish than team owners and television stations.*	**Counterarguments:** *Some argue that it's not that easy to succeed in sports.*

Which writer do you think makes a better argument? Why?

_____

_____

_____

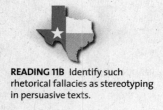

READING 11B Identify such rhetorical fallacies as stereotyping in persuasive texts.

Reading Skill: Evaluate Reasoning

As you read the articles, you may have noticed one or more rhetorical fallacies. Look back at your notes, and find examples of stereotypes. Then, in the chart below, write down each example, an explanation of why it is a stereotype, and how the writer could reword the statement to strengthen the argument. One example is completed for you.

Example of Stereotyping: *"I think pro athletes are selfish."*	Explanation: *A false judgment based on the actions of a few athletes*
Possible Rewording: *Some pro athletes may be selfish, but they aren't the only ones.*	
Example of Stereotyping:	**Explanation:**
Possible Rewording:	

Are people paid FAIRLY?

TURN AND TALK With a partner, discuss several jobs and whether you think people are paid fairly in those jobs. Take a position on how you think salaries should be decided.

Vocabulary Practice

Write *true* or *false* next to each statement.

_____ 1. An **appalling** situation is one that shocks and upsets you.

_____ 2. If you do volunteer work, you don't expect **compensation**.

_____ 3. The author of a 3,400-page book is probably known for her **brevity**.

Academic Vocabulary in Speaking

The word **objective** (uhb JEK tiv) is a noun that means *a goal* or *something that is aimed for or worked toward*.

Manuel studied hard because his **objective** was to get a full scholarship to college.

TURN AND TALK Do you think getting paid a high salary is the main **objective** of most professional athletes? Discuss your thoughts with a partner, and be sure to use the word **objective** in your discussion.

READING 3 Analyze genre in different cultural and contemporary contexts.
8 Analyze how an author's use of language suggests mood.

Texas Assessment Practice

DIRECTIONS Use both of the selections to answer questions 1–6.

1 A writer's main idea or position is called —

- **A** a claim
- **B** support
- **C** a point
- **D** a counterargument

2 Why should writers avoid using stereotypes?

- **F** Stereotypes are very persuasive.
- **G** No one will believe a stereotype.
- **H** Stereotypes will confuse readers.
- **J** Stereotypes can cause the subject to be judged unfairly.

3 What does Singletary believe about the future of professional sports?

- **A** Pro athletes will be paid less in the future.
- **B** Professional sports will become more popular.
- **C** People will stop going to games because of rising costs.
- **D** Professional sports will have to change or go out of business.

4 What counterargument does Singletary offer to oppose the idea that pro athletes are selfish?

- **F** Athletes are not selfish, but smart.
- **G** Athletes have to be selfish to protect their income.
- **H** Athletes are selfish only because fans allow them to be.
- **J** Athletes are no more selfish than team owners or television networks.

5 What message does Hjelm say athletes' salaries send to young people today?

- **A** Stay in school.
- **B** Money is all-important.
- **C** Athletes are selfish and overpaid.
- **D** Everyone can become a pro athlete.

6 According to Hjelm, who is partly to blame for athletes' huge salaries?

- **F** Fans
- **G** Owners
- **H** Television networks
- **J** Teammates

READING 11 Analyze persuasive text. **11B** Identify rhetorical fallacies in persuasive texts.

Why We Shouldn't Go to Mars
Based on the magazine article by **Gregg Easterbrook**

Do we have our PRIORITIES straight?

We all have a limited amount of time each day. And most people have a limited amount of money. What we spend our time and money on reflects our priorities, or what we consider most important. Setting the right priorities can be difficult.

TURN AND TALK On the lines at left, list several tasks that you have to do on an average school day. Then, work with a partner to decide which item on both of your lists is the most important task. Be sure to provide strong reasons for your choice.

Things I need to do:

1. Homework
2. _____
3. _____
4. _____
5. _____
6. _____
7. _____
8. _____

Elements of Nonfiction: Counterargument

A strong counterargument is an important part of any argument. A **counterargument** guesses what "the other side" might say and answers possible objections with reasons and evidence.

As this article's title suggests, the author believes that sending astronauts to Mars is a mistake. Rather than ignore those who disagree with him, he states his opponents' views and then tells why he disagrees. He uses facts and examples to make his points. As you read, search for examples of counterarguments.

Counterargument Technique		
Clearly state the opposing view	→	Show why that view is wrong using reasons and evidence
A journey to Mars would be like Lewis and Clark's journey of discovery.		*Lewis and Clark were going to a place where they knew people already lived.*

Reading Skill: Paraphrase

Easterbrook supports his argument with scientific facts. To make sure you understand his ideas you can **paraphrase** them, or restate them in your own words. A good paraphrase includes all the main ideas and supporting details of the original source. As you read, you'll be asked to paraphrase.

Passage from Article	Paraphrase
"Proponents of space exploration mock the mention of technical issues or the argument that needs on Earth should come first."	People who want to explore space make fun of the possible problems or the idea that Earth's needs are more important.

Vocabulary in Context

Note: Words are listed in the order they appear in the article.

Exhilarating (eg ZIHL uh ray ting) is an adjective that means *exciting* or *thrilling*.

> Our field trip to the space center was **exhilarating.**

Tantalizing (TAN tuh ly zihng) is an adjective that means *tempting but out of reach*.

> Space travel has long been a **tantalizing** idea for humans.

Rationality (rash uh NAL uh tee) is a noun that means *reasonableness* or *logic*.

> The key to a good experiment is **rationality:** Does it make sense?

Vocabulary Practice

Review the vocabulary words and their meanings. Then, circle *t* or *f* to identify each statement as true or false. Explain your answers.

1. An exciting thrill ride is usually **exhilarating.** t/f

_____

2. A dessert would be **tantalizing** if you wanted to eat it but couldn't. t/f

_____

3. One sign of **rationality** is a person's reliance on emotions. t/f

_____

SET A PURPOSE FOR READING
Read this magazine article to discover the author's opinion about sending astronauts to Mars.

WHY WE SHOULDN'T GO TO MARS

BASED ON THE
MAGAZINE ARTICLE BY
GREGG EASTERBROOK

BACKGROUND In 2004, President George W. Bush announced a new space program that would send people to Mars. This article responds to the president's announcement.

Ⓐ COUNTERARGUMENT
Reread the first paragraph. Circle the argument that President Bush makes for exploring Mars. Reread the second paragraph. Underline each of the counterarguments that the writer makes in response.

President George W. Bush announced his desire to send humans to Mars by talking about Meriwether Lewis and William Clark's exploration of new lands.[1]

Yet there are important differences between Lewis and Clark's expedition and a Mars mission. First, Lewis and Clark were headed to a place where people could live; thousands were already living there. Second, Lewis and Clark were *certain* to discover valuable places and things. Third, the Lewis and Clark
10 venture cost next to nothing by today's standards. In 1989 NASA estimated it would cost over $400 billion to send people to Mars. That would cost $600 billion today. A Mars mission might cost more than any undertaking besides war in U.S. history. Ⓐ

---

1. **Meriwether Lewis and William Clark:** American men who explored unmapped land west of the Mississippi River beginning in 1804.

IN OTHER WORDS President George W. Bush announced a plan to send humans to Mars, just as Lewis and Clark had been sent to explore the west.

The thought of travel to Mars is exciting and **exhilarating**. Surely men and women will someday walk on that planet and make wonderful discoveries.

But just because Mars is a **tantalizing** destination doesn't mean the journey makes sense. And Mars as a
20 destination for people makes no sense at all today.

Sending spacecraft to low-Earth orbit[2] is very expensive today. Finding the money to launch a spacecraft for a Mars mission—would require cutting other important programs or raising taxes. **B**

Once on Mars, scientists could do little more than analyze rocks and be amazed by looking at the sky of another world. Yet rocks can be studied by the instruments aboard automated probes without risk to human life, at a fraction of the cost of sending people.
30 President Bush listed some major achievements of space exploration: pictures of the rings of Saturn, evidence of water on Mars, and the study of Martian soil. All of these came from automated probes or space telescopes. A plan to send people to Mars might actually lead to less money for spacecraft operated without people on board. And yet that's the one aspect of space exploration that's working really well.

Rather than spend hundreds of billions of dollars to go to Mars using today's technology, why not take

The word **exhilarating** (ehg ZIHL uh ray tihng) is an adjective that means *exciting or thrilling*.

The word **tantalizing** (TAN tuh ly zihng) is an adjective that means *tempting but out of reach*.

B **COUNTERARGUMENT**
Reread lines 15–24. (Circle) the word that shows that the writer is making a counterargument. Then, in your own words, state his counterargument below. Be sure to include the facts and evidence the author provides.

Counterargument

---

2. **low-Earth orbit:** a region about 200 to 500 miles above Earth, the easiest area to reach in space.

40 ten or twenty years to develop better technology? If we could launch spacecraft affordably and speed up the long, slow trip to Mars, then stepping onto the Red Planet might become a reality. Mars will still be there when the technology is ready.

IN OTHER WORDS The idea of traveling to Mars is exciting, but it doesn't make sense right now. The best way to explore Mars is by using probes.

Proponents of space exploration mock the mention of technical issues or the argument that needs on Earth should come first. But they are wrong. The first concern is **rationality**. The second is setting priorities. Those who support sending people to Mars
50 should raise private funds and put together their own expedition. If they expect taxpayers to provide the money, then they must argue their case against the nation's many other needs. And the case for using money to send people to Mars—when weighed against the needs for healthcare, education, the reduction of poverty, and support of the military—is weak. **C**

The urge to explore is part of what makes us human. Dreams must be checked by reality, however. For the moment, going to Mars is unrealistic.

IN OTHER WORDS Supporters of a Mars mission should realize that taxpayers don't view it as a high priority.

The word **rationality** (RASH uh NAL uh tee) is a noun that means *reasonableness* or *logic*.

C PARAPHRASE
Reread lines 45–56. In the space below, paraphrase this paragraph.

My Paraphrase

Elements of Nonfiction: Counterargument

Reread lines 21–38. Some people say that it's necessary to send astronauts to Mars. Easterbrook, however, disagrees. Use the chart to show Easterbrook's counterargument.

READING 11 Analyze persuasive text. **11B** Identify rhetorical fallacies in persuasive texts.

Counterargument Technique		
Opposing View	→	**Objections, Reasons and Evidence**
Sending astronauts on a mission to Mars is necessary to make achievements in space exploration.	→	

Do you find Easterbrook's counterargument convincing? Why or why not?

_____

_____

_____

_____

_____

_____

_____

READING 11 Analyze persuasive text. **11B** Identify rhetorical fallacies in persuasive texts.

Reading Skill: Paraphrase

Review the article and the notes you made in the margins. Then, paraphrase the argument against sending astronauts to explore Mars that you find the most convincing.

_____

_____

_____

_____

Do we have our PRIORITIES straight?

Where do you think our priority should be—on a mission to Mars, or on something else? On what should our nation concentrate money and effort? Why?

_____

_____

_____

_____

_____

Vocabulary Practice

Circle the letter of the item most closely associated with each vocabulary word.

1. **tantalizing: (a)** an old pair of tennis shoes **(b)** the smell of chocolate-chip cookies baking

2. **exhilarating: (a)** a fast run **(b)** a boring chore

3. **rationality: (a)** a letter from an old friend **(b)** an explanation of a science experiment

Academic Vocabulary in Speaking

The word **hypothesis** (hy POTH ih sis) means *a reasonable guess that still needs to be proved true or false.*

> Sari planned to test the **hypothesis** that adding salt to water caused it to boil faster.

TURN AND TALK What is a hypothesis that supporters of sending astronauts to Mars might make? Discuss what astronauts might find with a partner. Be sure to use the word **hypothesis** in your discussion.

Texas Assessment Practice

DIRECTIONS Use "Why We Shouldn't Go to Mars" to answer questions 1–5.

1 A counterargument is —

- **A** a restatement of the facts
- **B** a question about an issue
- **C** an opinion
- **D** a response to an opposing view

2 A paraphrase should include —

- **F** your opinion about the information
- **G** the main ideas and details of the original passage
- **H** more details than the original source
- **J** only the most important ideas

3 Comparing the Mars mission to Lewis and Clark's expedition is misleading because —

- **A** both involve travel to an unexplored place
- **B** both require extremely long and dangerous journeys
- **C** Lewis and Clark's expedition was inexpensive; a Mars mission will be very costly
- **D** Lewis and Clark were asked to explore a region by the president; a Mars mission would not have presidential approval

4 A reason Easterbrook gives for opposing a mission to Mars is —

- **F** the money needed would be better spent on Earth
- **G** there are many areas still to be explored on Earth
- **H** it makes more sense to provide funding for a space station
- **J** scientists have already learned all that they can about Mars

5 Which is the best paraphrase of the article's final sentence?

- **A** Sending astronauts to Mars will never work.
- **B** The dream of going to Mars will be realized at any moment.
- **C** Right now, the idea of traveling to Mars doesn't make sense.
- **D** People who might go to Mars can't hope to find anything there.

READING 11A Analyze the structure of the central argument in contemporary policy speeches and identify the different types of evidence used to support the argument.

Remarks at the Dedication of the Aerospace Medical Health Center

Based on the speech by John F. Kennedy

What INSPIRES people?

Sometimes a leader comes along who really inspires people to think of new ways to make life better. This speech is by one such leader—President John F. Kennedy.

TURN AND TALK Think about people who have inspired you to make a change in your life. At left, make a list of these people. Then, with a partner, discuss one person and how he or she has inspired you.

Elements of Nonfiction: Argument in Speech

This speech is a **policy speech** (POL ih see speech). Policy speeches argue in favor of needed guidelines or rules. In this speech, President Kennedy presents an argument, or opinion. Then, he supports his argument by giving reasons and by providing evidence in the form of facts and examples.

As you read Kennedy's speech, look for these elements:

Elements of the Speech	Ask Yourself . . .
Main Argument	What plan of action does Kennedy recommend?
Reasons	What reasons does Kennedy give for his plan?
Evidence	What facts and examples does Kennedy use to strengthen his reasons?

Who has inspired me?

_____

_____

_____

_____

_____

_____

_____

_____

Reading Skill: Identify Persuasive Techniques

As you read this speech, look for **persuasive techniques** (puhr SWAY siv tek NEEKS) that Kennedy uses. A persuasive technique is the way someone tries to convince you of something. One example is included below.

READING 11A Analyze the structure of the central argument in contemporary policy speeches and identify the different types of evidence used to support the argument.

Persuasive Techniques	Examples from Speech
appeals to strong feelings	"We stand on the edge of a great new era of achievement and challenge."
appeals to the need to belong	

Vocabulary in Context

Note: Words are listed in the order in which they appear in the speech.

Endeavor (en DEV er) is a noun that means *an attempt to succeed*.

A recent **endeavor** of scientists is to explore Mars.

Disorientation (dis or ee en TAY shuhn) is a noun that means *a loss of direction, location, or time*.

Disorientation can make some people sick.

Impetus (IM pih tuhs) is a noun that means *a force that makes something happen*.

The speech was an **impetus** to more exploration in space.

Tedious (TEE dee uhs) is an adjective that means *long and tiring*.

Space exploration can be a very **tedious** task.

Vocabulary Practice

Review the words and sample sentences above. For each group of words below, circle the synonym of the blue Vocabulary word.

1. endeavor   failure   try

2. disorientation   confusion   clarity

3. impetus   energy   calm

4. tedious   exciting   boring

SET A PURPOSE FOR READING
Read this speech to find out what one American president thought about the importance of space exploration and research.

VOCABULARY

The word **endeavor** (en DEV er) is a noun that means *an attempt to succeed.*

VISUAL VOCABULARY

A **pioneer** is someone who is the first to explore a new place.

Ⓐ **LANGUAGE COACH**
Speeches often include **repetition**, or the repeating of words. Speakers use repetition to make their ideas easy to remember. Notice how Kennedy uses the word *era* three times in lines 6–9.

Remarks at the Dedication of the Aerospace Medical Health Center

Based on the speech by
President John F. Kennedy

BACKGROUND After becoming president in 1961, John F. Kennedy promised to increase America's knowledge about space. In 1963, Kennedy gave the following speech.

Mr. Secretary, Governor, Mr. Vice President, Senator, Members of the Congress, members of the military, ladies and gentlemen:

For more than 3 years I have spoken about the New Frontier. The New Frontier refers to this Nation's place in history. We stand on the edge of a great new era of achievement and challenge. It is an era which calls for action and the best efforts in the human <u>endeavor</u>. It is an era for explorers and **pioneers**. Ⓐ

10   Today, I honor an outstanding group, the people who operate the Brooks Air Force Base School of Aerospace Medicine and the Aerospace Medical Center. It is fitting and right that San Antonio should be the site of this center. It was here that Sidney Brooks,[1] whose memory we honor

---

1. **Sidney Brooks:** a young flyer who was killed in a training accident.

today, and many pioneers of the air trained. And history is being made every day by the men and women of the Aerospace Medical Center. **B**

IN OTHER WORDS America faces a new frontier, a new challenge: space research. San Antonio, Texas, is an excellent place for the Medical Center.

Many Americans think that space research has no value. Nothing could be further from the truth. . . .
20 Research in space medicine promises great benefits. Medicine in space is going to make our lives healthier and happier here on earth. **C**

I give you three examples: first, medical space research may help us better understand man's relationship to his environment. We can learn about <u>disorientation</u> and about changes in people's bodies. Space studies also can help us reduce air pollution in cities.

And second, medical space research can completely
30 change modern medicine. New devices created for astronauts will improve medical equipment. Heart patients, those who suffer from eye defects, and critically ill patients may all benefit from instruments developed through space research.

And third, medical space research may lead to new protections from dangerous materials. Astronauts will need new devices to protect them from radiation. These devices can change the practice of medicine in a major way. **D**

40 This center has the labs, the talent, and the resources to give new <u>impetus</u> to research. But I am not saying that medicine is the only reason for our space program.

Monitor Your Comprehension

B IDENTIFY PERSUASIVE TECHNIQUES
Reread lines 10–17. Put brackets [ ] around any sentences that might inspire people to want to belong to a group.

C ARGUMENT IN SPEECH
Reread lines 18–22. What **argument**, or claim, does Kennedy make in these lines? Discuss your answer with a partner.

VOCABULARY
The word **disorientation** (dis or ee en TAY shuhn) is a noun that means *a loss of direction, location, or time.*

D ARGUMENT IN SPEECH
In lines 23–39, what three examples does Kennedy give to support his claim that medicine in space will make life better? Put checkmarks ✔ beside the sentences that tell you.

VOCABULARY
The word **impetus** (IM pih tuhs) is a noun that means *a force that makes something happen.*

IN OTHER WORDS Research in space medicine will benefit everyone. This research can help scientists better understand the environment and can change medicine for the better.

The space program stands on its own as a part of our nation's strength. When our Saturn C-1 rocket booster is launched in December, it will carry the largest payload[2] that any country has ever sent into space.

I think the United States should be a leader in space research. We have a long way to go. Many years of long, <u>tedious</u> work lie ahead. There will be setbacks and
50 disappointments. There will be pressures to do less in this area, and temptations to do something else that is easier. But the research here must go on. This space effort must go on. That much we can say with confidence and certainty.

The Irish writer Frank O'Connor tells about walking across the countryside when he was a boy. When he and his friends came to an orchard wall that seemed too high to climb, they tossed their hats over the wall. Then they had no choice but to follow their hats.

This Nation has tossed its hat over the wall of space,
60 and we have no choice but to follow it. Whatever the difficulties, we will overcome them. Whatever the dangers, we must guard against them. With the help of this Aerospace Medical Center and others who work in the space endeavor, we will climb this wall—and explore the wonders on the other side. **E**

Thank you.

IN OTHER WORDS The United States must be a leader in space research, no matter how difficult it may be.

► With a partner, paraphrase, or put into your own words, what Kennedy says in lines 59–65.

2. **payload:** the load, such as equipment, carried by a rocket or other vehicle.

VOCABULARY

The word **tedious** (TEE dee uhs) is an adjective that means *long and tiring*.

What does Kennedy say will be *tedious*? ⟨Circle⟩ the answer.

E IDENTIFY PERSUASIVE TECHNIQUES

Reread lines 59–65. Identify one phrase that you think might cause people to feel proud. Write this phrase in the chart below.

Persuasive Techniques	Examples from Speech
appeals to strong feelings	

Elements of Nonfiction: Argument in Speech

Look back at how Kennedy builds his argument. Reread lines 18–38 from the speech. Then, in your own words, list each element.

READING 11A Analyze the structure of the central argument in contemporary policy speeches and identify the different types of evidence used to support the argument.

Elements of the Speech	Example in My Own Words
Main Argument (lines 18–19)	
Reason Given to Support the Argument	
Examples Given to Support the Reason	1. 2. 3.

Does President Kennedy's speech persuade you that America should continue space research? Why or why not?

_____

_____

_____

_____

What INSPIRES people?

Think back to Kennedy's speech and to your discussion on page 390. How might *you* inspire someone? Describe how you could inspire someone with words, actions, or both.

_____

_____

_____

_____

READING 11A Analyze the structure of the central argument in contemporary policy speeches and identify the different types of evidence used to support the argument.

Reading Skill: Identify Persuasive Techniques

In addition to structuring a strong argument, Kennedy uses persuasive techniques in this speech. Two techniques he uses are emotional appeals (appeals to feelings) and appeals to the need to belong to a group. Which technique do you think is more powerful? Explain.

_____

_____

_____

_____

_____

_____

Vocabulary Practice

Answer each question and give reasons for your response using the vocabulary words in bold.

1. What **endeavor** is worth your time and effort?

_____

_____

2. If someone has a feeling of **disorientation**, how does he or she feel?

_____

_____

3. What might be one **impetus** for making good grades?

_____

_____

4. Would you rather have a **tedious** experience or an ordinary one?

_____

_____

Academic Vocabulary in Writing

The word **resolve** (rih ZOLV) is a verb that means *to figure out, solve, or make clear.*

When you immediately **resolve** problems, life can be much simpler and easier for you.

WRITE IT Leaders, like President Kennedy, must **resolve** all kinds of issues or problems. What are some issues that you would like to **resolve**? On the lines below, write down one issue and a possible way to **resolve** it. Be sure to use the word **resolve** in your writing.

_____

_____

_____

READING 11A Analyze the structure of the central argument in contemporary policy speeches and identify the different types of evidence used to support the argument.

Texas Assessment Practice

DIRECTIONS Use "Remarks at the Dedication of the Aerospace Medical Health Center" to answers questions 1–5.

1 A policy speech tries to —
- **A** inspire people
- **B** entertain people
- **C** argue for rules
- **D** make people think

2 One persuasive technique used in Kennedy's speech is —
- **F** appeals to emotions
- **G** appeals to arguments
- **H** appeals to ideas
- **J** appeals to opinions

3 Kennedy's main argument is that America should —
- **A** do more research before exploring space
- **B** end all space exploration
- **C** always copy what other countries are doing in space exploration
- **D** continue to be the leader in space exploration

4 To support his argument, Kennedy uses all of the following except —
- **F** facts
- **G** statistics
- **H** examples
- **J** reasons

5 What does President Kennedy most likely want listeners to feel when he says, *Heart patients, those who suffer from eye defects, and critically ill patients may all benefit from instruments developed through space research?*
- **A** He wants listeners to feel that there is hope for these people.
- **B** He wants listeners to feel sorry for these people.
- **C** He wants listeners to feel angry that these people are not being helped.
- **D** He wants listeners to feel happy that they don't have problems like these.

Resources

Glossary of Academic Vocabulary in English & Spanish

The Glossary of Academic Vocabulary in this section is an alphabetical list of the Academic Vocabulary words found in this textbook. Use this glossary just as you would use a dictionary—to find out the meanings of words used in your literature class, to talk about and write about literary and informational texts, and to talk about and write about concepts and topics in your other academic classes.

For each word, the glossary includes the pronunciation, syllabication, part of speech, and meaning. A Spanish version of each word and definition follows the English version. For more information about the words in this glossary, please consult a dictionary.

Analyze (AN uh lyz) is a verb that means *to examine something by looking critically or closely at it.*
   Analizar es un verbo que significa *examinar algo críticamente o de cerca.*

Area (AIR ee uh) is a noun that means *a field of experience, activity, or knowledge.*
   Área es un sustantivo que significa *campo de experiencia, actividad o conocimiento.*

Attribute (AT ruh byoot) is a noun that means *an element or characteristic that is a natural part of someone or something.*
   Atributo es un sustantivo que significa *elemento o característica considerada como parte natural de alguien o algo.*

Aware (uh WAIR) is an adjective that means *realizing or knowing about.*
   Consciente es un adjetivo que significa *saber algo o darse cuenta de algo.*

Clause (klawz) is a noun that means *a group of words with a subject and a verb* or *a part of a legal document.*
   Cláusula es un sustantivo que significa *grupo de palabras con un sujeto y un verbo o una parte de un documento legal.*

Communicate (kuh MYOO nih kayt) is a verb that means *to tell ideas or information to others.*
   Comunicar es un verbo que significa *transmitir ideas o información a otros.*

Conduct (kuh DUKT) is a verb that means *to manage, direct, or control.*
   Conducir es un verbo que significa *administrar, dirigir o controlar.*

Contemporary (kuhn TEM puh rer ee) is an adjective that means *from the present time.*
   Contemporáneo es un adjetivo que significa *perteneciente a este momento.*

Context (KON tekst) is a noun that means *the conditions in which an event or idea happens or exists.*
   Contexto es un sustantivo que significa *condiciones en las que un evento o una idea ocurren o existen.*

Cultural (KUL chuhr uhl) is an adjective that means *relating to the entire way of life of a group of people.*
   Cultural es un adjetivo que significa *el modo de vida de un grupo de personas.*

Demonstrate (DEM uhn strayt) is a verb that means *to show clearly.*
   Demostrar es un verbo que significa *mostrar claramente.*

Describe (dih SKRYB) is a verb that means *to tell or write about in detail.*
   Describir es un verbo que significa *decir o escribir algo en detalle.*

Develop (dih VEL uhp) is a verb that means *to grow in a way that seems natural.*

> **Desarrollar** es un verbo que significa *crecer de manera que parece natural.*

Domain (doh MAYN) is a noun that means *a place or field of activity over which a person has control.*

> **Dominio** es un sustantivo que significa *lugar o campo de actividad sobre el que una persona ejerce control.*

Element (EL uh muhnt) is a noun that means *a needed or basic part of something.*

> **Elemento** es un sustantivo que significa *necesidad o parte básica de algo.*

Encounter (en KOWN tuhr) is a noun that means *a meeting, especially one that is not expected.*

> **Encuentro** es un sustantivo que significa *reunión, especialmente inesperada.*

Evaluate (ih VAL yoo ayt) is a verb that means *to judge the value or worth of something.*

> **Evaluar** es un verbo que significa *juzgar el valor o el precio de algo.*

Focus (FOH kuhs) is a noun that means *a point or center of attention.*

> **Foco** es un sustantivo que significa *punto o centro de atención.*

Goal (gohl) is a noun that means *something a person is trying to achieve.*

> **Meta** es un sustantivo que significa *algo que una persona intenta alcanzar.*

Hypothesis (hy POTH ih sis) is a noun that means *a reasonable guess that still needs to be proved true or false.*

> **Hipótesis** es un sustantivo que significa *suposición razonable que todavía tiene que ser demostrada como verdadera o falsa.*

Identify (eye DEN tuh fy) is a verb that means *to point out or recognize something.*

> **Identificar** es un verbo que significa *mostrar o reconocer algo.*

Illustrate (IL uh strayt) is a verb that means *to explain or make clear by using examples.*

> **Ilustrar** es un verbo que significa *explicar o aclarar por medio de ejemplos.*

Impact (IM pakt) is a noun that means *the effect of one thing on another.*

> **Impacto** es un sustantivo que significa *el efecto de una cosa sobre a otra.*

Influence (IN floo uhns) is a noun that means *the power of a person or thing to affect others.*

> **Influencia** es un sustantivo que significa *el poder de una persona o cosa para afectar a otras.*

Integrity (in TEG rih tee) is a noun that means *being honest and true to oneself.* It also can mean *the condition of being complete, whole, or undivided.*

> **Integridad** es un sustantivo que significa *ser honesto y sincero con uno mismo.* También puede significar *ser completo, entero o indivisible.*

Interpret (in TER prit) v. is a verb that means *to explain or make clear.*

> **Interpretar** es un verbo que significa *explicar o aclarar.*

Link (lingk) is a verb that means *to connect or join.*

> **Unir** es un verbo que significa *conectar o enlazar.*

Locate (LOH kayt) is a verb that means *to find where something is.*

> **Ubicar** es un verbo que significa *hallar algo.*

Objective (uhb JEK tiv) is a noun that means *a goal or something that is aimed for or worked toward.*

> **Objetivo** es un sustantivo que significa *finalidad o algo a lo que se aspira o se tiene como meta.*

Physical (FIZ ih kuhl) is an adjective that means *having to do with the body or material things.*

> **Físico** es un adjetivo que significa *perteneciente al cuerpo o a las cosas materiales.*

Primary (PRY mer ee) is an adjective that means *first* or *most important.*

> **Primario** es un adjetivo que significa *primero o más importante.*

Process (PROS es) is a noun that means *the steps to take in making or doing something.*

   Proceso es un sustantivo que significa *pasos que se deben tomar para hacer o fabricar algo.*

React (ree AKT) is a verb that means *to act in response to someone or something.*

   Reaccionar es un verbo que significa *actuar en respuesta a alguien o a algo.*

Resolve (rih ZOLV) is a verb that means *to figure out, solve, or make clear.*

   Resolver es un verbo que significa *sacar en claro, solucionar o esclarecer.*

Respond (rih SPOND) is a verb that means *to answer or reply.*

   Responder es un verbo que significa *contestar o dar una respuesta.*

Specific (spih SIF ik) is an adjective that means *definite, exact.* It describes *a certain thing and no other.*

   Específico es un adjetivo que significa *definitivo, exacto.* Describe *algo en concreto.*

Status (STAT uhs) is a noun that means *the position or rank of someone or something compared with others.*

   Estado es un sustantivo que significa *posición o rango de alguien o algo en comparación con otros.*

Structure (STRUK chuhr) is a noun that means *something made of parts put together* or *the way something is put together.*

   Estructura es un sustantivo que significa *algo que se construye uniendo varias partes.*

Style (styl) is a noun that means *the way in which something is said or done.*

   Estilo es un sustantivo que significa *manera en que se dice o se hace algo.*

Symbol (SIM buhl) is a noun that means *something chosen to represent or stand for something else, such as a mark or sign.*

   Símbolo es un sustantivo que significa *algo escogido para representar o apoyar a otra cosa, como una marca o signo.*

Task (task) is a noun that means *a job or piece of work to be done.*

   Tarea es un sustantivo que significa *trabajo o labor a realizar.*

Theme (theem) is a noun that means *the overall message or point of a piece of writing.*

   Tema es un sustantivo que significa *mensaje global o asunto del que trata un escrito.*

Tradition (truh DISH uhn) is a noun that means *a custom, belief, or practice that is passed down from one generation to the next.*

   Tradición es un sustantivo que significa *costumbre, creencia o práctica que se transmite de generación en generación.*

Undertake (un duhr TAYK) is a verb that means *to begin or agree to do a task.*

   Asumir es un verbo que significa *empezar o acordar hacer una tarea.*

Vary (VAIR ee) is a verb that means *to change or become different in some way.*

   Variar es un verbo que significa *cambiar o diferir de alguna manera.*

High-Frequency Word List

Would you like to build your word knowledge? If so, the word lists on the next six pages can help you. These lists contain the 600 most common words in the English language. The most common words are on the First Hundred Words list; the next most common are on the Second Hundred Words list; and so on.

Study tip: Read through these lists starting with the First Hundred Words list. For each word you don't know, make a flash card. Work through the flash cards until you can read each word quickly.

FIRST HUNDRED WORDS

the	he	go	who
a	I	see	an
is	they	then	their
you	one	us	she
to	good	no	new
and	me	him	said
we	about	by	did
that	had	was	boy
in	if	come	three
not	some	get	down
for	up	or	work
at	her	two	put
with	do	man	were
it	when	little	before
on	so	has	just
can	my	them	long
will	very	how	here
are	all	like	other
of	would	our	old
this	any	what	take
your	been	know	cat
as	out	make	again
but	there	which	give
be	from	much	after
have	day	his	many

SECOND HUNDRED WORDS

saw	big	may	fan
home	where	let	five
soon	am	use	read
stand	ball	these	over
box	morning	right	such
upon	live	present	way
first	four	tell	too
came	last	next	shall
girl	color	please	own
house	away	leave	most
find	red	hand	sure
because	friend	more	thing
made	pretty	why	only
could	eat	better	near
book	want	under	than
look	year	while	open
mother	white	should	kind
run	got	never	must
school	play	each	high
people	found	best	far
night	left	another	both
into	men	seem	end
say	bring	tree	also
think	wish	name	until
back	black	dear	call

THIRD HUNDRED WORDS

ask	hat	off	fire
small	car	sister	ten
yellow	write	happy	order
show	try	once	part
goes	myself	didn't	early
clean	longer	set	fat
buy	those	round	third
thank	hold	dress	same
sleep	full	tell	love
letter	carry	wash	hear
jump	eight	start	eyes
help	sing	always	door
fly	warm	anything	clothes
don't	sit	around	through
fast	dog	close	o'clock
cold	ride	walk	second
today	hot	money	water
does	grow	turn	town
face	cut	might	took
green	seven	hard	pair
every	woman	along	now
brown	funny	bed	keep
coat	yes	fine	head
six	ate	sat	food
gave	stop	hope	yesterday

FOURTH HUNDRED WORDS

told	yet	word	airplane
Miss	true	almost	without
father	above	thought	wear
children	still	send	Mr.
land	meet	receive	side
interest	since	pay	poor
feet	number	nothing	lost
garden	state	need	wind
done	matter	mean	Mrs.
country	line	late	learn
different	large	half	held
bad	few	fight	front
across	hit	enough	built
yard	cover	feet	family
winter	window	during	began
table	even	gone	air
story	city	hundred	young
I'm	together	week	ago
tried	sun	between	world
horse	life	change	kill
brought	street	being	ready
shoes	party	care	stay
government	suit	answer	won't
sometimes	remember	course	paper
time	something	against	outside

High-Frequency Word List

FIFTH HUNDRED WORDS			
hour	grade	egg	spell
glad	brother	ground	beautiful
follow	remain	afternoon	sick
company	milk	feed	became
believe	several	boat	cry
begin	war	plan	finish
mind	able	question	catch
pass	charge	fish	floor
reach	either	return	stick
month	less	sir	great
point	train	fell	guess
rest	cost	fill	bridge
sent	evening	wood	church
talk	note	add	lady
went	past	ice	tomorrow
bank	room	chair	snow
ship	flew	watch	whom
business	office	alone	women
whole	cow	low	among
short	visit	arm	road
certain	wait	dinner	farm
fair	teacher	hair	cousin
reason	spring	service	bread
summer	picture	class	wrong
fill	bird	quite	age

SIXTH HUNDRED WORDS

become	themselves	thousand	wife
body	herself	demand	condition
chance	idea	however	aunt
act	drop	figure	system
die	river	case	line
real	smile	increase	cause
speak	son	enjoy	marry
already	bat	rather	possible
doctor	fact	sound	supply
step	sort	eleven	pen
itself	king	music	perhaps
nine	dark	human	produce
baby	whose	court	twelve
minute	study	force	rode
ring	fear	plant	uncle
wrote	move	suppose	labor
happen	stood	law	public
appear	himself	husband	consider
heart	strong	moment	thus
swim	knew	person	least
felt	often	result	power
fourth	toward	continue	mark
I'll	wonder	price	voice
kept	twenty	serve	whether
well	important	national	president

UNIT ONE

Houghton Mifflin Harcourt: Adaptation from "Seventh Grade," from *Baseball in April and Other Stories* by Gary Soto. Copyright © 1990 by Gary Soto. Reprinted by permission of Houghton Mifflin Harcourt Publishing Company. All rights reserved.

Scholastic: Adaptation from "The Last Dog" by Katherine Paterson. Copyright © 1999 by Minna Murra, Inc. Published in *Tomorrowland: Ten Stories about the Future* compiled by Michael Cart. Copyright © 1999 by Michael Cart. Reprinted by permission of Scholastic, Inc.

UNIT TWO

William Morris Endeavor Entertainment: "Zebra," from *Zebra and Other Stories* by Chaim Potok. Copyright © 1998 by Chaim Potok. Used by permission of William Morris Endeavor Entertainment, LLC on behalf of the author.

Brent Ashabranner: Adaptation from "A Wall of Remembrance," from *Their Names to Live* by Brent Ashabranner. Copyright © 1998 by Brent Ashabranner. Used by permission of the author.

National Park Service: Mrs. Eleanor Wimbish's Letter to Her Son, William "Billy" Stock. Reprinted by permission of the National Park Service, Vietnam Veterans Memorial Collection.

Bilingual Press/Editorial Bilingüe: Adaptation from "The Scholarship Jacket" by Marta Salinas, from *Nosotras: Latina Literature Today* by María del Carmen Boza, Beverly Silva, and Carmen Valle, editors. By permission of Bilingual Press/Editorial Bilingüe, 1986, Tempe, AZ.

UNIT THREE

Piri Thomas: Adaptation from *Stories from El Barrio* by Piri Thomas. Copyright © 1978 by Piri Thomas. Reprinted by permission of the author.

Pantheon Books: "The War of the Wall," from *Deep Sightings and Rescue Missions* by Toni Cade Bambara. Copyright © 1996 by the Estate of Toni Cade Bambara. Used by permission of Pantheon Books, a division of Random House, Inc.

Random House: "Homeless," from *Living Out Loud* by Anna Quindlen. Copyright © 1987 by Anna Quindlen. Used by permission of Random House, Inc.

UNIT FOUR

Don Congdon Associates: "Dark They Were, and Golden-Eyed" as "The Naming of Names," from *Thrilling Wonder Stories* by Ray Bradbury. Copyright © 1949 by Standard Magazines, renewed 1976 by Ray Bradbury. Reprinted by permission of Don Congdon Associates, Inc.

Liveright Publishing: "maggie and milly and molly and may," from *Complete Poems: 1904–1962* by E. E. Cummings, edited by George J. Firmage. Copyright © 1956, 1984, 1991 by the Trustees for the E. E. Cummings Trust. 1904 "who are you,little i?" from *Complete Poems: 1904–1962* by E. E. Cummings, edited by George J. Firmage. Copyright © 1963, 1991 by the Trustees for the E. E. Cummings Trust. "old age sticks," from *Complete Poems: 1904–1962* by E. E. Cummings, edited by George J. Firmage. Used by permission of Liveright Publishing Corporation.

UNIT FIVE

Sterling Lord Literistic: "The Names" by Billy Collins. Copyright © 2002 by Billy Collins. Reprinted by permission of SLL/Sterling Lord Literistic, Inc.

HarperCollins Publishers: "A crow has settled," from *The Essential Haiku: Versions of Bashō, Buson & Issa,* edited and with an introduction by Robert Hass. Copyright © 1994 by Robert Hass. Reprinted by permission of HarperCollins Publishers.

HarperCollins Publishers: "Fireflies," from *Joyful Noise* by Paul Fleischman. Text copyright © 1988 by Paul Fleischman. Used by permission of HarperCollins Publishers.

Henry Holt and Company: "Fireflies in the Garden," from *The Poetry of Robert Frost* edited by Edward Connery Lathem. Copyright 1956 by Robert Frost. Copyright 1928, 1969 by Henry Holt and Company. Reprinted by permission of Henry Holt and Company, LLC.

Rodale: Adaptation from "Stars with Wings" by Therese Ciesinski, from *Organic Gardening,* July/August, 2000. Reprinted by permission of Organic Gardening magazine. Copyright Rodale, Inc., USA. All rights reserved. www.organicgardening.com

N. Scott Momaday: "The Delight Song of Tsoai-talee," from *The Gourd Dancer* by N. Scott Momaday. Copyright © 1976 by N. Scott Momaday. Reprinted by permission of the author.

Susan Bergholz Literary Services: "Four Skinny Trees," from *The House on Mango Street* by Sandra Cisneros. Copyright © 1984 by Sandra Cisneros. Published by Vintage Books, a division of Random House, Inc., and in hardcover by Alfred A. Knopf in 1994. Reprinted by permission of Susan Bergholz Literary Services, New York. All rights reserved.

UNIT SIX

Scholastic: Adaptation from *The Greek Gods* by Bernard Evslin. Copyright © 1966 by Scholastic, Inc. Reprinted by permission.

Houghton Mifflin Company: Adaptation from "The Great Musician," from *Greek Myths* by Olivia E. Coolidge. Copyright © 1949 and renewed 1977 by Olivia E. Coolidge. Reprinted by permission of Houghton Mifflin Harcourt Publishing Company. All rights reserved.

Dutton Signet: Excerpt from *Beowulf* translated by Burton Raffel. Copyright © 1963, renewed © 1991 by Burton Raffel. Used by permission of Dutton Signet, a division of Penguin Group (USA) Inc.

Barbara S. Kouts: Adaptation from *Young Arthur* by Robert D. San Souci. Copyright © 1977 by Robert D. San Souci. Reprinted by permission of Barbara S. Kouts, Literary Agent.

UNIT SEVEN

Atheneum Books for Young Readers: Adaptation from "Eleanor Roosevelt," from *Great Lives: Human Rights* by William Jay Jacobs. Copyright © 1990 by William Jay Jacobs. Reprinted with the permission of Atheneum Books for Young Readers, an imprint of Simon & Schuster Children's Publishing Division.

G. P. Putnam's Sons: "Chemo," from *It's Not About the Bike* by Lance Armstrong. Copyright © 2000 by Lance Armstrong. Used by permission of G. P. Putnam's Sons, a division of Penguin Group (USA), Inc.

Da Capo Press: Adaptation from *23 Days in July* by John Wilcockson. Copyright © 2004 by John Wilcockson. Reprinted by permission of Da Capo Press, a member of Perseus Books, LLC.

PLAYS: "Clara Barton: Battlefield Nurse" by Jeannette Covert Nolan, from *Plays of Great Achievers.* Copyright © 1992. Reprinted by permission of the publisher Plays/Sterling Partners, Inc., P.O. Box 600160, Newton, MA 02460. Performance rights must be obtained in writing from the publisher.

UNIT EIGHT

National Geographic: Adaptation from "Great White Sharks" by Peter Benchley, from *National Geographic,* April 2000. Copyright © 2000 by National Geographic. Reprinted with permission from The National Geographic Society.

Cobblestone Publishing: Adaptation from "Like Black Smoke—The Black Death's Journey" by Diana Childress, from *CALLIOPE,* March 2001. Copyright © 2001 by Cobblestone Publishing, 30 Grove Street, Suite C, Peterborough, NH 03458. All rights reserved. Used by permission of Carus Publishing Company.

Cobblestone Publishing: Adaptation from "A World Turned Upside Down: How the Black Death Affected Europe" by Mary Morton Cowan, from *CALLIOPE,* March 2001. Copyright © 2001 by Cobblestone Publishing, 30 Grove Street, Suite C, Peterborough, NH 03458. All rights reserved. Used by permission of Carus Publishing Company.

GCOEM: Adaptation from "Emergency Supply Kit," from the Galveston County Office of Emergency Management web site. Used with permission.

D. Mark Singletary: Adaptation from "Pro Athletes' Salaries Aren't Overly Exorbitant" by Mark Singletary, from *New Orleans CityBusiness,* March 25, 2002. Copyright © 2002 by D. Mark Singletary. Used with permission.

Justin Hjelm: Adaptation from "Do Professional Athletes Get Paid Too Much?" by Justin Hjelm, from *the Horizon.* Copyright © 2004 by Justin Hjelm. Used by permission of the author.

Time: Adaptation from "Why We Shouldn't Go to Mars" by Gregg Easterbrook, from *Time,* January 26, 2004. Copyright © 2004 by TIME, Inc. Used by permission.

RESOURCES

McGraw-Hill Companies: from *Elementary Reading Instruction* by Edward Fry. Copyright © 1977 by McGraw-Hill Companies, Inc. All rights reserved. Reprinted by permission of the publisher.

The editors have made every effort to trace the ownership of all copyrighted material found in this book and to make full acknowledgment for its use. Omissions brought to our attention will be corrected in a subsequent edition.

COVER

Cattle Ranch, Texas © Joseph McNally/Getty Images; *background* © George Ostertag/Superstock.

HOW TO USE THIS BOOK

xiii *top* © Ken Hurst/istockphoto.com; *center* © Photodisc/Getty Images; *bottom* © Comstock Images/Jupiterimages Corporation; **xiv** © Ken Hurst/istockphoto.com.

UNIT 1

2 © Comstock Images/Jupiterimages Corporation; **6–12** *top* © Ken Hurst/istockphoto.com; **6** *center* © PhotoDisc/Getty Images; *bottom* © Comstock Images/Jupiterimages Corporation; **8** *center* © Ken Hurst/istockphoto.com; **11** *center* © PhotoDisc/Getty Images; *bottom* © Ken Hurst/istockphoto.com; **18–28** *top* © Roman Sigaev/ShutterStock; **18** *center* © Daniel van de Kamp/istockphoto.com; **19** *center* © Javier Larrea/Age Fotostock America, Inc.; **27** *bottom* © Daniel van de Kamp/istockphoto.com; **34–40** *top* © Jupiterimages Corporation; **34** *center* © Heuclin Daniel/Age Fotostock America, Inc.; **36** *bottom* © Radka Tesarova/ShutterStock.

UNIT 2

44 *Bond of Union* (1956), M. C. Escher. Lithograph. The Granger Collection, New York. © 2009 The M. C. Escher Company-Holland. All rights reserved. www.mcescher.com; **48–74** *top* © Christopher Elwell/ShutterStock; **48** *center* © Photos.com/Jupiterimages Corporation; **69** *center* © Brand X Pictures; **79** Photo by Lawrence Jackson/AP/Wide World Photos; **81** © Romanchuck Dimitry/ShutterStock; **85** *left* © Leif Skoogfors/Corbis; *right* © Buffon-Darquennes/Sygma/Corbis; **90** *center* Photo by Sharon Hoogstraten; **100–108** *top* © Corbis; **100** *center* © Dynamic Graphics/Jupiterimages Corporation; **105** *center* © Jupiterimages Corporation; **107** *center* © BW Folsom/ShutterStock.

UNIT 3

112 © Elsa/Getty Images; **116–120** *top* © Terraxplorer/istockphoto.com; **116** *center* © Brand X Pictures/Jupiterimages Corporation; **118** *center* © Corbis/PunchStock; **126–136** *top, ink splats* © Kirsty Pargeter/ShutterStock; *top, brick wall* © Tobias Machhaus/ShutterStock; **126** *center* © Agb/ShutterStock; **133** *center* Don Couch/HRW Photo; **141** © Bill Pierce/Time & Life Pictures/Getty Images; **144** *bottom* © PhotoObjects.net/Jupiterimages Corporation.

UNIT 4

148 © Lara Jo Regan/Liaison/Getty Images; **152** *center* © AbleStock/Jupiterimages Corporation; **165** *center* © Lepas/ShutterStock; **166** *center* © Alessio Ponti/ShutterStock; **178–181** *top* © Studio_Bateman/ShutterStock; **178** *center* © Smit/ShutterStock; **180, 181** *center* © rickt/ShutterStock.

UNIT 5

184 © Cosmin Manci/ShutterStock; **188–191** *top* © Rob Byron/ShutterStock; **188** *center* © Ruth Fremson/Pool/Reuters/Corbis; **189** © Susan Quinland-Stringer/ShutterStock; **196–206** *top* © Katrina Leigh/ShutterStock; **196** *center* © Photos.com/Jupiterimages Corporation; **197** *bottom* © Olemac/ShutterStock; **199** *center* © nix/ShutterStock; **211** *left* © Comstock Images/Jupiterimages Corporation; *right* © M.a.u./ShutterStock; **212–215** *top* © Tatjana Strelkova/ShutterStock; **212** *center* © Henk Bentlage/ShutterStock; **213** *center* © Anita Patterson Peppers/ShutterStock; **215** *center* © Satoshi Kuribayashi/Oxford Scientific/photolibrary; **219** *left* Illustration by Ken Oliver/Wildlife Art/The Art Agency; *right* © Anita Patterson Peppers/ShutterStock; **226** *center* © Corbis; **228** *center* © Elena Elisseeva/ShutterStock.

UNIT 6

232 © Photos.com/Jupiterimages Corporation; **236–242** *top* © Jupiterimages Corporation; **236** *center* © Agb/ShutterStock; **240** *center* © Vallentin Vassileff/ShutterStock; *bottom* Museo della Civilta Romana, Rome. © Alfredo Dagli Orti/The Art Archive; **248–251** *top* © Sally Wallis/ShutterStock; **248** *center* Anglo-Saxon helmet. British Museum. Photo © Image Asset Management Ltd./SuperStock; **250** *center* © Sally Wallis/ShutterStock; *bottom* © Mel Longhurst/Age Fotostock America, Inc.; **256–260** *top* © Aleksandar Todorovic/ShutterStock; **256** *center* © William Attard McCarthy/ShutterStock; **260** *center* © Arte & Immagini srl/Corbis.

UNIT 7

264 © Morton Beebe/Corbis; **268–276** *top* © osubuckeye/istockphoto.com; **268** *center* Eleanor Roosevelt in Calgary, Canada. March 1949. Courtesy of the Franklin D. Roosevelt Library Digital Archives; **270** *center* © Alexander Kalina/ShutterStock; **281** © Hulton Archive/Getty Images; **282** © Bettmann/Corbis; **288–293** *top* © Andrei Malov/istockphoto.com; **288** *center* © Reuters/Corbis; **291** *center* © vndrpttn/istockphoto.com; **294–296** © slobo mitic/istockphoto.com; **294** *center* © Wolfgang Rattay/Reuters/Corbis; **302–324** *top* Illustration by David McHargue; **302** *center* Illustration by David McHargue; **308** *center* © PhotoObjects.net/Jupiterimages Corporation; **325** Library of Congress, Prints and Photographs Division [LC-USZC4-6307/LOT 8494].

Unit 8

332 © Digital Vision/PunchStock; **336** © Jeff Rotman/Getty Images; **338** © frantisekhojdysz/ShutterStock; **346** Illustration by Stephen R. Wagner; **347** *center* © SMC Images/The Image Bank/Getty Images; *bottom* Illustration by Stephen R. Wagner; **350–351** © GeoNova LLC; **353** The Granger Collection, New York; **361, 362** Photo by Dave Martin/AP/Wide World Photos; **366** *bottom* © photostogo.com; **372** © Chad McDermott/ShutterStock; **384** NASA Jet Propulsion Laboratory (NASA-JPL); **392** *left* © liquidlibrary/Jupiterimages Corporation; *right* © patrimonio designs limited/ShutterStock.